F. O. Matthiessen and the
Politics of Criticism

THE WISCONSIN PROJECT ON AMERICAN WRITERS
A SERIES EDITED BY FRANK LENTRICCHIA

F. O. Matthiessen and the Politics of Criticism
WILLIAM E. CAIN

In Defense of Winters: An Introduction to the Poetry and Prose of Yvor Winters
TERRY COMITO

A Poetry of Presence: The Writing of William Carlos Williams
BERNARD DUFFEY

Lionel Trilling: The Work of Liberation
DANIEL T. O'HARA

Visionary Compacts: American Renaissance Writings in Cultural Context
DONALD E. PEASE

"A White Heron" and the Question of Minor Literature
LOUIS A. RENZA

The Theoretical Dimensions of Henry James
JOHN CARLOS ROWE

Specifying: Black Women Writing the American Experience
SUSAN WILLIS

F. O. Matthiessen and the Politics of Criticism

William E. Cain

THE UNIVERSITY OF WISCONSIN PRESS

The University of Wisconsin Press
114 North Murray Street
Madison, Wisconsin 53715

The University of Wisconsin Press, Ltd.
1 Gower Street
London WC1E 6HA, England

5   4   3   2   1

Printed in the United States of America

Library of Congress Cataloging-in-Publication Data
Cain, William E., 1952–   .
    F. O. Matthiessen and the politics of criticism/William E. Cain.
    246 pp.   cm. — (The Wisconsin project on American writers)
    Bibliography: pp. 217–232.
    Includes index.
    ISBN 0-299-11910-6   ISBN 0-299-11914-9 (pbk.)
    1. Matthiessen, F. O. (Francis Otto), 1902–1950—Criticism and
interpretation.   2. American literature—History and criticism—
Theory, etc.   3. Criticism—United States—History.   4. Politics
and literature—United States.   I. Title.   II. Series.
PS29.M35C35   1988   88-17275
810'.9—dc 19   CIP

To Barbara and Julia

Contents

Preface

IN WHAT FOLLOWS I situate F. O. Matthiessen's books in various contexts—biographical, institutional, literary critical, political; and I deal with them in what I judge to be their order of interest and importance. This means that I depart somewhat from the chronological line that Giles Gunn and Frederick Stern have basically pursued in their studies of this critic. *American Renaissance* was, and remains, Matthiessen's central achievement, and so I have chosen to examine it last. One of the advantages of this is that I can then devote more attention to *Henry James: The Major Phase*, *From The Heart of Europe* (Matthiessen's memoir of his experiences at the Salzburg Seminar in 1947), and *Theodore Dreiser*. Coming as they do after his masterpiece, these final three books are often treated briefly and are described as essentially marking a "decline" in Matthiessen's critical and scholarly power. But though they are flawed in certain key respects, they also show important, if uneven and sometimes contradictory, signs of growth. Matthiessen is struggling in them to express his political radicalism more directly in his literary criticism. This leads him, among other things, to be both surprisingly severe on James and remarkably generous—some have said too much so—to Dreiser.

The issue of perhaps central focus in Matthiessen's career concerns the complicated relations between criticism and politics, scholarship and the public sphere, pedagogy and social activism. How much or how little should politics enter into critical writing about and teaching of literature? Matthiessen judged his own work to be political, a means by which to advance the cause of "democracy." But, at the same time, he repeatedly maintained that the critic and teacher should first and foremost sympathetically interpret "the object as it is" and should ward off interferences that his own social and political views might create. Matthiessen labored tirelessly for political change and involved himself in many controversial left-wing causes during the 1930s and 1940s; he was also a great admirer of T. S. Eliot and aligned himself with the formalist enterprise that Eliot inaugurated and that the New Critics developed and institutionalized. He was a fervently political man who yearned to make his criticism "political" but whose fundamental literary assumptions required that politics be kept out of criticism.

Leo Marx and others have stated, often compellingly, that the tensions and inconsistencies in Matthiessen's books give them strength. These, it is said, were enabling and empowering, furnishing Matthiessen's criticism with a range and suggestiveness that distinguish it from the writing done by both his New Critical and his Marxist/socialist/Communist contemporaries. Yet I don't think, finally, that this assessment gets at the whole truth. Matthiessen's books suffer from questions that he raised, but never truly confronted and resolved, about politics and criticism: the unanswered questions lead to confusions and ambiguities that linger even in the later, more politically emboldened studies of James and Dreiser.

In taking note of Matthiessen's limitations, I don't mean to indicate that critics and teachers today have integrated their literary and political loyalties any better than he did. What makes Matthiessen, in fact, so absorbing to consider is that he reveals how hard it is to be politically engaged in the teacher/critic's craft, particularly so long as we cling to the view that politics should enter into the discussion only after the literary critical job has been cleanly undertaken. This is the view Matthiessen embraced, though not always unequivocally, and it led to scholarship that was both extraordinary and sometimes badly skewed. In my Conclusion, I will suggest, going against the grain of *American Renaissance* and other writings, that democrats and socialists—Matthiessen was one himself—should acknowledge the primacy of their political commitments and proceed to teach and write accordingly. Politics, in a word, should explicitly shape literary and critical choices. Not all will welcome this proposal, and I am not wholly comfortable with it myself, for it entails major reorientations of texts and the approaches for examining them. But it nevertheless seems to me to state the lesson that Matthiessen's career teaches. This critic dramatizes for us the personal, professional, and intellectual costs that result when we persist in separating politics from literary work even as we simultaneously strive to make them somehow coincide.

A few additional words about my procedure in this book. Primarily I concentrate on Matthiessen's writings and the contexts within which they figure. But I do offer some detailed commentary on Thoreau, Dreiser, James, and Melville where it seems warranted. At the risk of appearing occasionally to divert attention from Matthiessen himself, I believe it is only fair to provide a clear indication why I dissent from, or would want to supplement, certain readings of texts that he presents. Sometimes in Matthiessen's work, as in his intriguing failure to examine *Benito Cereno*—a text he praised very highly—the question is not why a reading is wrong or incomplete but, instead, why Matthiessen did not undertake a particular analysis and what it might have looked like, and the consequences it might have generated, if he had.

Even sympathetic readers may judge that I digress too much in my final chapter and Conclusion, where I consider Matthiessen's inability to see Afro-American literature as significant and note W. E. B. Du Bois' theory and practice of intellectual/political work as a better alternative to Matthiessen's own. My account certainly marks a limitation in Matthiessen's criticism, but it is intended, more generally, to illustrate the kind of separation of literary and political realms that has often afflicted radicals, who tend to believe that some things are not political (or to be politicized). I mean the alternative I offer to be a challenging one: it challenges, I know, loyalties I have long adopted and which critics like Matthiessen have helped to instill in me. I regard this book, then, not really as a judgment upon Matthiessen, but, rather, as an opportunity to seek enlightenment through him—to gauge where his work, if seriously pondered and absorbed and argued with, leads.

Acknowledgments

I AM INDEBTED, first of all, to a number of scholars, including Richard Ruland, Giles Gunn, Frederick Stern, Leo Marx, Jonathan Arac, and George Abbott White, who have written well about F. O. Matthiessen. Their books and essays have allowed me to follow related, but finally different, paths in my own study of this critic and his career. These supplement the moving testimonies, written by friends, students, and literary and political colleagues, that Paul M. Sweezy and Leo Huberman assembled soon after Matthiessen's death, in *F. O. Matthiessen: A Collective Portrait*.

In addition, I want to express my special thanks to a number of scholars who carefully read an earlier version of this manuscript: Art Casciato, Gerald Graff, Ross Posnock, Patrick Quinn, Richard Ruland, and Eric Sundquist. I also greatly appreciate the words of advice and encouragement I received from Giles Gunn, Irving Howe, Alfred Kazin, and Mark Krupnick. For their support of this study from its beginnings, and for their reading of the manuscript, I am also grateful to Allen Fitchen, Director of the University of Wisconsin Press, and Frank Lentricchia, editor of the Wisconsin Project on American Writers series.

Neither George Dardess nor Stanley Fish read my manuscript, but both of them helped me to write it through what they taught me about literature and criticism: I remain deeply in their debt. Along these general lines, I want to mention, too, how much I have learned, especially about writing, from Eric Sundquist, with whom I have been sharing work-in-progress since graduate school. Jerry Graff has also been a good friend and steady source of support; he has always been extremely generous with his time and helpfully tough-minded and insightful in his criticisms.

In its finished form, this book is lovingly dedicated to my wife, Barbara Leah Harman, and my daughter, Julia, the most important people in my life and, in one way or another, the informing presences of and central audiences for everything I write.

Portions of this book first appeared, in a somewhat different form, in *New England Quarterly* and *South Atlantic Quarterly*, and I am grateful for their permission to reprint.

F. O. Matthiessen and the
Politics of Criticism

Introduction

The common reader . . . does not live by trends alone; he reads books, whether of the present or past, because they have an immediate life of their own.

—American Renaissance x

I WOULD LIKE to begin by reprinting a polemical paper that I presented at an American Studies conference in the fall of 1985. It will help me to explain my aims in writing this book, and will indicate the nature of my thinking about literature, criticism, and teaching when I realized I needed to return to F. O. Matthiessen, a critic I had often read and learned from but had never studied in detail.

"American" Study: One Way to Revise the Humanities

In recent years, critics and teachers in the humanities have increasingly been pressured to "justify" what they do. Administrators, parents, and students stress jobs, careers, financial comfort and security, and often they grow impatient with academics whose pastimes appear fanciful and even otherworldly. Students, in my experience at least, are enterprising and eager to learn—they are not so programmed for success that they spurn hard work and knowledge about "impractical" subjects. But they are also very attentive to the realities of the world around them, a world of limited opportunities where only the well trained and well equipped will survive the demanding competition. Students justifiably fear this world, and anxiety about it dramatically colors their parents' and their own attitudes toward education, particularly in literature, history, philosophy, and other branches of the humanities. What is the rationale for studying these disciplines? How do they connect with the rigors of American life in the 1980s? Why should a student invest time and energy in perusing novels and poems when economics and the hard sciences beckon?

The response of those in the humanities to these questions has, for the most part, been clumsy and confused. This judgment holds true, I believe, for all of the humanistic fields, but I will focus my commentary here on literature and criticism, which is what I know best. When asked to justify literary study and explain how it bears on contemporary life, many critics and teachers simply become irritable or even enraged, as though the request were in bad taste and mirrored the vulgarity of the person who advances it. Literary study in the college and university, it appears, justifies itself, and it should continue because it has existed for decades. End of discussion.

Others do attempt to describe and defend literary study, but usually they fare poorly. Their efforts are earnest, but lapse quickly —as can be readily seen in the various panel and commission reports on higher education—into misty pieties about the "great books of the Western tradition" and "the best that has been thought and said." Such an echoing of Matthew Arnold and his heirs, however, is no longer compelling to people outside the small circle of readers who take their intellectual cue from *Culture and Anarchy* and "The Function of Criticism" and other Arnoldian texts: it lacks the immediacy and relevance that we need to make contact with—and truly instruct—our public constituencies.

Still other faculty in literature departments, unable to embrace Arnoldian terms and values, unfortunately bow to the economic facts of life. They urge their colleagues to seek survival and perhaps even prosperity by shearing off literature courses and replacing them with an imposing array of courses in business and technical writing, journalism, and practical composition (which shows a student how to assemble a resumé, craft a good personal statement, and apply for employment in winningly modulated prose). This option makes a certain sort of utilitarian sense, but it is guaranteed to induce self-loathing among the faculty. And it defaults on the responsibilities of criticism in its refusal to contest or even ponder the reasons for injurious tendencies in American education, and in its surrender of intellectual standards to the bidding of the marketplace.

There is a fourth group of spokespersons for literary study, a group that is both more admirable and more misguided than the others. Here I have in mind the teachers and critics who have adopted structuralism, poststructuralism, semiotics, or one of the other feisty methodologies from Europe. These are the American disciples, explicators, and celebrants of Roland Barthes, Jacques Derrida, Michel Foucault, Louis Althusser, and Jacques Lacan, to cite the most luminous of the big names. Americans have been drawing upon the beguilingly complex texts of these Continental writers for nearly two decades, and have managed to provoke some valuable inquiry into the nature of criticism. We have seen, for example, worthwhile questioning of any absolute distinction between literary and nonliterary works, and this has led to profitable interdisciplinary scholarship on diaries, autobiographies, travel narratives, and other kinds of texts not ordinarily classified as "literature." In addition, most people now acknowledge the limitations of the New Criticism, the "close reading" approach that privileged a steady focus on the text as a discrete object or "verbal icon" and hence discouraged efforts to develop what were considered extrinsic contexts—social, political, historical—for criticism. Literary study has gained a good deal from the intense, often waspish, debates about theory and methodology. It is in certain respects more open, adventurous, and flexible than before, and this is to be welcomed.

But curiously, these changes have not made literary study seem more defensible or justifiable, nor have they helped critics and teachers to gain access to an audience more numerous than the captive students in the seminar or classroom. Indeed, the vaunted difficulty of many current modes and approaches has cut off criticism almost entirely from nonacademic readers. What goes on in many literature departments, at conferences, and in vanguard journals is high-powered and contentious, but it concerns only the experts and professionals in the field—they produce and consume a commodity that few others care about or understand. To an outsider, literary study today looks rather impressive, unsparingly dense and technical in its poststructuralist probings of texts from *Hamlet* to *Ulysses*. But it is incomprehensible and unrelated to the needs and interests of people who do not make their living "doing criticism."

There are, in my view, rich, ample projects for literary study that will enable us to justify it and make it contribute to the en-

Introduction

richment of American cultural discourse. We should be grateful to
the structuralists, poststructuralists, and their brethren from abroad
who have forced us to reexamine how we conduct interpretive business, but we must now go beyond their stunted technicality. And we
go beyond it by laboring to fashion a criticism and pedagogy that lie
directly in the American grain. For philosophical support and sus-
tenance, we should now be reading Emerson, Dewey, and William
James; and for exemplary critical performances, we should be re-
newing our acquaintance with Randolph Bourne, Van Wyck Brooks,
Edmund Wilson, Kenneth Burke, and R. P. Blackmur. America has
a noble tradition of critics and intellectuals (there are many more
besides those I have named) that has pretty much been ignored in the
rush to pay fealty to the latest methodologies from France. It is this
tradition that we should aim to rediscover, in order to remind ourselves of and show our students the resilience and range of American
criticism ("criticism" that is both keenly particular and capaciously
general), and to offer examples of oppositional theory and practice
("oppositional" in conservative, liberal, and radical senses).

Students—and far too many teachers and critics—know almost
nothing about this tradition. For every graduate student and assistant professor who is eloquent about William James, there are no
doubt hundreds who can speak today with aplomb about the dis-
quisitions of Derrida. For every person who has encountered Burke,
there are innumerable others well versed in Foucault and his commentators. Derrida and Foucault are obviously important. But they
alone will never be able to direct us toward a better critical and
pedagogical practice in America. If we ever hope to justify teaching
and writing about literature; if we seek in fact to give the humanities
a marked relevance to American society; if we want our constituencies to value what we do, then we should take as a central mission a
renewed commitment to informing ourselves and our students about
the literature, philosophy, and history of the United States.

We have our own "great tradition" in literature and criticism, and
it consists of writers who speak in many different tones and textures.
One thinks, for example, of statesmen such as Paine, Jefferson, and
Lincoln; of poets, autobiographers, and novelists such as Thoreau,
Whitman, Twain, and Faulkner; of social critics and reformers such
as Douglass, Cable, Tourgée, and Jane Addams; of powerful story-
tellers, mythmakers, and public speakers such as Du Bois, Wright,

6

Baldwin, and Malcolm X. This is, clearly, a disparate group, and one would not want to endorse everything—Du Bois' self-deluded fantasies about the marvels of the Soviet Union are a case in point —that these men and women said and did. And this listing would appear even more various if one were to add to it, for instance, Henry James and Edith Wharton, both of whom impress us with the force of their deeply held conservatism, and who teach us much —as of course Emerson and Wilson do as well—about the mediations between America and Europe. By taking note of James and Wharton, I mean to stress that an American great tradition is not a body of writers exclusively liberal or radical, nor is it "purely American," whatever that might mean. It is, instead, a heterogeneous order of extraordinarily gifted men and women who display rare forms of public, social, and national consciousness and address both the aspirations and dissolutions of—to quote Lincoln's and Whitman's phrase—"American Union." They are curious about and appreciative of other cultures, yet attend persistently to American culture— its distinctiveness, its successes, its glaring omissions and how these might be remedied.

Some might counter this proposal by saying that it is provincial, but this strikes me as a misleading charge. At the present time, especially in the college and university, there is no danger that an "American" literary and cultural criticism will overwhelm and lead to the banishment of "foreign" terms, texts, and approaches. Too many people have too much invested in subindustries devoted to poststructuralism for any dangerously wholesale narrowing of perspective to occur. More significantly, it would be foolish and self-defeating not to refine our own enterprise by taking what we can from Orwell, Leavis, Raymond Williams, and other English and European critics, historians, and men-of-letters—anyone, in short, who can be of use. I am not making an argument for cultural nationalism, not advocating that we survey *only* American traditions and deny their intimate bonds to England and Europe; Emerson himself, after all, grafts his own project as a writer to Montaigne's and Bacon's, and he pairs illuminatingly with Coleridge and Carlyle. Rather, I am recommending that we take these traditions seriously enough to learn about and cherish them, and that we strive more willingly to foreground them in criticism and pedagogy. Patriotic feeling, national pride, love of country—it is easy to scoff at these things, and political campaigns regularly testify to the manner in which they can be distorted and abused. But faith in and fondness for America are *real,* a current of spirit and emotion that teachers and critics should draw upon. "America," we need to make clear, means both an invigorating set of ideals and a relentless critique of them. We have no reason to invoke and cite Marx and Mao Zedong to highlight our failures as a nation and sharp departures from our best ideals. We have our own critical tradition; it has always been there, waiting to be restored.

Let me be more specific about the kind of course work I have in mind. A natural subject for literary study is slavery and race relations: What could be more potent as a way of relating criticism and teaching to past and present problems in contemporary America? Yet this is a subject that is too rarely taught, and it figures infrequently in scholarly journals and at conferences. It is a startling fact that says much about the isolation and irrelevance of the humanities today that critics have been writing about the American Renaissance for many years and regularly teaching the texts of this period without discussing abolitionism, types of proslavery and antislavery argument, slave narratives, antebellum culture and politics. Thanks to Ann Douglas, Nina Baym, Eric Sundquist, and others, this situation has begun to improve somewhat, at least in scholarship, but it is still far from satisfactory. *The Scarlet Letter, Billy Budd,* and a handful of other symbolic and allegorical classics bear the weight of annual reading and explication, while a considerable amount of provocative material by William Lloyd Garrison, Frederick Douglass, Martin Delany, Theodore Weld, the Grimké sisters, Lydia Maria Child, and others remains ignored.

I am saying not that we should cease reading Hawthorne, but that it makes sense to read his texts and scrutinize their language in relation to the texts and verbal strategies that Douglass, Garrison, and other sociocultural critics devised. Similarly, reading and talking about Emerson proves most fruitful if we locate *Nature,* "The American Scholar," and other familiar works from the American Renaissance syllabus in conjunction with Emerson's comments about slavery and race in his letters, journals, and essays on the Fugitive Slave Law, John Brown, and the Emancipation Proclamation. This is what a committed American literary and cultural pluralism obliges us to do. And this is how we show students (and remind ourselves) that the American past contains vital examples of men and women who developed ideas and a language for speaking about (and against) their society.

Literary study will never justify itself by deploying new theories and methodologies to process, yet once more, canonical literary texts stripped of their historical immediacy and impact and severed from their relation to other forms of speech and writing. We do not desperately need Russian Formalist accounts of narrative in Hawthorne's stories, Derridean forays into the antics of metaphor and metonymy in Poe's poetry, or Lacanian meditations on the signifier in Melville's tales. These come perilously close to being make-work enterprises that seem very avant-garde but are dated the moment they appear. To justify literary study and make the humanities meaningful, we must persuade audiences—using lucid, forceful prose that makes statements—that the texts we study do engage issues which actually matter to people. What is the historical context of the texts we write about and teach? What can they tell us about American society, culture, politics? How do they instruct us about race, religion, family, and community? What, furthermore, do our writers reveal about the potential of language as a means of social criticism and protest? Who are the dissenting American voices—conservative, liberal, and radical—and how successfully do they still speak to us? How can we draw upon the resources of Emerson, Douglass, Garrison, Bourne, and Burke to renew and define our own place within an American critical tradition?

Here are obvious questions that can help us to articulate and lay claim to the authority of literary work, but these are, at the present time, questions that few in the humanistic disciplines are asking. It is time to treat our country and culture with greater seriousness by undertaking acts of American study that will renew, as they demonstrate, the energetic idiom of this nation's speech and writing.

This still strikes me as a useful polemic, but its shortcomings are obvious. My grouping of writers and critics is loose, my tone is too strident, and my efforts to guard against the charge of cultural nationalism are not wholly convincing. In addition, some things that I criticized were already, even then, in 1985, changing for the better. Much good work continues to be done on "expanding the canon," and the many new anthologies of literature, which include a great deal of writing by women and minorities, attest that this work is

9

having a productive impact. Literary critics as well as philosophers have also begun to reassess William James and John Dewey, noting in particular that pragmatism, with its emphasis on the practical consequences of ideas, enables us to move beyond limited debates about structuralist and poststructuralist theory.

My central concern in this paper, however, had less to do with the impact of literary theory than with my effort to develop firmer bonds between literature, criticism, and teaching that would make my own work better equipped to respond to the American social and political scene. As I saw it, I think essentially accurately, if self-righteously, America in the first half of the 1980s was increasingly growing morally callous and becoming ever more contentedly accepting of a cruel, if extraordinarily powerful, political discourse. This was the discourse—backed by action—of Ronald Reagan and the new conservatism, and it appeared to me dispiritingly to be without an effective competing discourse. Liberals occasionally mounted protests, but 1980s liberalism appeared unable to connect with its old coalition, and on most key domestic and foreign policy issues, it usually ended up meshing with what Reagan called for.

Particularly in the academy, Marxism offered one kind of language to answer Reagan's, and it was indeed one of the results of the conservative revolution that it revitalized (and enlarged the number of) Marxists on college and university campuses. But Marxism seemed then, and basically still seems, too marginal to the American situation as a whole to be truly worthwhile as a cause to rally around (Cain, "English in America"). It charted valuable lines for critique and questioning of capitalist and corporate society, but as Edmund Wilson said long ago, it is not, and never has been, a "language" that Americans can really hear. In my paper I wanted to advocate the study of an American critical language, a "native tradition" of literary and social protest. My students did not know (nor did I know as well as I should have) the writings of Garrison, Douglass, Du Bois, and others, writings directed in some fashion or other against the dominant order. Students were more familiar with Twain and Whitman, but usually they had read these writers with little awareness of historical context and contemporary relevance. My intention, then, was to make teaching and criticism more socially engaged and responsible. I hoped with my students to learn an oppositional discourse informed by the voice and vision of radicals, revolutionaries, and reformers in America's past.

Given that this was my aim, it now seems all the more peculiar to me that I omitted the name of F. O. Matthiessen from my roll call of exemplary figures. Here was a critic who had urged his readers in *American Renaissance* to repossess a "literature for our democracy" and "feel the challenge of our still undiminished resources" (xv). Here, too, was a critic who had maintained, even as the New Criticism was establishing itself in the 1930s and 1940s, that teachers and critics should reject the "new scholasticism"; become knowledgeable about other fields, techniques, and theories (including Marxism); and recognize the inescapable connections between intellectual and political life ("Responsibilities" 5, 10, 11).

I realized that I had omitted Matthiessen a few weeks after the conference when I was reviewing secondary materials on Dreiser for a class on *Sister Carrie*, and came across some notes I had taken on his critical biography of this writer. I had simply forgotten about Matthiessen, a critic whose credentials and commitments made him a clearly pertinent figure for my interests. This was a bad but interesting mistake. I recalled that no one else had cited him at the conference where I gave my paper. Nor did anyone there point out the obvious fact—Jane Tompkins, Donald Pease, and others have since done so forcefully—that Matthiessen had himself established the conception of the "American Renaissance" that I recommended we should challenge.

Matthiessen has not figured prominently in discussions of criticism and literary theory. Derrida, Foucault, Lacan, and other philosophers and historians influential on the current scene have received exorbitant attention during the past two decades, but their predominance has not by any means ruled out detailed, extensive treatment of the important makers of modern literary criticism. To take a few notable instances: contemporary scholars, theorists, and critics regularly examine (and usually attack) Cleanth Brooks as the embodiment of the New Criticism, admire William Empson for his shrewd mix of commonsensical and sophisticated thinking about language, and encourage us to reacquaint ourselves with the more-than-mere formalists Blackmur and Burke. Still others often refer positively to Edmund Wilson and the New York intellectuals (Philip

Rahv, Lionel Trilling, Irving Howe) for practicing a trenchant cultural journalism that contrasts with the aridity and specialization of so much of the writing now being done by academic professionals. Yvor Winters, F. R. Leavis, I. A. Richards—these figures, too, in all their provocative eccentricity and unevenness, have been the subject of frequent study and debate. In their different ways, they, too, have their place in critical controversies. Matthiessen does not.

This is not to say that Matthiessen has been altogether ignored. Giles B. Gunn (1975) and Frederick Stern (1981) have written informative surveys of his life and career. Richard Ruland (1967) has perceptively situated him in the context of twentieth-century assessments of America's literary past. Jonathan Arac (1985) has sensitively explored the conflicts between Matthiessen's scholarship in *American Renaissance* and his socialist politics; and René Wellek (1986) has offered a cogent summary in his history of American criticism from 1900 to 1950. Scattered essays, reviews, and testimonials have also appeared, the most noteworthy being the rewarding critical/biographical essay by George Abbott White that was published in *Tri-Quarterly* in 1972.

Nevertheless there does seem to be a disproportion between the relatively small amount of this scholarship and the affirmations—brief but outsized—of Matthiessen's importance that one encounters everywhere. In *American Literature: A Study and Research Guide*, for example, Lewis Leary describes *American Renaissance* as "a major work in literary scholarship, and perhaps the single most influential study of literature in America at the middle of the nineteenth century" (17). Gunn and Stern themselves both remark that Matthiessen's book revolutionized the study of American literature. Richard Brodhead observes that *American Renaissance* "did more than any other book to set the American canon as it would be taught in American universities after World War II" (210); and William L. Hedges, in tracking relations between Progressive historiography and modernist criticism, goes so far as to state that it still stands as "the key work in American literary theory" (105).

These major claims acquire an even fuller body when one recalls Matthiessen's significance for an entire generation of students during the 1930s and 1940s who viewed themselves as carrying on and extending his legacy in their own careers. Leo Marx, Kenneth Lynn, and Quentin Anderson have spoken vividly about Matthiessen's

teaching; and the "collective portrait" of Matthiessen edited by
Sweezy and Huberman that appeared soon after his death in 1950
contains additional, equally eloquent, reports. And the group of
writers, poets, and intellectuals—including Harry Levin, Arthur M.
Schlesinger, Jr., Richard Wilbur, Robert Coles—Matthiessen influenced and inspired in his teaching and stimulating tutorials at Harvard is very impressive indeed. Laurence B. Holland, author of perhaps the best book on Henry James, studied under Matthiessen, as
did J. C. Levenson, author of one of the best books on Henry Adams.
Three of Matthiessen's other students produced central books in
American studies and literary criticism: Henry Nash Smith, *The Virgin Land* (1950); R. W. B. Lewis, *The American Adam* (1955); and
Leo Marx, *The Machine in the Garden* (1964). One could easily add
to this list, and could justifiably conclude that, inside and outside
the academy, Matthiessen effectively *made* the study of American
literature possible and prestigious.

But has Matthiessen's actual work held up well? He was a great
man and teacher, and a fine scholar and editor, but was he a great
critic? Does his criticism still stimulate new thinking about literature? The work he accomplished in his tragically short life, particularly *American Renaissance* and the books on Eliot, James, and
Dreiser, was crucial in legitimating and advancing certain kinds of
reading, study, and scholarship. Yet when one returns to them, ex-
pectations high, one is perhaps disappointed. Matthiessen's style
often lacks energy and punch, and even in *American Renaissance*,
there are fewer ideas and insights than one had hoped to find.

One test of a critic's greatness (few of us could survive it) is how
well he or she sustains rereading. Empson—incisive and entertaining
—is very much worth rereading, even when he is at his most cranky
and perverse in *Milton's God* and his other later writings. Blackmur, too, is a critic to whom one can profitably return; his essays
on modern poetry, in *The Double Agent* (1935) and *The Expense of
Greatness* (1940), have an enviable economy and precision. One goes
to them not only for Blackmur's intimate sense of Eliot's or Pound's
strengths and limitations, but also for the model that these essays
represent—probing "close readings" of texts in the context of beautifully articulated arguments about imagery, language, poetic structure, and authority. Though here I am in more disputed territory, I
would hazard that much of Leavis also repays a second and third

reading. He makes instructive errors, as when he condemns the later James in *The Great Tradition*; and his blasts against received opinion, as in his critique of A. C. Bradley's "sentimentalized" Othello in *The Common Pursuit*, still help to focus important features of major texts. He possesses an idiosyncratic, but challenging, style of intellectual attack—fierce, uncompromising, highly dogmatic.

It is not evident to me that Matthiessen, however much I admire him, provides such rewards. His work has many virtues, among them an exemplary patience with complex materials, an absence of self-advertising gestures, and a deep sympathy and respect for the writers and subjects he addresses (he had a bad temper in person, but rarely exhibited it in print). But his books do not always appear compelling today. *American Renaissance* is a critical landmark—a diligent scholarly performance that did salient work for American criticism and culture. But perhaps like other landmarks of one sort or another—Brooks and Warren's celebrated 1938 text, *Understanding Poetry*, comes to mind—it is a book that one finally esteems for what it indubitably "did," for the effects that it had. It is not a book that spurs the imagination to the degree it did back in the 1940s.

Of course there is more than one very good reply to this line of argument. One could say, first of all, that Blackmur, Empson, and Leavis are three of the finest critics of this century. It is hardly a badge of shame that Matthiessen falls short when placed alongside of them; it would still be possible to identify him, at his best, as an outstanding critic who provides his own kind of intellectual rewards on both first and later readings. One could also maintain, more tellingly still, that Matthiessen's critical language lacks potency for us because it *is*—largely owing to him—now the language that we speak: in his books on Eliot, James, Dreiser, and the writers of the American Renaissance, he laid the discursive ground that other past and present critics and scholars build upon, and that those who urge an opening up of the canon now seek to break up. From this angle of approach, Matthiessen might well pair with Eliot himself, who is also difficult for many to reread today, largely because his critical essays on Milton, Marvell, and the metaphysical poets have so deeply saturated the language we instinctively employ about literature and criticism. What is irritating about Eliot, and possibly about Matthiessen as well, is the extent of their influence. So much has their language become our language that it does seem at moments slightly repellent: we see, with some discomfort, how much we owe to them, how powerfully they have structured our perceptions, how painfully familiar their terms have become. Both unsettlingly remind us, when we discern the infiltration of their voices into our speech, of the difficulty of being original.

To make a point like this one is to appreciate Matthiessen's distinction, his very rare kind of influence that continues to guide American literary study. As Leo Marx has said, "no writer in the last half century has had a greater influence on the prevailing conception of American literature and its relation to our history" ("Double Consciousness" 34). One might make a similarly forceful point by noting several key datelines. In 1929, Matthiessen (he was just twenty-seven) announced "it is time for the history of American literature to be rewritten" ("New Standards" 181); in 1935, 1941, and 1944, he published books on Eliot, the American Renaissance, and James that effectively *did* rewrite American literary history and that sparked others to initiate their own acts of rewriting and revision; and in 1948, Robert E. Spiller and others issued the *Literary History of the United States*, a massive enterprise that testified to the success of what Matthiessen (who himself contributed chapters on Poe and modern poetry to the Spiller volume) had, more than anyone else, inaugurated and made prevail.

If an additional marker is needed, there is, published in 1951, the *Report of the Committee on Trends in Research in American Literature, 1940–1950,* which announced the surge of criticism and scholarship on Emerson, Thoreau, Whitman, Hawthorne, and Melville, and the greatly diminished quantity of writing on Whittier, Longfellow, Holmes, Lowell, and other distinguished but no longer canonical New England worthies. To be sure, others had engaged the writers of the American Renaissance before Matthiessen got to them. D. H. Lawrence (1923), Constance Rourke (1931), and Yvor Winters (1938), to name just three, had studied Melville. Lawrence, Parrington (1930), and Newton Arvin (1938), among others, had explored social and political themes in Whitman. And there was abundant secondary material on Emerson, Thoreau, and Hawthorne. But it was Matthiessen, with unparalleled scholarship and the credentials that came with a Harvard professorship, who mapped the contours of the American Renaissance and identified, once and for all, its authors and their masterworks.

Despite all of this, however, I think Matthiessen does persist as a "problem" and is harder to appraise than these signs of his achievement indicate. One could after all contend that Leavis also established a critical discourse by virtue of his "revaluations" of English poetry and studies of "the great tradition" in the English novel from Jane Austen to D. H. Lawrence. One could reasonably suggest, too, that Empson, particularly in *Seven Types of Ambiguity* (1930) and *Some Versions of Pastoral* (1934), also launched an extensive incursion into the languages of literature and criticism. And yet their work often enjoys a vigorous contemporaneity, whereas Matthiessen's does not. It is insufficient simply to accent Matthiessen's influence—not if one wants really to understand him and measure the true caliber of his critical production. He deserves a more rigorous kind of scrutiny.

Why, then, does Matthiessen regularly receive accolades but relatively few detailed analyses and even fewer statements of his value for the present? Why, indeed, is he absent from most anthologies and histories of modern criticism? In his ample account of "post-war American literary opinion," Grant Webster treats Eliot, Brooks, Tate, Blackmur, Austin Warren, Winters, Burke, Wellek, Murray Krieger, Trilling, Howe, Rahv, and Wilson, but he gives only scant mention to Matthiessen (105–6). Other books that investigate or gather samples of modern literary criticism tell the same perplexing story. And if one turns to books on American intellectual history, one finds only brief references or outright absences there as well. In the standard work, Robert Allen Skotheim's *American Intellectual Histories and Historians* (1966), there are substantial chapters on Vernon Louis Parrington, Merle Curti, Samuel Eliot Morison, Perry Miller, Ralph Gabriel, and others, but not even a single reference to Matthiessen. Nor does he show up, except for one or two comments in passing, in Cunliffe and Winks's *Pastmasters: Some Essays on American Historians* (1969), which includes thorough analyses of Parrington, Miller, Richard Hofstadter, and others. Not only does Miller, a colleague and friend of Matthiessen's at Harvard, occupy a central position in such books, but his magisterial inquiries into the Puritan origins and intellectual traditions of America seem alive and controversial in ways that Matthiessen's examinations of his authors do not. Miller is an informing presence in Higham and

Conklin's *New Directions in American Intellectual History* (1979); Matthiessen is not cited even once.

As before, lines of response to this evidence quickly suggest themselves. Matthiessen did not see himself as an intellectual, social, or economic historian, remarking in *American Renaissance* that his focus is instead on the aesthetic theory and practice of the writers he examines (vi–viii). But what then does this aim make him: a critic? a literary historian? a "scholar-critic"—which is what Wellek labels him (74–84)? To ask such a question is not merely to fret about classification. It takes us more closely to the center of the Matthiessen "problem," and it needs to be raised if we want to know, first, "what Matthiessen wrote," and, second, "what wrote Matthiessen," what were the literary/critical, social, and political forms and forces that propelled his work.

To take a case in point, one that I will address more fully in my first chapter: what is Matthiessen's relation to the New Criticism? How did it help to form his critical identity, and how, in turn, did he respond to, participate in, and fashion its discourse? Matthiessen, who came of age as a critic in the 1930s, both is and is not a New Critic, it seems to me. He often speaks as though he indubitably is; his masterwork, *American Renaissance*, "was written during the accession of the New Criticism" (Sutton 92); and he was familiar with the poetry and prose of Ransom, Tate, Warren, and others instrumental throughout the 1930s and 1940s in developing New Critical theory and practice. But early and late in his career, he also appears edgy and uncomfortable about the risks of critical and textual isolation that accompanied the New Criticism. Matthiessen was forever mindful of the acts of worldly attention that an unmonitored and unchecked New Criticism could discredit or deny. Perhaps this helps to account for the failure of Brooks and Wimsatt to mention Matthiessen—except in a footnote to a chapter on Ben Jonson and John Dryden!—in their mammoth history of literary criticism: they did not recognize him as one of their kin.

Looked at one way, Matthiessen's achievement was to learn from the New Critics' skills in "close reading" texts and then to supplement them with broader emphases on the individual and society and the "possibilities of democracy" (*American Renaissance* ix). He presents, one could propose, a fertile combination of historical knowledge and formalist criticism. He neither lapses into the dead-ening summaries of "backgrounds" that characterized the work of previous literary historians, nor does he exclusively spotlight the ambiguity of words and play of metaphors as do some of the New Critics and their followers.

This may sound persuasive at first hearing, but it is not really satisfactory. For it slides over what is in fact an unresolved tension in Matthiessen's work that is *there* in his writing, as responses to it frequently testify. In *Symbolism and American Literature* (1953), published a little more than a decade after *American Renaissance*, Charles Feidelson, Jr., observes that Matthiessen's book was "the first large-scale attempt to define the literary quality of American writing at its best." "Yet," he adds,

> even in this magnificent work, which reorients the entire subject, the sociological and political bent of studies in American literature makes itself felt indirectly. Despite Matthiessen's emphasis on literary form, his concern with the "artist's use of language" as "the most sensitive index to cultural history" tends to lead him away from specifically aesthetic problems. The "one common denominator" which he finds among the five writers treated in his book is not, in the final analysis, a common approach to the art of writing but a common theme—"their devotion to the possibilities of democracy." (3–4)

Compare this with the diagnosis given by Larzer Ziff in *Literary Democracy: The Declaration of Cultural Independence in America* (1981):

> F. O. Matthiessen's *American Renaissance* remains the standard work on the purely literary quality of the writings of the period. Subtitled "Art and Expression in the Age of Emerson and Whitman," his book analyzes the way in which the major writers (Poe excluded) fused form and content. Concerned with the aesthetics of American Romanticism, it does not deal with the cultural context of the works it examines. (viii)

"One sees what one brings," Henry Adams once reflected mordantly, and it may be that Feidelson and Ziff are simply perceiving ten-dencies in Matthiessen's seven-hundred-page book that bring into relief their own, different commitments. Nevertheless it is a significant index to something not directly addressed and worked through in Matthiessen that while Feidelson criticizes him for drifting into sociology and politics, Ziff admonishes him for sticking too much to purely literary and aesthetic issues. These contrasting judgments of *American Renaissance* highlight a dual aim on Matthiessen's part that he was not able to make cohere.

This conflict in *American Renaissance* is very similar to one that is evident in much criticism and scholarship today; and when we witness and explore it in Matthiessen, it may help to give an illuminating contemporary relevance to his work after all. In strict honesty, I cannot claim that *American Renaissance* and the other books necessarily will become excitingly animated again when seen from my perspective. But I do believe that what I have said will give them an educationally valuable, if limited, new life. Matthiessen has a noble ideal—an organic relation between the writing of literary criticism and the goal of a more "democratic" politics. It is an ideal of a scholarship that is truly serviceable to society, that seeks to mobilize critical and historical discoveries which bear on the reformation of the American scene.

It is also an ideal that hopes to blend two currents in American criticism. The first, beginning with Coleridge as an English source and reaching forward at its most authoritative to James and Eliot, is primarily aesthetic and formalist in its orientation; and the second, of perhaps more recent vintage and including Van Wyck Brooks, Parrington, Lewis Mumford, and, in his own boisterous fashion, H. L. Mencken, invests its energy in a search for a "usable past" that will rouse the nation from its literary and political lethargy. One current fosters an intelligent appreciation of art primarily for its own sake, for the special intensities it brings to experience. The other is more militant, its goal being to prompt Americans to see limiting conditions in the culture and to hear the liberal, progressive, visionary voices that assailed these conditions (and who perhaps may have been destroyed by them). The first is exaltedly high-minded but elitist, sometimes exasperatingly indifferent or even reactionary in its politics. The second is admirably populist—its sympathies are usually "for democracy," "for the people"—but it can also be crudely provincial and reductive, allegorizing art and artists, as Brooks does in his studies of Twain and James, in order to exhibit ailments in the society.

Particularly since the 1960s, critics and theorists have often been drawn to the second critical tradition, and have called for a more historically aware and socially responsible kind of literary study. Yet they have done so with only mixed success; and some of them have now sought to return to the formalist aims of the New Criticism or have sailed down certain streams of poststructuralism and deconstruction. Neither tradition has seemed wholly satisfactory. If you concentrate on the texts themselves "as works of art" (*American Renaissance* vii), you may achieve disciplined local insights at the expense of larger literary, social, and political generalizations. If, instead, you fix on a larger mission of reform or revolution, you may rather rapidly look like a fool—someone who hungers to do something he or she is not trained to do, someone who ends up in pools of muddled discourse, someone who reads badly and has moved away from specific texts before understanding them. You may, on the one hand, draw the verdict that your overrefined literary sensibility represents a flight from the demanding tests of political life. Or, on the other hand, you may be told that your political language and values are at odds with truly "literary" criticism—which seems to be the verdict that Wellek renders on Matthiessen's reference to "the possibilities of democracy" in *American Renaissance* when he gruffly declares it "a trivial conclusion obsessively repeated" (74).

There is, of course, a third alternative that insists on frequent transits between texts and contexts, circuitings between particular works of art and society, culture, history. Another way of evoking this alternative is to imagine a mind truly interested in, and able to appreciate, the virtues of both James and Dreiser, two writers who have served (and continue to serve) as focal points for debates about critical responsibility and literary judgment, sociopolitical relevance and artistic standards. Lionel Trilling criticized Matthiessen in "Reality in America" for aligning himself with the artistically crude Dreiser, but Matthiessen wrote about Dreiser *and* James. He saw the choice that Trilling sets out, "the dark and bloody crossroads where literature and politics meet" (24), and, in an act that was the opposite of an inert acceptance, he sought to choose both writers. I do not believe he succeeded in his efforts—which were balked, confused, and contradictory—to integrate criticism and politics. There were not only intellectual and imaginative barriers to these efforts, but also, no doubt, personal and institutional ones as well. But Matthiessen did strive toward an alternative—incompletely and intermittently glimpsed—that would somehow democratically harmonize hard conflicts and apparently competing choices. To his credit, he was dedicated to defining, though could not finally fashion, terms for American study.

Yet even this way of making the point is not entirely satisfactory, for perhaps it still does not wholly acknowledge the full power of the "organic" ideal Matthiessen celebrated and took as his guide for conduct. As part of the institutionalization of the New Criticism, the organic principle became a familiar term, but a reduced one that suggested primarily the organic relation between the form and content of a text; as one commentator on the critical scene put the matter as early as 1951, "organic unity" seemed to be serving as a "mere intensive" that connoted a poem had "lots of unity" (Benziger 24). For Matthiessen, and the critics and students whom he inspired, however, "organic" meant much more than this. It not only concerned the organization of the text itself, but also implied and evoked the whole relation between writer, work, and social context that classic texts aspired toward and dramatized. "The major desire" among all five authors treated in *American Renaissance* was, Matthiessen stresses, "that there should be no split between art and the other functions of the community, that there should be an organic union between labor and culture" (xiv–xv). Vitalized by the tonic injunctions of Emerson, Horatio Greenough, Whitman, and Louis Sullivan, Matthiessen sought to see American literature and art as the expression of a democratic people, and, furthermore, wished his own criticism and teaching to extend that expression so that it might live potently in the present. Matthiessen knew the English and European sources—Goethe, Coleridge, Schlegel, Wordsworth, and Carlyle—for the American writing he explored, and recognized their significant informing presence in Emerson and the rest. But he wanted to foreground the American translation of these sources and its distinctive casting—one that was eloquently democratic—of the organic tradition.

For Matthiessen, "organic" thus intimated natural bonds between the personal and the political, the literary and the social. Such a vision is, in many respects, surely a bracing and alluring one. It is an unalienated vision that imagines the writer, critic, and teacher as integrated with the society and culture. And it is a vision that

Matthiessen strove to fulfill in his life as a radical activist, endeavoring to realize the organic ideal in twentieth-century America. But the democratic sentiments and values which Matthiessen cherished, and which, to an extent, he embodied, did not emerge with full success, blocked as they were by both private and public resistances. Matthiessen felt the rightness of his ideal deeply, and he fought fiercely for it, yet he also seems, more deeply still, to have felt himself in opposition to it. Though he wanted to furnish literary study with political resonance and force, he also insisted on a formalist separation between art and politics, between the text in its own right (to be judged on its own terms) and the social/political contexts within which it developed and with which it might intersect. Criticism, for him, simultaneously did and did not have a social/political component, was organic yet unorganically grained and articulated. In a finely drawn distinction that led to vexing splits in his enterprise, Matthiessen maintained that critics should not be political but that they could nevertheless be politically inspired and politically relevant in their scholarly mission and findings. He made the case evocatively, but not without violating his organic ideal, assuming as he did that there would always be the critical imperative to examine literature as literature and that, consequently, a truly organic, integrated conception of literature and politics would at the outset inevitably have to be suspended or, worse, denied.

Ironies abound. One is that Matthiessen, a socialist, would look to T. S. Eliot, a royalist, as a compelling authority. Another is that he would dispute the narrowness of New Critical methodology, and also rebuke Agrarian conservatism, yet often sound decidedly like a New Critic himself in his remarks about his own approach to literature. Such ironies tell us something about conflicting tendencies in Matthiessen's work, but may point, too, toward the ambiguities of organicism as an ideal and empowering attitude. Eliot, the Agrarians, F. R. Leavis, and other critics whom Matthiessen read closely all embraced versions of an organic view, yet in each case their political assumptions diverged sharply from Matthiessen's: these men were not democrats. Matthiessen perceived himself in a line of democratic visionaries who regarded the organic society more capaciously and generously, and he aimed to incorporate their fortifying meanings of "organic" into literary study so that these would propel and promote liberal and radical goals. But he persisted in defining literary criticism basically as New Critical formalists did, and hence ended up dismantling a bridge between literature and politics even as he labored to build it. His work was heroic, tragic, admirable, but fissured by contradiction, limited by the temperament of the man himself, the historical conditions within which he lived and wrote, and the double-edged assumptions about literature, criticism, and politics he embraced. What were his strengths? His limitations? As we answer these questions, we can illuminate the rewarding but finally flawed—if widely shared—understanding of literary study to which Matthiessen's career bears painful witness.

ONE

Matthiessen and the New Criticism

> The poet perpetuates in his poem an order of existence which in actual life is constantly crumbling beneath his touch.
> —Ransom, *The World's Body* 348

A MEMORABLE MOMENT in *American Renaissance* occurs when Matthiessen examines Thoreau's "thinking in images" in "the best known passage" in *Walden*. Here is the passage, followed by Matthiessen's analysis of it:

"I went to the woods because I wished to live deliberately, to front only the essential facts of life, and see if I could not learn what it had to teach, and not, when I came to die, discover that I had not lived. I did not wish to live what was not life, living is so dear; nor did I wish to practice resignation, unless it was quite necessary. I wanted to live deep and suck out all the marrow of life, to live so sturdily and Spartan-like as to put to rout all that was not life, to cut a broad swath and shave close, to drive life into a corner, and reduce it to its lowest terms, and, if it proved to be mean, why then to get the whole and genuine meanness of it, and publish its meanness to the world; or if it were sublime, to know it by experience, and be able to give a true account of it in my next excursion."

The measured pace seems in exact correspondence with [Thoreau's] carefully measured thoughts, and serves, as effective rhythm always does, to direct the fullest attention to the most important words. The satisfaction that we have seen him taking in the feel of syllables in the muscles of his mouth and throat is carried across to us by the placing of "deliberately": as the first long word in the sentence, followed by a marked pause, it compels us to speak it as slowly as possible, and thus to take in its full weight: deliberate = *de* +

librare, to weigh. A kindred desire to bring out the closest possible relation between the sense of a word and its sound seems to operate in his placing of "resignation," for again the pause emphasizes its heavy finality. A clearer instance of his "philological" interest is the pun on "dear," which is not distracting since its basic sense of "beloved" is no less relevant than its transferred sense of "expensive." Hence it encompasses something of what Coleridge praised in the puns of the Elizabethans, a compressed and thereby heightened variety.

But the chief source of power here seems to lie in the verbs of action: "front," barer than the more usual "confront," is also more muscular. Behind Thoreau's use of it is his conviction that the only frontier is where a man fronts a fact. The extension of its range is reserved for the third sentence, where his metaphors shift rapidly but not in a way to interfere with one another, not until each has released its condensed charge. For the primitive act of sucking out the marrow is not incompatible with the military image, appropriate to this Spartan intensity, of putting to rout life's adversaries. And as the campaign returns from the enemy to the pursuit of the essence, both the range and pressure of Thoreau's desire are given fuller statement by the widened image of harvesting and the contracted image of closing in on a hunted quarry. With that final dramatic concentration, we are able to feel what it would really mean to reduce life to its lowest terms. The phrase is no longer a conventional counter since we have arrived at it through a succession of severe and exhilarating kinesthetic tensions. After which a characteristic turn for Thoreau is not to leave the impression of anything grim, but, by mentioning his "next excursion," to suggest its relaxed pleasure. (94–95)

Matthiessen does not remark on the insistent negatives with which Thoreau begins. Nor does he note the undercurrents of troublesome meaning that here, as often in *Walden*, Thoreau creates by laying words together that both give the reader an obvious sense and play against it. Thoreau plainly goes to the woods to learn what they have to teach, but the negative construction (which he could have avoided) pressures the reader to hear the words in an opposite direction—"and see if I could *not* learn." Thoreau loves to move the literal meaning of his sentences against their rhythm, so that he can prompt us to reflect upon the affiliations between language, action, and intention. He wishes to "learn," but he urges us to weigh how the language he uses to express this desire counters it. This exemplifies one facet of Thoreau's unsettling form of instruction. His aims and his language sometimes move at cross-purposes: words resist and cut against intention; language leads away from the deed's purpose.

Matthiessen also misses the potent pun in "excursion." The word, as he states, does evoke "relaxed pleasure," but this is only part of its meaning. "Excursion" also implies going beyond bounds, overstepping propriety; it signals Thoreau's repeated interest in testing limits. These limits concern not only the limits of behavior but those that pertain to discourse as well. "Excursion" also connotes a break or deviation in one's speech, a digression, a departure from custom and rule. Thoreau's enterprise in *Walden* ties together what he did with how he writes about it; and seen in this light, "excursion" does double duty, implying relaxation yet also a tense resounding of the behavioral and writerly risks entailed in the pursuits that Thoreau takes up. Excursions, too, have their demands and obligations; they can even be unpleasant, as anyone knows who has gone on a family vacation. Departures from the conventional path are not always easy and comfortable.

This is a modest supplement to the analysis given in *American Renaissance*, intended not to flag Matthiessen's shortcomings but, rather, to indicate the ever-enriching lines of thought about Thoreau that he encourages. One can feel in Matthiessen's own writing his enjoyment in responding to Thoreau as a craftsman, and in unfolding the verbal resources that the style of *Walden*, with its linkages to the Elizabethans, marvelously displays. Matthiessen is very close to the words on the page (he sounds their depths, down to their etymologies), and he controls his elucidation of Thoreau's art with a critical and literary/historical expertise that manages to retain, and convey to us, Matthiessen's own original enthusiasm as a gratified reader. What is exciting about criticism like this is that it teaches particular lessons about a complex work even as it deftly locates them within a more general statement of intersecting structural motives and patterns—Thoreau's "philological" interest, his fondness for puns and verbs of action, his interanimated vocabulary ("front" and "frontier," leading to "fronting a fact").

Yet deliberate analysis of this invigorating kind is rare in *American Renaissance*, and, for that matter, in Matthiessen's other books. It was Cleanth Brooks, in fact, who first noted a version of this when he observed about Matthiessen's study of Eliot that Matthiessen occasionally supplies astute readings of passages from *The Waste*

Land but "no complete consecutive examination of the poem" (136). It is surprising that he describes the verbal behavior of a writer's language so infrequently, given the maxim he sets out in the section on "method and scope" in *American Renaissance*: "The critic knows that any understanding of the subtle principle of life inherent in a work of art can be gained only by direct experience of it, again and again. The interpretation of what he has found demands close analysis, and plentiful instances from the works themselves" (xi). "Close analysis," however, is more policy than practice for Matthiessen; he can do it adroitly, as in the section about *Walden* and in a few other places, such as his commentary on the final chapter of *White Jacket* in *American Renaissance* (390–95). But he usually shies away from or maneuvers around it and attends to symbolism, thematic patterns, and influences, as when, in addressing *Moby Dick*, he provides "a kind of slow-moving picture" of the structure of the novel "as a whole" (417–21).

To make this observation marks one way of getting at Matthiessen's vexed relation to the New Criticism, surely the dominant Anglo-American critical movement in this century. *American Renaissance*, it is worth remembering, appeared in the same year, 1941, as did Ransom's *The New Criticism*, the book that named the pedagogical, critical, and disciplinary undertaking that had been developing throughout the 1920s and 1930s (Cain, *Crisis in Criticism* 85–103; Graff). Though committed to "close analysis," Matthiessen is apprehensive about the ways in which explication of texts can distract the critic from other, more urgent, kinds of work. Matthiessen sees something necessary but finally self-regarding about the close reading of texts. As he once said about R. P. Blackmur: this critic asks "the right questions" but is guilty of a "tedious overelaboration, as though he couldn't keep his fingers out of the dictionary" ("Record of Our Education" 285). Articulating how a writer handles language is important, but so, too, is guarding against a fussing about words that disserves art and prevents understanding of fundamental relationships between text and context, literary art and art conducted in other media, literature and life, criticism and history.

Matthiessen thus worries about the New Criticism and mostly refrains from lengthy explications, but is, at the same time, indebted to New Critical attitudes about literature, in particular the belief that the critic must focus on the work "as it is," as "an object in its own right." This is one of several key paradoxes that cause problems in Matthiessen's criticism. This is also why it is both accurate and inaccurate to describe *American Renaissance* as "the first study of American literature to apply New Critical analytic tools to American writing as a whole" (Reising 170).

Of course there is another way to look at this paradox. One could maintain that Matthiessen capitalizes upon, yet is not bound by, the New Criticism. He is not a pure New Critic, is more of a historian, and is, furthermore—unlike the reactionary New Critics—a man of the left. These things are basically true, but Matthiessen never quite unified his disparate loyalties in his critical practice. As I hope to show in this book, he is not a socialist cultural historian, but a socialist *and* a historian *and* a New Critic—each of these identities exists in uneasy relation to the others.

On one important point, the not-quite-New Critical Matthiessen was correct: whatever its strengths, the New Criticism did not deal well with history. It did not manage to connect its skills for "close reading" particular texts with the study of historical contexts. Defenders of the New Criticism, to be sure, deny that the New Critics "left out" history, and hence they might quarrel with the dissenting role to which I partially want to assign Matthiessen. René Wellek, for example, contends that "the New Criticism embraces a total historical scheme, believes in a philosophy of history, and uses it as a standard of judgment" (148). Yet Wellek is not replying to the exact antihistorical charge that Matthiessen directed against the New Criticism. It is one thing to say that the New Critics exhibit in their books and essays an abiding concern for historical traditions. But this differs from agreeing that the New Critics truly established ties between literary and nonliterary history, between texts and the specific social, economic, and political conditions from which they emerged.

As Wellek reminds us, the founders of the New Criticism often did write "about" history. Allen Tate, for instance, authored biographies of Stonewall Jackson (1928) and Jefferson Davis (1929) and a vivid novel, *The Fathers* (1938), about the pre–Civil War South, and Robert Penn Warren has produced a body of work in prose and poetry that includes a biography of John Brown (1929); a "tale in verse and voices"—*Brother to Dragons* (1953, 1979)—that depicts the Kentucky frontier; studies of the Civil War and segregation; and novels like *All the King's Men* (1946) that are anchored in American history. No one could accurately say that Tate and Warren, or Ransom or Brooks, are uninterested in historical subjects, controversies, crises. But all of this does not amount to proving that the New Critics actually sought to bond close reading *to* history and invested their energies in defining how critics and teachers could effectively contextualize their forays in explication. This is what the New Critics and their successors overlooked; this explains why Matthiessen noted the absence of "history" from New Critical theory and practice.

Admittedly, many today sell the New Critics short, underestimating their advance beyond earlier scholars and critics, especially in the academy, and forgetting that Ransom and the others had to fight for what we now take for granted. We do not often recall, in the midst of oppositional sallies against the New Criticism, that it was very much an oppositional movement itself in the 1930s and 1940s. A colleague once remarked to me that when he read *Understanding Poetry* soon after its publication in 1938, he found the experience thrilling and angering, for it made him realize how badly his own professional training in fact-based literary history had served him. The New Critics stood against philology, impressionism, and source-and-influence hunting. Even more, they stood steadfastly against Marxism and the New Humanism, both of which threatened to make art captive to dogma and doctrine. It is worth recalling, too, that the core group of New Critics did not undertake many "close readings" themselves. You could read many essays by Tate and Ransom before locating one that dedicates its main attention to analyzing "the words on the page" in the lemon-squeezing fashion we associate with New Critical exegesis. There are, of course, exemplary "close readings" in Blackmur's criticism, and plentiful evidence of detailed textual scrutiny in such English brethren of the New Critics as Richards, Empson, and Leavis. But the New Critics are significant less for the practical criticism they sometimes did—and which Matthiessen both drew upon and disputed—than for the assumptions about criticism and literary study that they propagated and popularized—and which Matthiessen shared.

A very interesting line can be drawn from the writings of the Agrarians in the late 1920s and early 1930s to the writings of the New Critics in the late 1930s; and we need to trace it in order better to understand Matthiessen's own ambiguous position in the history of modern criticism and its institutionalization. Roughly speaking, this line extends from Ransom's essays on Agrarianism and *I'll Take My Stand: The South and the Agrarian Tradition* (1930) to Ransom's *The World's Body* (1938)—which "formally launched" the New Criticism—and Brooks and Warren's *Understanding Poetry* (1938; rev. ed. 1950), the book that "revolutionized the way literature is taught in the classroom" (Young 408, 411; cf. Bradbury 134). In the earlier, Agrarian work, whatever its flaws and ideological errors, Ransom and his colleagues seek an integrated critical enterprise that is as much social and cultural (and explicitly so) as it is literary. In the later work, they limit themselves to literary criticism, particularly as it should be taught in colleges and universities. Much of our present difficulty in making criticism socially responsible and historically sound—it was Matthiessen's difficulty, too—stems from the New Critics' narrowing of their original aims.

It would not have been a simple matter for Ransom and the others to win acceptance for cultural studies rather than English studies. But whether the causes were primarily personal, institutional, or political, what we witness when we look backward to the 1930s is a reduction of scope. In developing sensitive instruments for reading texts, the New Critics gave "English" a strong statement of purpose and self-definition. But in doing this, the New Critics sacrificed something else—the "general" criticism they envisioned in their Agrarian books and essays. And it was such a general criticism, which included but did not confine itself to *literary* criticism, that Matthiessen wanted to fashion even as he resolutely aligned himself with New Critical principles. Like the New Critics, he stressed in the 1930s and afterward the "close study" of texts and sought to rescue art from disfiguring ideologies. Like them, as I will explain in more detail in the next chapter, he learned much from T. S. Eliot, seeing this eminent poet-critic as his central guide and inspiration. Matthiessen also knew the New Critics (and Eliot) personally, published often in their journals (*Kenyon Review, Sewanee Review*, and *Southern Review*), and, along with Ransom and Lionel Trilling, was one of the founders and first fellows of the Kenyon School of English that was established in 1948 (Webster 105–6). But Matthiessen made clear that he did not wish critics to become so restricted in their perceptions and in their understanding of their role that they failed to see how art figured in society and how the close study of literary texts led to cultural history.

Cultural history is very much what the Agrarians themselves wrote in *I'll Take My Stand* (which appeared about the time Matthiessen was starting his teaching career at Harvard). Hardly an unequivocal success, the Agrarians' book is dreamily deluded and offensive in many respects, mixing its bracingly radical criticisms with nasty reactionary sentiments. There is, for example, a notable air of unreality to Ransom's depictions of those southern "farms and native provinces" that distinguished life before the North unleashed its military/industrial dragons during and after the Civil War. As John L. Stewart has pointed out, the Agrarians failed—and Ransom conceded as much later in his life—"to provide a substantial and believable image of life on a Southern farm that was capable of satisfying to the degree they claimed for it the spirit and aspirations of man" (131). Ransom and the others also inclined toward polarities—North and South, reason and sensibility, industrialism and farming, prose and poetry—that transformed history into an allegorical scheme. And the attitudes toward slavery and race relations expressed in some of the essays, notably in Frank Owsley's "The Irrepressible Conflict" (*I'll Take My Stand* 61–91), are ugly. Even Ransom was capable of remarking, in a 1934 essay on "the esthetic of regionalism," that "the darkey," like the climate, "is one of the bonds that make a South out of all the Southern regions" (119).

The Agrarians also did not understand the drift of the South to which they preached: they did not perceive that their audience had already converted to industrialism and the materialism of the "New South" creed. In evoking and appealing for rural communities and farming as a vocation, a way of life like that they had known at the turn of the century when they were growing up, the Agrarians were fighting for a lost cause that failed to match up with the realities of the contemporary South:

> The Agrarians never spelled out the balance they wanted between agriculture and industry or urban and rural life, or explained how an agrarian South could be insulated from forces of nationalization, standardization, and industrialization. They never grappled realistically with the problems of the rural South—not even tenancy, one-crop agriculture, poor health, and poor housing, to say nothing of racial and class prejudice, religious bigotry, illiteracy, violence, and dema-

goguery, all of which tended to correlate with the degree of ruralism. (Newby 451)

The South of the 1930s was afflicted with economic problems that the Agrarian appeal for small, independent farmers could not answer:

> By the mid-thirties nearly seventy-five per cent of the farmers in the South were sharecroppers or tenants, with eighty per cent of these Negroes; sharecropping which was increasing yearly was in reality a subtle form of enslavement rather than a step toward farm ownership; at this time the mass of Southern sharecroppers in cotton country could no longer manage to be even moderately efficient with the pro-verbial "forty acres and a mule." (Rock 429)

The reviews of *I'll Take My Stand* by the southern as well as the northern press were generally hostile, and events during the depression years quickly outpaced the Agrarians' arguments and proposals. "Within a few years' time," the New Deal "so changed the relationship of government and of economic and social planning to the problems and possibilities of southern life that many of the specific hypotheses upon which the essays of *I'll Take My Stand* had been predicated had been significantly altered" (Rubin 206).

Despite these grave failings, the notion of criticism that *I'll Take My Stand* manifests is generally an admirable one. In its critique if not in its prescriptions, it is a rich contribution to southern literature and to American conservative thought. The essays gathered in the book, which itself first took shape as a response to attacks upon southern beliefs and values by Joseph Wood Krutch, H. L. Mencken, and other Northerners during the 1925 Scopes trial, total up to "a scathing criticism of the dehumanizing consequences produced in a society organized around an industrial mode of production" (Havard 419–20). In the introduction, Ransom—he wrote the draft of the introduction, though it did undergo some revision by the others—attacks the "Cult of Science" and presents an interesting account of the modern degradation of labor:

> The contribution that science can make to a labor is to render it easier by the help of a tool or a process, and to assure the laborer of his perfect economic security while he is engaged upon it. Then it can be performed with leisure and enjoyment. But the modern laborer has

not exactly received this benefit under the industrial regime. His labor is hard, its tempo is fierce, and his employment is insecure. The first principle of a good labor is that it must be effective, but the second principle is that it must be enjoyed. Labor is one of the largest items in the human career; it is a modest demand to ask that it may partake of happiness. (xl)

The bad "tempo" of labor, Ransom contends, brutalizes thought and hardens feeling. Men are forced by industrialism either to labor or to consume goods; they have no time for leisure and contemplation, and their religion and art suffer as a result:

> Religion can hardly expect to flourish in an industrial society. Religion is our submission to the general intention of a nature that is fairly inscrutable; it is the sense of our role as creatures within it. But nature industrialized, transformed into cities and artificial habitations, manufactured into commodities, is no longer nature but a highly simplified picture of nature. . . . Nor do the arts have a proper life under industrialism, with the general decay of sensibility which attends it. Art depends, in general, like religion, on a right attitude to nature; and in particular on a free and disinterested observation of nature that occurs only in leisure. Neither the creation nor the understanding of works of art is possible in an industrial age except by some local and unlikely suspension of the industrial drive. (xlii–xliii)

Some of this is quaint, such as the note about nature "transformed into cities and artificial habitations." And a key shortcoming to Ransom's analysis is evident in his focus on industrialism rather than capitalism (Fekete 69–70): he and the others object to industrial blight, not to class privilege and private property and ownership, which are the underpinnings of industrialism. His critique did not burrow deeply enough, largely because the Agrarians were at odds as much with the socialist theorizing of leftist groups as with the celebrants of the new industrial South. Allen Tate and Robert Penn Warren, in fact, were determined not to give comfort to Communists and socialists, and they attempted to change the title of the volume to *Tracts against Communism*. Tate later made clear just how at odds were Communism and Agrarianism in his mind: "The communist solution doesn't lend itself to the South. Communism does not grow out of rural life" (Cutrer, "Conference on Literature and Reading" 271). One can hardly wish that the Agrarians had turned

Red; indeed, their opposition to Communism, during a period when many intellectuals were hymning the Soviet experiment, is rather refreshing. But the Agrarians' focus on industrialism was askew; they wanted to maintain systems and distinctions that were entangled with the conditions they loathed.

This to the side, Ransom's insistence on the economic bedrock of the culture remains forceful and positive. Speaking from a conservative position, his indictment of capitalism converges intriguingly at moments with a leftist critique—which helps to explain in part why Matthiessen readily found features in the Agrarian/New Critics' arguments that he could endorse. "The trouble with the life-pattern," Ransom continues,

> is to be located at its economic base, and we cannot rebuild it by pouring in soft materials from the top. The young men and women in colleges, for example, if they are already placed in a false way of life, cannot make more than an inconsequential acquaintance with the arts and humanities transmitted to them. Or else the understanding of these arts and humanities will but make them the more wretched in their own destitution. . . . We cannot recover our native humanism by adopting some standard of taste that is critical enough to question the contemporary arts but not critical enough to question the social and economic life which is their ground. (xliii–xliv)

Ransom's argument, especially the final sentence, is astonishing; these are the sorts of things he regularly said in the days before he became a New Critic. Compare what Ransom says here with his words in the preface to *The World's Body*, published just eight years later:

> Where is the body and solid substance of the world? It seems to have retired into the fulness of memory, but out of this we construct the fulness of poetry, which is counterpart to the world's fulness.
>
> The true poetry has no great interest in improving or idealizing the world, which does well enough. It only wants to realize the world, to see it better. . . . Men become poets, or at least they read poets, in order to atone for having been hard practical men and hard theoretical scientists. (x–xi)

By 1938, Ransom had turned his attention from the "economic base" that seemed crucial to him in 1930 and toward poetry, which provides occasions for acts of atonement. Poetry, Ransom suggests, restores memories of a nature that men violate in their daily occupations: we cannot hope to change the world, but at least we can express sorrow for what we have done and will continue to do to it. Here and elsewhere, Ransom describes his views about poetry elegantly. But he gave up too much as he sought to distance himself from his Agrarian views, moving farther from his "original position" than any of the others (Rock 418). It was better—deeper and more decisive—to speak, as he did before, about the economy and culture in general and their relation to literature. In *I'll Take My Stand*, Ransom's terms have more resonance because he situates them in a richer, if problematic, context. His angle of vision is wider: he sees more possibilities for criticism and its polemical and recuperative powers.

By the time of *The World's Body*, Ransom judges society to be beyond redemption. Society is degraded, but somehow we must learn to live within it and adjust to its mechanized momentum. What we have is poetry, a sacramentalized tactic for accommodating ourselves to a sadly scarred world. It is the mission of literary men in colleges and universities to be responsive to poetry and to teach young people to do the same in college and university classrooms. As "Criticism, Inc.," the concluding essay in *The World's Body*, testifies, criticism is now to mean an academic discipline. Criticism engages the verbal economy of poems, not an "economic base" that conceivably could clarify the poetry men and women write and the opportunities they do or do not have for contemplative reading. Academics should "professionalize" criticism, Ransom maintains, and identify their "product" as the "close analysis" of literary texts.

> It is really atrocious policy for a department to abdicate its own self-respecting identity. The department of English is charged with the understanding and the communication of literature, an art, yet it has usually forgotten to inquire into the peculiar constitution and structure of its product. . . . Strategy requires now, I should think, that criticism receive its own charter of rights and function independently. (335, 346)

What precisely should members of English departments do? What is involved in true literary criticism?

> Studies in the technique of the art belong to criticism certainly. They cannot belong anywhere else, because the technique is not peculiar to any prose materials discoverable in the work of art, nor to anything else but the unique form of that art. A very large volume of studies is indicated by this classification. They would be technical studies of poetry, for instance, the art I am specifically discussing, if they treated its metric; its inversions, solecisms, lapses from the prose norm of language, and from close prose logic; its tropes; its fictions, or inventions, by which it secures "aesthetic distance" and removes itself from history; or any other devices, on the general understanding that any systematic usage which does not hold good for prose is a poetic device. (346–47)

"Removes itself from history" is the crucial phrase. All of the things that Ransom names are essential to an analysis of a poem, but why is it necessary that poetic fictions be perceived as "removed" from history? The implications are alarming, not only because the historical circumstances of a text would seem, at the least, one of its central elements. Even more, what about the history of the late 1930s, the period in which Ransom is defining a certain style of criticism and identifying special values for the study of poetry? What about economic depression at home and abroad, the Fascist menace, the cultural and political impact of the Popular Front? One could slant Ransom's paragraph differently, and could return it to the emphases of *I'll Take My Stand*, if one asked: How are poems situated in history? How do they fictionalize history? How do historical forces shape the types of "aesthetic distance" that writers and literary movements favor and employ? How do poems teach us about history, and do so in a fashion that distinguishes them from prose works? What is it about a certain history that leads poets (and critics) to wish to remove poems from it? How do the vocabularies and values of commerce and business enter into poetry and criticism? How, finally, do poems exist in, and influence our understanding of, the present—the history in which we live (and which we make) as we read, discuss, debate, and appraise them?

By not raising these questions and others like them, and by divorcing literary criticism from social-cultural criticism, Ransom and the New Critics launched "English" on the course which Matthiessen both resisted and reinforced. Their arguments made an immediate sense as an alternative to New Humanism, philology, and varieties of Marxism afloat in the 1930s. These arguments, however, were guaranteed to produce—and rapidly they did produce—unfortunate consequences. Ransom and his colleagues established a set of explicative skills (which revolutionized pedagogy) and criteria for professional competence and expertise, but not a rationale for criticism in a broadly meaningful sense. They brought about the triumph of technique, one that triggered a managerial revolution within English studies, simultaneously consolidating the discipline and restricting it. "Criticism" meant *literary* criticism only.

That this statement is not too strong becomes clear from a reading of Ransom's interesting letters of the late 1930s, where he emphasizes that it is a strictly literary enterprise to which he now seeks to devote himself. To Edwin Mims, Ransom states that he has "contributed all I have" to regionalism and agrarianism and has "of late gone almost entirely into pure literature. . . . At my time of life it seems legitimate for me to work at literature a little more single-mindedly than I have been doing" (8 June 1937; *Selected Letters* 223). A few months later, writing to Allen Tate, he relates his desire, in the new "Review" he is hoping to inaugurate at Kenyon College, "to stick to literature entirely," adding that "there's no consistent group writing politics. . . . In the severe field of letters there is vocation enough for us: in criticism, in poetry, in fiction" (4 November 1937; *Selected Letters* 233). Again writing to Tate, this time about his 1941 book *The New Criticism*, Ransom insists that he wants to "repel any idea of a 'political' strategy behind it. I wanted it to have *no politics at all*" (23 May 1941; *Selected Letters* 282). In view of the superb work that Ransom did, and, too, of the impressive issues of the *Kenyon Review* that he and his colleagues and friends prepared, it is hard to quarrel too much with his taut appeal for purely literary studies. But the achievements of the New Critics, made possible by this highly focused commitment, did exact a cost. Something important was gained, much was lost.

One need only glance at the "Postscript" to the 1950 edition of Brooks and Warren's *Understanding Poetry*—the book Ransom cited as a "monument" to "the Age of Criticism" ("Teaching of Poetry" 80, 81)—to grasp what the New Critics had wrought. Committed to the principle, expressed in the 1938 "Letter to the Teacher," that critics should stick to "the poem in itself, if literature is to be studied as literature" (xi), Brooks and Warren find themselves in a bind when they ponder "What Good is Poetry?" To students, this is the ultimate question, and it of course bears on the entire point of embarking upon literary criticism and work in the academic discipline of "English." But in framing the definition of poetry and criticism as they do, Brooks and Warren disable their efforts to deal with the question.

Brooks and Warren contend, first, that poetry organizes itself differently from science. They then offer a lengthy quotation from Bertrand Russell about the practical "power-knowledge" that informs the scientist's statements and activities. The remainder of Brooks and Warren's answer consists of vague assertions about the compensatory manner in which poetry ministers to us when we are not about our daily business. We have "other interests and impulses," the authors insist:

> Why and how good poetry, and good literature in general, give a fuller satisfaction to these impulses and interests is a matter which can best be stated in connection with concrete examples before us, and the attempt in this book to state this matter will be gradually developed by the study of examples. But the fundamental point, namely, that poetry has a basis in common human interests, must not be forgotten at the beginning of any attempt to study poetry. (lvi)

It is fine to profess that poetry satisfies "impulses and interests" and dovetails with aspects of "common" experience. But since Brooks and Warren have urged throughout their preceding discussion that texts should be analyzed "in themselves," they do not possess a language for speaking about a poem except in a self-enclosed fashion: they cannot get outside the poem's language to other languages that might delineate and contextualize the "impulses" and "interests" and hence explain convincingly why poetry is "good."

Like Ransom in "Criticism, Inc.," Brooks and Warren evade the basic issue in the guise of engaging it: their notion of what criticism "is" puts it beyond their grasp. "The question of the value of poetry," Brooks and Warren conclude,

> is to be answered by saying that it springs from a basic human impulse and fulfills a basic human interest. To answer the question finally, and not immediately, one would have to answer the question as to the value of those common impulses and interests. But that is a question

which lies outside of the present concern. As we enter into a study of poetry it is only necessary to see that poetry is not an isolated and eccentric thing, but springs from the most fundamental interests which human beings have. (lvi)

This is what Brooks and Warren leave teachers and students with —reiterated terms and dodged questions. They locate "outside" the boundaries of their discussion probably the most pressing question of all, and the one that they supposedly have been tackling: what, finally, *is* the "value" of poetry?

These passages from *Understanding Poetry* are worth lingering over as a critical credo that Matthiessen—who "not only approved of *Understanding Poetry* but immediately adopted it and profited by it in his own classroom" (Cutrer, *Parnassus* 185)—both abided by and opposed. *Understanding Poetry* demonstrates that the New Criticism had put itself in the awkward position of being unable to justify criticism. To justify it, the critic would need to have recourse to social, ethical, and other kinds of terms that a concentrated literary-critical focus "on the page" prohibits.

Brooks and Warren had taken a different tack in their editorial duties for the *Southern Review*. When Brooks sent out his first letter to potential contributors in 1935, he stated that he and Warren were seeking "to provide a large quarterly which will be a ready index to the most vital contemporary activities in fiction, poetry, criticism, and social-political thought, with an adequate representation in each of the departments" (quoted in Cutrer, *Parnassus* 52). Brooks and Warren sought the "best voices" in both literature and politics, and despite their own Agrarian sympathies, they published ample material that was neither southern nor conservative in its orientation —so much so that some of their Agrarian comrades complained to them about the direction of the magazine. The *Southern Review* under Brooks and Warren was, in a word, a more multifaceted journal than the one that Ransom later established at Kenyon. They assumed that educated readers would want stimulating essays and reviews about society and politics as well as short fiction, critical pieces, and poetry. Brooks and Warren, as Thomas Cutrer aptly remarks, "engineered debates among the best minds representing all sides of an argument, thus revealing the strengths and weaknesses of contending political and literary dogmas" (*Parnassus* 78–79). The range of the theory and practice of the *Southern Review* brings out the undue limits of what Brooks and Warren envisioned for the classroom in *Understanding Poetry*.

For a final indication of the price of the New Criticism for pedagogy and criticism in general, compare "Criticism, Inc." and the "Postscript" to *Understanding Poetry* with the views that Donald Davidson sketches in his contribution to *I'll Take My Stand*:

> Under ideal circumstances education can probably accomplish a great deal, and even under the worst handicaps it produces intangible results in which we can well afford to rejoice. However, again we encounter the old difficulty. Education can do comparatively little to aid the cause of the arts as long as it must turn out graduates into an industrialized society which demands specialists in vocational, technical, and scientific subjects. The humanities, which could reasonably be expected to foster the arts, have fought a losing battle since the issue between vocational and liberal education was raised in the nineteenth century. (37)

Davidson mounts a direct assault on industrial society, the performance of the humanities, and the educational system as a whole. He has a shrewd, disturbing insight into the dilemmas that the humanist faces in a world dedicated to science and specialization. Today, he observes, the humanities either

> will appear as decorative and useless to the rising generations who know that poetry sells no bonds and music manages no factories, and hence will be taken under duress or enjoyed as a pleasant concession to the softer and more frivolous side of life. Or, the more successfully they indoctrinate the student with their values, the more unhappy they will make him. For he will be spoiled for industrial tasks by being rendered inefficient. He will not fit in. The more refined and intelligent he becomes, the more surely will he see in the material world the lack of the image of nobility and beauty that the humanities inculcate in him. The product of a humanistic education in an industrial age is most likely to be an exotic, unrelated creature—a disillusionist or a dilettante. Lastly, there is the almost overwhelming difficulty of communicating the humanities at all under systems of education, gigantic in their scope, that have become committed to industrial methods of administration—the entire repulsive fabric of standards, credits, units, scientific pedagogy, over-organization. (38)

Davidson inveighs in 1930 against the very educational structure within which Ransom, Brooks, and Warren will seek to lodge English as "Criticism, Inc." They will still claim to resist science and industrialism, but, as the only half-ironic title of Ransom's essay betrays, their vocabulary and orientation will become geared toward the administrative and bureaucratic terms which, as Agrarians, they despised.

Davidson remained an unreconstructed Agrarian whose racial views were still woeful as late as the 1950s: he is not a figure one can wholeheartedly admire (Rock 262–67, 433–37, 482–83). But he does show us a crucial failing of the New Criticism. The unsettling truth seems to be not merely that the New Critics gave up something when they left Agrarianism behind. They appear in addition to have taken strides toward an embrace of the enemy, filtering their notion of criticism, the English department, and the academic discipline through commercial and professional/managerial values that they once strove to delegitimize and displace. Interestingly, Davidson urged teachers and critics to take their cue from the Victorian sages, who were "drawn irresistibly toward social criticism" and committed to remake "the conditions of life." "Industrialism can be deposed as the regulating god of modern society," he declares (50, 51). The later New Critics pretty much accepted these "conditions," and, through an upgraded and marketable commodity, labored to make the best of a bad situation.

Somewhat like the Agrarians, Matthiessen aspired toward social/ cultural goals that incorporated literature and criticism. As a Christian socialist, he dedicated his life's work to fighting against the industrial-capitalist order and all that it had done to all aspects of life. Yet in his actual academic and critical activity, Matthiessen placed himself in a literary and political fix. Refusing to allow his politics to propel his critical agenda, he put the critical agenda first, making the formalist approach and method his central focus. He claimed to be moving beyond the disabling apolitical and ahistorical limitations set by formalism; and he made this claim even as he persistently invoked and remained obeisant to New Critical, formalist principles. As we shall see, Matthiessen insisted upon the essential rightness of these principles while lamenting their consequences, as though the two didn't go hand-in-hand, as though the consequences did not flow inevitably from the principles themselves.

This paradox in Matthiessen's conception of criticism runs throughout his work, though signs of its disrupting effects start to become manifest in the books he wrote in the 1940s. I now turn to the beginnings of his scholarly career, where his literary attitudes and allegiances can be seen emerging, and where his indebtedness to T. S. Eliot is pronounced. Eliot's authority, established early, never really waned for Matthiessen or for the New Critics whom Eliot influenced. It did not even subside for Matthiessen in the 1940s when his painful response to the American and international political scene intensified, and when he found himself, as a result, disconcertingly at odds with Henry James (whose sensibility Eliot so esteemed) and in surprising, if uncomfortable, alliance with Dreiser.

TWO

The Labor of Translation: From Sarah Orne Jewett to T. S. Eliot

The important thing, as Richards has reaffirmed, is "not what a poem says, but what it *is*."

—*The Achievement of T. S. Eliot* 110

FOR ANY ASSESSMENT of Matthiessen's work, it is important to set down some biographical details. Matthiessen was born in 1902 in Pasadena, California. His father, Fredric William Matthiessen, Jr., never settled upon a career and moved his family frequently. His mother, however, often managed to stay, with her four children (Francis Otto was the third son and the youngest child), in her father-in-law's home in La Salle, Illinois. This father-in-law, Frederich Wilhelm Matthiessen, an interesting figure in his own right, had arrived in America in 1850 as a poor immigrant and proceeded to become a multimillionaire factory owner. Francis Otto's youth in La Salle led him to view himself as a "small town boy" from "the mid-west" (Summers and Summers 559), and later in his life, he pointed to his lack of knowledge as a young man of Parkman's *La Salle and the Discovery of the Great West* as an "appalling" sign of what was absent from his early education. "No school that I attended," he observed, "went at all imaginatively into the American past" (*From the Heart of Europe* 73–74).

After spending four years at Hackley School in Tarrytown, New York, Matthiessen went on to Yale, graduating in 1923, and then studied at Oxford as a Rhodes Scholar. He completed his advanced training at Harvard very quickly, receiving his M.A. in 1926 and his Ph.D. in 1927. Except for an early two-year stint at Yale as an instructor (1927–29), he spent his entire teaching career at Harvard, serving as a member of the English department and as a tutor in history and literature. One of the numerous intriguing facts of Matthiessen's career is that he led a life of privilege and distinction at major institutions yet was a radical in both political theory and practice. At Yale, when still an undergraduate, he had heard Norman Thomas and, more important, Eugene Debs speak. Matthiessen was inspired by their rhetoric, and felt a special admiration for Debs's capacity, as a socialist leader, "to command a mass movement" (*From the Heart of Europe* 76). Matthiessen was a leader himself at Yale, one of the "prophets" and "rebels" who in 1922 stirred up lively debates on campus by protesting against the disorganized curriculum and apathetic student body. "Short, compact, powerful," and "speaking with characteristic lunge and confidence," Matthiessen "attacked paternalism and materialism all along the line" (Pierson 61).

During his student days, Matthiessen had also responded deeply to Tawney's *The Acquisitive Society*, a book he came across by accident when doing a report for an economics class. He claimed that "there could have been no luckier opening of the door into social theory": "Tawney's ideas about equality have remained more living for me than anything else, except Shakespeare, that I read at college" (*From the Heart of Europe* 72). His reading and political friendships at Yale may also have helped to sharpen his sense of the dangers of wealth which his father's life had epitomized (Hyde 386–87). Matthiessen's father had been raised as a rich boy, had wasted his life, and had eventually deserted his wife and children, and this example of corruption doubtless spurred the son's disciplined attitude toward his work and his steady movement to the left. It was not until the late 1940s, near the end of his life, that Matthiessen managed a partial reconciliation with his father.

While a teacher at Harvard during the 1930s and 1940s, the intensely political Matthiessen worked vigorously for a host of radical causes. He was a key member of the Harvard Teachers' Union, serving as its vice-president when the Union was founded in 1935 and as one of its representatives to the Boston Central Labor Union, the Massachusetts State Council of Teachers Union, the Massachusetts Federation of Labor, and the American Federation of Teachers. He campaigned tirelessly for the Progressive party, and presented one of the seconding speeches for Henry Wallace's nomination in 1948. There is much more that could be noted, but maybe the most cogent piece of evidence is the list of defense committees and organizations to which Matthiessen belonged. This list was published as a political smear in the *Boston Herald* just two days after Matthiessen's suicide in 1950:

> American Russian Institute, American Committee for the Protection of the Foreign Born, Artists' Front to Win the War, American Youth for Democracy, Citizens' Committee to Free Earl Browder, Civil Rights Congress, Committee for Citizenship Rights, Committee for a Democratic Far Eastern Policy, Committee for Equal Justice for Mrs. Recy Taylor, Committee to Sponsor the Daily Worker, Committee of Welcome for the Very Reverend Hewlett Johnson, Conference on Constitutional Liberties in America, Defense of Communist Schools, Denunciation of the Hartley Committee, Educators for Wallace, Friends of Italian Democracy, National Council of Arts Sciences and Professions, National Federation for Constitutional Liberties, New Masses, New Masses Dinner Committee, Open Letter for Closer Cooperation with the Soviet Union, Samuel Adams School for Social Studies, Schappes Defense Committee, Sleepy Lagoon Defense Committee, Supporters for Samuel Wallach, Testimonial Dinner to Carol King, Veterans of the Abraham Lincoln Brigade, Win-the-Peace Conference, Writers for Wallace. (Sweezy 74)

Clearly Matthiessen did what he could in his life to oppose political injustice and economic inequality. Some have judged him pathetically naive—above all in his inability or unwillingness to assail Stalinism in the 1940s—and they have remarked that his commitment to socialist solidarity may simply reflect an effort to relieve his loneliness. Some have commented, too, on the somewhat strained manner in which Matthiessen tried to be a Christian as well as a socialist; and I think there is a problem here, as I will argue in Chapter 4. But there have been other Christian socialists besides Matthiessen. The link is not intrinsically perverse; Tawney himself, whatever his final verdict on Christianity in *Religion and the Rise of Capitalism*, maintained that Christ's lessons of love in the Gospels could empower a socialist mission. Like everybody else, Matthiessen made bad judgments in his politics, but to say this differs from impugning his motives or tallying up his activities as the manifestation of a psychological need (they could be that, but also more than that). For my purposes, what counts is that Matthiessen held certain socialist principles, acted as his conscience instructed him, and often risked much in publicly fighting for unpopular causes.

Matthiessen was also homosexual, which made him aware of another set of limits to personal choice and social freedom, and sensitive to another form of injustice and inequality (White, " 'Have I Any Right' "). He had met the painter Russell Cheney in 1924 on his return voyage to England for his second year as a Rhodes scholar, and these two men spent their lives together as lovers until Cheney's death in 1945. Their letters, which were published in 1978, are sometimes embarrassing to read—who would expect otherwise about love letters?—but Matthiessen's frequently reveal an admirable strength and courage. They do exhibit gushes of sentiment, yet they are also tough-minded, persistent, and persevering—Matthiessen is zealously determined to carry his and Cheney's love through hard times and tensions. His fondness for Whitman's poetry also comes through in the letters; his language is akin to that found in *Leaves of Grass*, and it displays a similarly elated passion and overwhelming of boundaries. Here is one example, taken from a 1925 letter in which he expresses how his love for Cheney (nicknamed "Rat") vitalizes his consciousness of the English landscape in springtime:

> I bicycled twenty miles this morning through fallow rolling hills with an occasional glimpse of the sea. It was soft and balmy, and the rooks kept up a constant racket in the treetops. Being alone, I could feel my heart swelling like the seeds in the ground, and I kept shouting over and over to the wind: "Rat, Rat, my God feller how I love you." I felt my life absolutely expressed in the fulness of the spring: every opportunity in the world, energy and hope abundant, and the road leading straight ahead and true with you. I realize that in these last months I am a whole man for the first time: no more dodging or repressing for we gladly accept what we are. And sex now instead of being a nightmare is the most sacred, all-embracing gift we have. Now I can see, as this morning while riding along, a husky labouring feller asleep on a bank one hand lying heavy across his thighs, and I can thrill at the deep earthiness and blood of him. For I know that I am of blood and earth too, as well as of brain and soul, and that my whole self waits—and waits gladly—for you. (Hyde 115–16)

Matthiessen had begun to read Whitman, his "first big experience" of American literature, in 1923. The "Children of Adam" and "Calamus" poems were, he said, especially meaningful in teaching him "to trust the body," and he recalled "the excitement of starting to read the small edition [of Whitman] I had bought in London, in a dreary tearoom near the British museum" (*From the Heart of Europe* 23). The feeling, imagery, and rhythm of much of his phrasing seem to echo not only these groups of poems but also "Song of Myself":

> I mind how once we lay such a transparent summer morning,
> How you settled your head athwart my hips and gently turn'd over
> upon me,
> And parted the shirt from my bosom-bone, and plunged your tongue
> to my bare-stript heart,
> And reach'd till you felt my beard, and reach'd till you held my feet.
> (Lines 87–91)

> You will hardly know who I am or what I mean,
> But I shall be good health to you nevertheless,
> And filtre and fibre your blood.
> Failing to fetch me at first keep encouraged,
> Missing me one place search another,
> I stop somewhere waiting for you.
> (Lines 1341–47)

Aware of it or not, Matthiessen tapped his passionate reading of Whitman to voice his love for Cheney. He communicated, and indeed sought to embody, the sexual and emotional vibrancies of the poet's words. As a sign of the manner in which institutions encroach on the personal, it is worth noting that the authorities at Harvard denied Matthiessen permission to write his dissertation on Whitman. There was nothing more to be said about Whitman, he was told.

Matthiessen spoke lovingly about Cheney in *From the Heart of Europe* (22), and he had earlier prepared a "record" and catalogue of Cheney's work. But despite his glad acceptance of his love for Cheney, Matthiessen seems to have been extremely uncomfortable with his homosexuality, and sometimes he even goes oddly out of his way to speak disapprovingly about homosexual leanings expressed in literary texts. This is especially the case in the long chapter on Whitman in *American Renaissance*, which contains a number of puzzling rebukes of, and complaints about, the poet's sexuality. At one point, Matthiessen quotes the very lines 87–91 from "Song of Myself" I have cited above, in order to reprimand the immaturity of Whitman's attitudes. "Moreover," he adds, "in the passivity of the poet's body there is a quality vaguely pathological and homosexual" (535). Matthiessen cannot engage this aspect of Whitman's verse except to criticize it or distance himself from it, and the effect, for those who know Matthiessen's own sexual preference, is quite disorienting. His critical gestures in the public form of his book feel like expressions of self-disapproval, as though he wanted not to be what Whitman was, or else wanted readers who knew he was homosexual to see that he spurned "abnormal" homosexual attitudes in poetry.

In one sense these facts of Matthiessen's sexual and political life may seem irrelevant: what bearing do they have on his actual literary criticism? They do not have much direct bearing at all, and that is why they are significant and warrant attention. Matthiessen always emphasizes "wholeness" and "integrity" in life and work, saying repeatedly that the teacher and critic must bring the rich range of his entire experience to his pedagogical and scholarly labors. This was the belief by which Matthiessen lived: it made him the great, if difficult and demanding, teacher and man that he unquestionably was. But part of Matthiessen seems missing from his books. In his first three books—*Sarah Orne Jewett* (1929), *Translation: An Eliza-bethan Art* (1931), and *The Achievement of T. S. Eliot* (1935; rev. ed. 1947)—Matthiessen forges his critical identity but also exposes for us conspicuous absences and limitations of perspective. There is development, but also the settling in of assumptions that handi-cap Matthiessen, and especially curtail his attempts to engage the political. As so often when appraising this critic, one ends up—un-fairly but not unreasonably—wanting Matthiessen to have done his work differently. It is difficult to keep from wishing that he had not only learned lessons in New Critical explication, but also moved to relate these to social-cultural organic critique of the sort that Ran-som and the others, by the late 1930s, had unfortunately rejected. Through Tawney and Debs, and his own experiences, Matthiessen had formed a more inclusive vision than the Agrarians of what was wrong with America. Conceivably he could have angled his criticism in a radical direction and made it political as well as literary. Socialist politics would then have entered into and energized his literary criticism and scholarship.

This, obviously, is easy to say: it is to slight the Matthiessen who was, and to dream of a Matthiessen who might have been. No doubt there is much to be said for returning from visions of unrealized possibilities to an assessment of what he actually wrote early and late. Still, one might be forgiven for asking what American criticism might have been like, what alternative directions it might have taken, if Matthiessen had connected his analytical skill and historical knowledge to a broadly based literary/political/cultural enterprise. As his first two books intimate and as his third book, devoted to T. S. Eliot, confirms, Matthiessen came to define his critical work in terms that tended to disengage it from politics and precluded a general cultural address.

Matthiessen's 1929 book on Jewett—who was related to Matthiessen's mother, Lucy Orne Matthiessen—displays a type of impressionistic criticism that he would soon surpass. For understandable reasons, it has not enjoyed a good reputation. The terms regularly and rightly used about it include sentimental, soft, and self-indulgent. One commentator has accurately observed that Matthiessen yielded "to his subject, and especially to the charm of her milieu; he was writing a back-to-the-womb lullaby to himself and his readers, not challenging them to exploration and judgment" (Bowron 49). Matthiessen's descriptions of Jewett's life and works are thin, and he continually dabbles in atmospherics:

> Her stories caught the flavor not only of the birches, but of the salt marshes, the roadside chicory and Queen Anne's lace. (64)

> Its pages [those of *The Country of the Pointed Firs*] are as direct as the rays of the sun, and as fresh as a breeze across the water. They envelop the mingled charm and sadness of the countryside just as you feel it on the summer day that brings the first hint of autumn, when, in the midst of the wild roses along the dusty road, you are suddenly aware of the first fateful spray of goldenrod. (101–2)

Matthiessen does not apply his full critical intelligence to examining Jewett, preferring to speak in an evocative and deliberately unanalytical voice. But his voice keeps sounding falsified, and not only because the lucid, forthright prose in *American Renaissance* dramatizes its shortcomings. In *Sarah Orne Jewett*, Matthiessen descends into mannerism; his diction and stylistic devices (the alliterative touch and Tennysonian vowels in "first fateful spray") draw notice to themselves in a maudlin way. The reader senses that the critic is in control of the sounds, but not the substance, of his words. There are too few ideas, and too much special pleading. Later in his career, Matthiessen would sternly quarrel with the impressionism of Van Wyck Brooks's Makers and Finders series, and his own strictures about these volumes—elegiac, wistful, critically infirm—guide us toward the proper judgment of *Sarah Orne Jewett*.

One means by which to save *Sarah Orne Jewett* is to view it as Matthiessen's version of pastoral, as his evocation, through Jewett, of New England village settings that the Civil War and industrialism had in most cases destroyed. Such rural simplicities, one could take Matthiessen to be suggesting, remain available through Jewett's acts of imagination and the responsive reader/critic's attempts to recreate them in his prose. But though Matthiessen admires Jewett's writing and accords it a respectful, appreciative treatment, he does not appear to take her with real seriousness. Her stories, he implies, however adeptly they beckon us to a time gone by, cannot finally sustain analysis. When, in the final chapter, Matthiessen notes the limits of Jewett's art, he makes brief but pointed judgments that, if he had pressed them, would have effectively called Jewett's stature very much into question. She does not "portray passion in her books," nor does she depict what in New England countryside life is "sordid, bleak, and mean of spirit" (144, 149). Another rendering of this second observation might be that Jewett is not articulate—to cite a chapter heading from Tawney's *The Acquisitive Society*—about "the nemesis of industrialism." What, one wonders, were Matthiessen's thoughts when he stated that in the years of Jewett's youth, at the time of the Civil War, "throughout New England the invigorating air that Emerson and Thoreau had breathed was clogged with smoke" (20)?

Sarah Orne Jewett is not a good book, but it is a labor of love and affection for another kind of life and landscape. Significantly, Matthiessen dedicated the book to his deceased mother, to whom he had been devoted, and he included in it illustrations by Cheney, with whom he had set up a household in Kittery Point, Maine, in 1927. The Jewett book was also an exercise in form, a holiday from the constraints of scholarship and teaching. Even more, it was a declaration against the type of work and credentials that academic professionalism demanded, a declaration—firm in the pleasures and loyalties it embraced—against the career within established institutions to which Matthiessen had decided to devote his life.

As an undergraduate at Yale, Matthiessen had already begun both to succeed within, and to resist, his home institution, and this pattern seems to thread through his life. Somewhat like F. R. Leavis, who was militantly inside and outside Cambridge University in England, Matthiessen felt himself to embody values that his institution should have endorsed but had scorned. Matthiessen loved certain features of his life at Harvard, especially his contact with students, yet he also saw himself as estranged from it and, in the postwar period, even considered resigning his professorship to take a position at Brandeis. He was, in a similar vein, a tireless, dedicated professional, one who achieved great success, yet he staunchly disliked scholarly meetings, notably those held by the Modern Language Association, where the atmosphere of "pure professionalism" struck him as totally unchallenging (quoted in Vanderbilt 475).

In a minor chord, *Sarah Orne Jewett* shows Matthiessen's determination not to be ensnared by the folkways of professional scholarship. It hence glances backward to the dissertation on Elizabethan translation that Matthiessen had written at Harvard under J. L. Lowes in 1926–27, and forward to the revised version of it that he published in book form as *Translation: An Elizabethan Art* in 1931. *Sarah Orne Jewett* affirms personal and familial commitments that the dissertation does not, but the publication of that dissertation makes apparent Matthiessen's ability to place the form in which he had embodied them. *Translation* portrays Matthiessen as a more rigorous worker, intent upon getting his scholarly discoveries into print. Matthiessen's private commitments obviously continued to mean much to him, and he often spoke affectionately of the period when he wrote *Sarah Orne Jewett*, but he was surely alert to the weaknesses of the book as a piece of criticism.

Translation is lively and interesting, written with a robust conscientiousness that demonstrates Matthiessen's enthusiasm for his texts. The book consists primarily of many meticulously conducted studies of passages from Hoby's translation of *The Courtier* (1561), North's translation of Plutarch's *Lives* (1579), Florio's translation of Montaigne's *Essays* (1603), and Holland's translations of Livy's *Roman History* and Suetonius' *History of Twelve Caesars* (1606). What holds together the specific analyses is Matthiessen's general argument that the Elizabethans sought to give contemporaneity to the texts they translated: "The feeling prevailed that these new books would have a direct bearing upon daily life, that they would bring new blood and vigor to the stock of England" (26). In describing translation, Matthiessen is also describing patriotism—the ways in which the literary imagination is vitally connected with the desire to rally and serve one's country. The translator does not simply "repeat" what is in the original, but reconceives the original in order to knit it to the ideals and actualities of the nation.

> Florio's greatest gift was the ability to make his book come to life for the Elizabethan imagination. Approximately the same forces surged through France and England in the Renaissance, but if Montaigne was to be fused into an integral part of the English mind and not left as a foreign classic, not only his spirit but the form of his expression had to be naturalized. And throughout his translation, sometimes consciously, more often instinctively, Florio creates a Montaigne who is an actual Elizabethan figure. (141)

> Everything that Florio does to Montaigne is calculated to bring the *Essays* closer to the spirit of his time. Words and expressions of Elizabethan flavor crowd every page: "mumpes and mowes," "block-ish asses," "meere bug-beares and scar-crowes, to scare birdes with all" appear in place of Montaigne's plain "grimaces," "des asniers," "vrais epouvantails de cheneviere." "I doe beware and keepe myselfe from such treasons, and cunny-catching in mine owne bosome" is the wholly characteristic version of "Je me sauve de telles trahisons en mon propre giron." Nouns are used for verbs or adjectives: "in a strange and foe country" for "en terre ennemie." Constant alterations are made in Montaigne's phrasing to introduce native idioms. "Respondirent à sa barbe" is shifted to "answered him to his teeth"; "sans suitte" is given the fullness of "without rime or reason, sans head or foot." Even more striking is the colloquial tone that Florio adopts. "God wot," "Well," "Marry, what you list" come frequently, and never with any counterpart in the original. " 'Tut-tut,' said he, 'it is alreadie finished' " for the simple "Elle est composée & preste"

reveals at a glance the greatness of this change. To the same purpose
is the translator's varied use of rich proverbial phrases where none
had appeared in the French: "to set the foolish and the wise, us and
beasts all in one ranke: *no barrell better Hering*." (151–52)

The critic who wrote passages like this about the rich colloquial-
ism of the Elizabethans and their unified sensibility is the same one
who would soon "translate" American writers of the nineteenth and
twentieth centuries for contemporary audiences. Here, in *Translation*, Matthiessen is locating examples of scholarly work undertaken
for more than just personal and professional purposes. Renaissance
translation, he affirms, did lofty work for a particular society and
culture: it was the opposite of pedantry.

Everywhere in *Translation* Matthiessen emphasizes the concrete
language that distinguishes the translators' rendering of their original texts. He states this point crisply in his introduction:

> The Elizabethan translator did not write for the learned alone,
> but for the whole country. He possessed a style admirably fitted to
> this end. Popular in the best sense, it took advantage of all the new
> richness of the language. His diction was racy and vivid, thronged
> with proverbial phrases, the slang of the streets, bold compounds,
> robust Saxon epithets, and metaphors drawn from English ports and
> countryside. The structure of his sentences reveals the growing ten-
> dencies of the time—the passionate delight in fullness of expression,
> the free use of doublets and alliteration, the building up of parallel
> constructions for the sake of rhythm. Perhaps his greatest gift, that
> which more than any other accounts for the freshness and vigor of
> his work, was one which he shared with the dramatists of his day.
> He had an extraordinary eye for specific detail. Whenever possible he
> substituted a concrete image for an abstraction, a verb that carried
> the picture of an action for a general statement. (3–4)

Matthiessen's argument closely resembles one that Leavis offered
several years later, in 1936, in *Revaluation*, his statement of "tradition and development in English poetry." Leavis, too, praises the
suppleness and strength of Elizabethan language, noting especially
the dramatic force and vivid colloquial idiom of Donne and Jonson.
But the connection between *Translation* and *Revaluation* is ultimately less pertinent than the influence of T. S. Eliot that shapes

both books. In speaking for the fertile bonds between language and everyday life in the Elizabethan age, both Matthiessen and Leavis root their arguments in Eliot's descriptions of metaphysical poetry, wit, and metaphor, and the later-seventeenth-century dissociation of sensibility that sundered the wholeness manifest in Donne and his contemporaries.

Matthiessen states his debt to Eliot explicitly:

> The most important fact in accounting for the freshness of both the poetry and prose of the early seventeenth century is that the men of that day possessed what Mr. T. S. Eliot has so accurately called "the direct sensuous apprehension of thought." . . . Holland's thoughts came to him with the same immediacy as the odor of a rose. . . . Knowledge was fresh, language could be bent to one's will, thoughts swarmed so eagerly that they could not be separated from emotions. The language was more fully alive than it has ever been, which means that the people were also. (226, 232)

Eliot's conception of history, particularly the lines he traces between history and language, structures Matthiessen's own account as he tells in *Translation* a story of loss roughly similar to that which he left implicit in *Sarah Orne Jewett*. In the later book, though, the crucial moment is not the industrial revolution but is, instead, the perceptual, linguistic, and cultural crisis that, according to Eliot, afflicted the England of Dryden and Milton. Modernist writers and intellectuals like Matthiessen, indebted to Eliot as a guide and authority, judged this crisis to define (and delimit) the twentieth century as well. In its reliance, then, on Eliot's myth of history and deployment of it to pattern observations about the style of the Elizabethan translations, *Translation* is a modernist text in its own right. Based in the academy, Matthiessen is supplying Eliot with formidable buttressing for the arguments advanced in *The Sacred Wood*. In these translations, Matthiessen reports, lie abundant evidence for the verdict Eliot has presented on our language and history. Here, too, is bountiful evidence for the verbal practice that Eliot, a craftsman burdened with modernity, now strives to recover.

Translation is also valuable for what it indicates about the sources for New Critical "close reading." One source was the work of I. A. Richards, in *Principles of Literary Criticism* (1925) and *Practical Criticism* (1929), and his pupil, William Empson, in *Seven Types of*

Ambiguity (1930). More relevantly for the American context, there were R. P. Blackmur's subtle analyses of the poetry of Eliot, Stevens, and others that had appeared in *Hound and Horn* and *Direction* in the late 1920s and early 1930s. But Matthiessen's *Translation* demonstrates that Eliot's role was also a formative one. Eliot rarely engaged in close readings himself, yet in his critical prose he highlighted an understanding of language to which he gave complex form in his poetry. Matthiessen grasped what it might mean to read closely by witnessing Eliot's language in action in his early poems. It was not merely that the New Critics invented techniques for reading Eliot and his fellow modern poets. Eliot's poetry, supported by the theoretical thrust of his criticism, encouraged readers to behave in ways that altered their general response to texts. Modern poetry and modern criticism reinforced one another.

Matthiessen, for one, was superbly suited to read in this fashion —and not only because Eliot's writing, with its invocations of unity and wholeness keyed to language, so appealed to him. As a scholar grounded in (and toughened by) philology and working on problems of translation, he was ready to attend analytically to language because he had been immersed in it all along. This may seem a minor point, but it reveals that New Criticism, while a new movement, may not have been so radical a break from philology after all. Many philologists stayed what they were—they opposed the new generation of critics in the academy, and the New Critics in turn assailed the philologists. Other philologists, however, and graduate students schooled in this discipline, took what they had learned and fitted it to the purposes of the newer kind of close reading. The New Criticism represented a significant departure from what had been done before, but it managed its reorientation effectively because philology had furnished it with something positive: philology was more than a bad practice waiting to be corrected.

Given Matthiessen's own talents as a reader and his interest in Eliot, it seems inevitable to us that he would devote his next book to Eliot's poetry. But it is still startling that this young assistant professor at Harvard and author of a slight study of Jewett and a scholarly monograph on Elizabethan translations would dare to commit himself to defining and defending the work of a difficult modernist writer. *The Achievement of T. S. Eliot: An Essay on the Nature of Poetry*, first published in 1935, and reissued in a revised and enlarged edition in 1947, is a book that now appears uncritical. Matthiessen, who had met Eliot when the poet came to Harvard to deliver the Norton Lectures in 1932–33, never attains a detached relation to Eliot. He treats sources, influences, themes, ideas, attitudes in Eliot's own terms. He does not hone a language of his own— there is no competitive dialogue between the critic and his author. As Giles Gunn cogently puts it, *The Achievement of T. S. Eliot* "is so dependent upon Eliot's own standards for a critical evaluation of his poetry that it never quite escapes from the shadow cast by its subject" (31).

All of this is true enough, and *The Achievement of T. S. Eliot* also suffers from serious problems caused by Matthiessen's developing formalist ideology, as we shall see. But before going further, we must appreciate the importance of this book for audiences in the 1930s. Richards, Pound, and Conrad Aiken had resolutely backed Eliot's poetry; Edmund Wilson had devoted a chapter to Eliot's poetry and criticism in *Axel's Castle* (1931); and Blackmur had published his estimable two-part essay in *Hound and Horn* (1928). There was a scattering of other reviews and essays, and even several books. Still, no one before Matthiessen—and certainly no one with his institutional credentials—had laid out so expertly the main lines of Eliot's accomplishment in his verse. This was a great work of "translation," one tied too closely to the original, but still a translation of distinction that displayed Matthiessen's desire to teach his countrymen how to honor and approach a modern master.

Matthiessen does a number of very worthwhile things, summarizing, for instance, Eliot's view of "tradition" and bonds to Arnold, James, Dante, Donne, and Baudelaire. He also provides helpful analyses of passages, including a three-page exploration of the lines about the "typist" and "young man carbuncular" from "The Fire Sermon" (30–32). Curiously, if revealingly, Matthiessen places nearly all of his relatively few close readings in the footnotes; and this marginalization of the workings of Eliot's language will strike many as a disappointing aspect of *The Achievement of T. S. Eliot*. However, the real disappointment—and fault—in the book is Matthiessen's overinsistence on poetic form and refusal to come to terms with Eliot's religion and politics. In studying Eliot, Matthiessen fastens so exclusively upon questions of poetic form that he is prohibited from making larger social and political connections he often claimed he wanted to make.

In the first paragraph of his preface to the 1935 edition, Matthiessen states his intention:

> My double aim in this essay is to evaluate Eliot's method and achievement as an artist, and in so doing to emphasize certain of the fundamental elements in the nature of poetry which are in danger of being obscured by the increasing tendency to treat poetry as a social document and to forget that it is an art. The most widespread error in contemporary criticism is to neglect form and to concern itself entirely with content. The romantic critic is generally not interested in the poet's work, but in finding the man behind it. The humanistic critic and the sociological critic have in common that both tend to ignore the evaluation of specific poems in their preoccupation with the ideological background from which the poems spring. (vii)

Though he refers here to New Humanist and romantic critics, it is the sociological and political critics who are Matthiessen's chief foes. He respected the foremost New Humanist, Irving Babbitt, noting on one occasion that "by far the most living experience in my graduate study at Harvard came through the lectures of Irving Babbitt, with whose neo-humanistic attack upon the modern world I disagreed at nearly every point. The vigor with which he objected to almost every author since the eighteenth century forced me to fight for my tastes, which grew stronger by the exercise" (*From the Heart of Europe* 74; see also Nevin 11–32). When he attended Babbitt's lectures and read such books as *Literature and the American College* and *Rousseau and Romanticism*, Matthiessen doubtless admired this New Humanist's firm point of view, the prophetic urgency of his voice, the sense of history, and perhaps too the fierce isolation and identity as "outsider" within the institution. Matthiessen probably also respected Babbitt's concern for educational reform and his attack on the impersonality and mechanization of American colleges and universities. These had been Matthiessen's sturdy interests at Yale during his undergraduate days, and they remained with him all his life.

By the mid-1930s, however, New Humanism was no longer an influential force. Its key text, *Humanism and America*, published in 1930, was less a declaration than a last gasp, and it was effectively demolished by the rival volume, *The Critique of Humanism*, which was published in the same year. Romantic, psychological, and psychoanalytic types of criticism, sparked by Freud's *Three Contributions to a Theory of Sexuality* (translated in 1910) and Ernest Jones's oedipal study of *Hamlet* (published in 1910), had also won some champions on the critical scene since the first decade of the century, but none of these were as prominent during the 1930s as Marxist, sociological, and other kinds of political approaches. It is certainly important to remember such delvings into psychoanalytic or psychological criticism as Joseph Wood Krutch's *Edgar Allan Poe: A Study in Genius* (1926), Lewis Mumford's *Herman Melville* (1929), and Ludwig Lewisohn's *Expression in America* (1932)—these books did have an impact. Yet while Matthiessen regretted this trend in criticism, he seems never to have judged it likely to endanger literary art to anything like the degree that the "sociological" did. Psychoanalyzing Shakespeare or Twain may have appeared crude and wrongheaded to Matthiessen, but it was not as subversive of literary categories as a political critique that, in his opinion, coarsely ranked art and artists according to their serviceability for the class struggle.

The motley performance of Marxist, socialist, radical, and leftist criticism during the 1930s may make most readers sympathetic to Matthiessen's complaints about the "mechanical rigidity" of V. F. Calverton's and others' books and his emphasis on literature as an art ("An Excited Debater" 185). But the vehemence with which Matthiessen adheres to this principle is nettling. On the one hand, he acknowledges in his Eliot monograph that "in the last analysis content and form are inseparable" (vii), yet he does not then proceed to take their interdependence seriously. He claims that "the error" that distorts criticism is the "neglect" of form and the exclusive preoccupation with content. Why then not seek a middle ground? Why not advocate a method that shows the ways in which form and content are interwoven? Why not inquire into technique *and* ideas?

These were exactly the questions Granville Hicks raised in his review of *The Achievement of T. S. Eliot*. "Mr. Matthiessen very properly regards both form and content as important. What disturbs me is that he fails to investigate the relation between the two"

("Eliot in Our Time" 103). Matthiessen at times implies that the study of this relation is indeed his goal, but his procedure is finally much more narrow. Something happens to Eliot's ideas, Matthiessen suggests, through the forms that the poet shapes for them: technique transforms ideas. Invoking Coleridge, Matthiessen identifies this process as "organic form," a perfect fusion of form and content achieved through the artistic imagination. Here, Matthiessen may have been drawing upon the work of Richards, who had begun teaching at Harvard in 1931 and whose influential book *Coleridge on Imagination* appeared in 1934. He was more likely, though, evoking and elaborating upon insights he had acquired through J. L. Lowes, who was not only Matthiessen's dissertation supervisor but also the author of *The Road to Xanadu*, a 1927 study of Coleridge's "poetic imagination." Matthiessen, I suspect, interpreted and responded to Lowes's emphasis on "imaginative creation" and "controlling Form" (*Road to Xanadu* 395) by way of Eliot's more austere voice and views. He read Lowes and Coleridge through Eliot, retaining Lowes's passion for learning but eliminating the scholar-adventurer's sometimes mystical tone and impressionism. Eliot helped to give Matthiessen's own grasp of Coleridge's doctrine of "organic form" a special modernist valence and sanction, and authoritatively led Matthiessen to identify the flowering of this doctrine in the writings of the American renaissance.

"Organic form" also mattered greatly to Matthiessen because it connected the man and the work—the poet wholly at one with his art, the critic at one with his subject. But if the critic is going to praise Eliot's "wholeness," "integrity," and "authenticity," as Matthiessen does repeatedly, then should he not at some stage inquire into the nature of the content, into the substance of the ideas? Hicks appeals to Matthiessen to probe what poetic form "does" to ideas, how technique alters them, how the poet's verbal resources make them more or less palatable to readers. To be sure, Matthiessen, following Eliot, also understood organic form as a metaphor for, or representation of, the ordered society. In this respect, the form itself does signify a social content. But the difficulties that Hicks raises remain, for Eliot's notion of the ordered society differs starkly from Matthiessen's. As he made abundantly clear in *American Renaissance*, Matthiessen judged himself to be a worker for "the people"

(xvi) who sought to further the expansive cause of democracy. Organic form figured forth for Matthiessen a social content that Eliot would never have espoused.

More generally, organic form seems conceptually geared, for Matthiessen and others, to evoke a content that cannot literally be named and detailed. To name the content would not only dramatize the conflict between an Eliot and a Matthiessen—a conflict which the generalized references to order and wholeness conceal—but also oblige critics to articulate the contested politics embedded in their apparently similar formalist views. Organic form is, in truth, a politically charged term, but an extremely variable one. It intriguingly functions to suspend political debate, forestalling particularity and implying a consensus that exists only superficially.

Matthiessen thus hardens the distinction between form and content where he might instead have tried to articulate a dialectical mode of response to texts, a mode that does not privilege technique over ideas and that strives to blend literary and sociopolitical analysis. Hicks again provides a sharp counterstatement:

> Every critic, no matter how far to the left, acknowledges, even if he sometimes appears to forget, that there is no ideological equivalent for a poem. He also knows that there is a difference between good expression and bad expression. But what some of us hold is that a thing well expressed and a thing badly expressed are two different things. . . . I think Eliot is important because he says something. That "something," I will repeat, cannot be reduced to ideas. The way he says it, I will add, is important. But the way he says his "something" is part of what he says. The form of his verse, in other words, is in large measure determined by the subtlety of his perceptions, and his artistic mastery in no small degree lies in his understanding of their demands. ("Eliot in Our Time" 103, 104)

Throughout his career, Matthiessen sometimes says this himself, yet his practice usually reflects a different policy. This inconsistency is highly troubling: one wants the socialist Matthiessen to query the formalist Matthiessen's terms for examining Eliot and other writers. Even as he is working on, and later revising and reissuing, his book on Eliot, Matthiessen is, after all, deepening his radicalism and developing the political interests that had first captivated him at Yale. He is an admirer of Tawney and Debs, a defender of the union leader Harry Bridges, a supporter of Harvard professors (Ray Walsh and Paul Sweezy) denied tenure because of their radical politics—the list could be easily extended. What follows is Matthiessen's own account, written in the late 1940s, of his politics during the early 1930s:

> In '32, with the depression at its worst, I thought that here at last was a chance for the Socialists to regain the broad base they had developed under Debs, and I joined the party. Roosevelt's speeches during that campaign struck me as little more than the promises of a Harvard man who wanted very much to be President, and I had not gauged the sweep of middle and lower-middle class reaction against Hooverism that turned the rascals out. Roosevelt in office was something quite other than I had foreseen, and after he began to effect even some of the things for which Thomas had stood, I voted for him enthusiastically, though always from the left, until his death. . . . Whatever objective reasons compelled towards socialism in the nineteen-thirties seem even more compelling now, and it is the responsibility of the intellectual to rediscover and rearticulate that fact. (*From the Heart of Europe* 76, 79)

When it comes to literary criticism, however, Matthiessen often sounds much more like Ransom and Brooks than like Granville Hicks and others on the left. Some might reply that this is all to Matthiessen's distinction, but one might answer them by saying that this allegiance tended to impel Matthiessen to work, as a literary critic, *against* his own political convictions. It lodged a limiting contradiction at the heart of Matthiessen's labors: he was an active socialist who wanted to be purely literary yet somehow still be politically engaged in his criticism. Whenever he refers to politics in his books on Eliot and other writers, his comments are invariably distancing and unspecific. They do not fulfill his organic rhetoric, as the activities of his life help make us see.

Matthiessen seems never to have asked himself whether it was really desirable to keep his socialism outside—or, at best, on the margins of—his literary criticism, and this failure led to repeated dissonance in his writing and his expressed hopes for it. This is a hard charge for me to direct against Matthiessen because I concede that my first impulse is to commend his tolerance and pluralism: he is willing to take great poetry wherever he can find it, even if it does not suit his own politics. But to admit this would imply that Matthiessen actually resolved, or at least directly faced, the ambiguities in his criticism and politics, and I don't believe that he did. With the possible exception of his work on James and Dreiser in the 1940s, he avoided the ambiguities, left them hanging.

By the 1947 edition, Matthiessen seems to have sensed that his views about Eliot contained a political problem, but he refers to it only briefly and underestimates its urgency:

> My growing divergence from his view of life is that I believe that it is possible to accept the "radical imperfection" of man, and yet to be a political radical as well, to be aware that no human society can be perfect, and yet to hold that the proposition that "all men are created equal" demands dynamic adherence from a Christian no less than from a democrat. But the scope of my book remains what it was before. I have not written about Eliot's politics or religion except as they are expressed through his poetry. (ix)

Can a critic with Matthiessen's political loyalties shield himself from engaging Eliot's politics and religion? How does a committed radical manage to bracket Eliot's religious and political beliefs when he reads the poet's work? Are there not fertile opportunities and obligations for the radical, as Edmund Wilson had shown in *Axel's Castle*, when he engages and tests Eliot's and the modernists' ideas? How does such a radical detach—*why* should he detach?—his response to *Four Quartets* from his knowledge of Eliot's vision of "a Christian society," with its "positive distinction—however undemocratic it may sound—between the educated and the uneducated," between the elect body of Christian intellectuals and "the mob" (*Idea of a Christian Society* 33)? Just how does a socialist who is also, like Matthiessen, a Christian measure Eliot's expression of Christianity in his poetry and prose? These are some of the questions Matthiessen sidesteps in his quest for purity of method.

"You begin to understand Eliot," Matthiessen insists,

> precisely as you begin to understand any other poet: by listening to the lines, by regarding their pattern as a self-enclosed whole, by listening to what is being communicated instead of looking for something that isn't. . . . One of the surest ways to fail to understand a poem is to begin by trying to tear the thought from the context in order to

approve or disapprove of what it seems to express. For the important thing, as Richards has reaffirmed, is "not what a poem says, but what it *is*"; and the only way of knowing what it does express is by a sustained awareness of all the formal elements of which it is composed. Only in this way, by experiencing the poem as a whole, and then by evaluating it "from the inside," so to speak, by trusting the evidence of your senses for its effect, can you determine whether or not the poem is alive; and thus, in turn, whether or not the poet has a sense of his age, whether what he believes and imagines about human destiny springs from a direct contact with life. (46, 110)

The New Criticism, with Matthiessen's help, has so woven these notions about poems as "self-enclosed wholes" into our readerly being that it is difficult to interrogate them. But surely it is a very risky business to profess that one knows when a poet's writing "springs from a direct contact with life" and when it does not. The ground for such a discrimination would seem all the more problematic for Matthiessen, who presumably takes issue with Eliot's conception of what constitutes "human destiny" and what "a direct contact with life" means. Eliot does not believe the same things that Matthiessen does; he does not know the world the same way.

Matthiessen's position appears to be flexible and open, receptive above all to literature as an art and concerned to protect it from the damaging intrusions of ideology. But his position is actually quite prescriptive, and there is finally something unnatural about his ardent call—which he brands "the chief assumption of my essay"— for separating poetry and politics, art and philosophy. This is one of many puzzling examples, slight but significant, which he invokes to prop up his approach:

> Milton's pamphlets are read for the importance of their ideas in relation to the development of seventeenth-century political theory; but readers are drawn to *Samson Agonistes* by a quality that still enables it to be a moving experience whether or not one is a special student of the seventeenth century. For, although many of Milton's same ideas are voiced in *Samson Agonistes*, what gives the poem its life is its quality of emotional expression through its expert fusion of content and form. (127)

These are exasperatingly dogmatic claims. How does Matthiessen reply to readers who differ with him? What about readers who believe that the pamphlets Milton wrote on the eve of the Restoration are as "moving" or even more "moving" than *Samson Agonistes*? An advocate of a Christian society himself, Milton knew that the Revolution had failed, yet he endangered his life by continuing his steadfast opposition to the monarchy. Readers could propose (and have proposed) that the pamphlets possess literary value and "move" us as artistic as well as political performances. "Moving experience" is an extremely fluid category, and some readers would in fact bicker with Matthiessen's assessment of Milton's verse. Here is Leavis' verdict on *Samson Agonistes* in *Revaluation*: "One can grant that it might possibly help to form taste; it certainly could not instil or foster a love of poetry. How many cultivated adults could honestly swear that they had ever read it through with enjoyment?" (67).

Like many New Critics, Matthiessen frequently seems unable to consider nonfictional prose like Milton's as more than a gloss for poems and novels. When Matthiessen does this, he is refraining from a real confrontation with a writer's ideas, the ideas that the writer seeks to express in his verse or his fiction. And the problem is especially vexed in Eliot's case, where the ideas the writer presents so often call for dissent, and particularly from people whose politics resemble Matthiessen's.

The difficulties worsen when one realizes just how selective Matthiessen's reading of Eliot's prose is. He reads it for its "literary" relevance—he sees "tradition," for instance, only in a literary sense —and he ignores explicitly social and political dimensions in the prose altogether. This has alarming consequences, notably the fact that *After Strange Gods*, which appeared in 1933 and which even Eliot did not see fit to reprint, receives respectful mention. Matthiessen also avoids confronting disturbing passages in Eliot's contributions to the *Criterion*, such as the following from a July 1929 piece:

> Fascism is . . . nationalistic, and communism internationalistic: yet it is conceivable that in particular circumstances fascism might make for peace, and communism for war. The objections of fascists and communists to each other are mostly quite irrational. I confess to a preference for fascism in practice, which I dare say most of my readers share; and I will not admit that this preference is itself wholly irrational. I believe that the fascist form of unreason is less remote from my own than is that of the communists. (Quoted in Aaron 265)

Matthiessen never comes to grips with statements like this one. In the midst of a tumultuous decade, both politically and socially, and several years before the appearance of *The World's Body, Understanding Poetry*, and *The New Criticism*, Matthiessen hews to a formalist line and celebrates a self-proclaimed classicist in literature, royalist in politics, and Anglo-Catholic in religion. A strange position for a socialist to find himself in!

"I am not concerned," Matthiessen says at one point,

> with the direct applicability of Eliot's political ideas; indeed, he frequently confesses himself an amateur in such matters, and yet defends the valid and valuable distinction between political ideas and actual politics, a distinction particularly necessary in a time of social disruption, when practice lags behind theory, when, indeed, the only way of clarifying the chaotic jungle of events is by subjecting them to the scrutiny of an articulated theory. But what is important to understand in the present context is that the strain of thought which characterizes Eliot's conception of the ideal state also runs throughout his conception of the nature of art. (143)

Again an array of questions pose themselves. Why not inquire into what society would "look like" if it were built upon the foundation that Eliot describes in *The Idea of a Christian Society* and other writings? Why not analyze, too, what it implies about Eliot—to reverse Matthiessen's final remark—that throughout his conception of art runs his conception of the ideal state? Matthiessen shuns these questions and many others like them. One suspects that he *has* to do so, or else he will be forced to adjust the high valuation of Eliot he is committed to maintaining. To put this in a more general way: Matthiessen has to devote himself to preserving a methodological purity in his criticism, or else consider the full implications of his socialism for literary studies. These would be painful and disarming: he would have to give up a great deal, including, perhaps, much literature he loves.

In the Eliot book and elsewhere, Matthiessen's language takes strange turns when he deals with the relation between literature, criticism, and politics. Several years after the appearance of *The Achievement of T. S. Eliot*, he reviewed Newton Arvin's book on Walt Whitman, strenuously objecting to Arvin's praise of Whitman's "optimism" in contrast to the pessimism of Poe and Melville:

Is the availability of a poet to be made to correspond to the degree in which his opinions chime in with our hopes? Is it not rather the function of the artist to bring to concentrated expression every major phase of human experience, its doubts and anguish and tortured defeats as well as its cheerful confidence? Indeed, is not one measure of the great artist his refusal to yield us any innocent simplification, his presentation of an account of life as intricate in its harsh tragic matching of good and evil, as complex in its necessities of constant struggle as the life that we ourselves know? Will any less dense past correspond to our usages as mature human beings? ("Whitman" 217; see also *Achievement of T. S. Eliot* 107)

This crucial passage reveals how Matthiessen's sense of the "tragic" shadows his politics. It is striking to witness the shift he makes from "our hopes" to "innocent simplification," as though the second phrase more accurately registers the essence of any desire for social change. For Matthiessen, life mixes good and evil, and this dimension of his Christian belief leads him in the final analysis to be deeply skeptical about the potential of socialism to convert minds and reorder society and its institutions. Admittedly going somewhat beyond direct evidence, I will risk saying that Matthiessen is a courageous, earnest fighter for socialism who does not believe that his cause could ever succeed: men and women are radically imperfect, and this hard fact always colors his sense of the likely prospects for change. You must struggle *against* the capitalist system and *for* economic equality, but you cannot assume, Matthiessen seems to be maintaining, that by changing external conditions you will change human nature. Matthiessen was a Christian, not a materialist. Literature, for him, is not so much political as formal—a form of expression that, especially in the tragic masterpieces of Shakespeare and Melville, exposes the limitations of the political.

Matthiessen invested much in categories he seems unable to question. In his book on Eliot and even in the later books, he circles around contradictions in his critical approach and musters defenses for views that he might have queried. It is partly true, but not wholly adequate, to say that he is admirably resisting the Marxists and the "sociologists" of the 1920s and 1930s who fail to value literature for its own sake. He is doing something for literature at the expense of a criticism that might conceivably move and mediate between literature and politics. Matthiessen makes it impossible to examine literature politically—the socialist has no option but to set aside his principles when he does literary criticism. I think we see here the self-alienating effects of Matthiessen's embrace of the New Criticism, formidably bolstered by Eliot's literary ethics. Possibly, too, we glimpse Matthiessen's sense of the limits of the socialist cause— which might alter conditions, but not essences—for which he fervently fought. He counsels "integrity" and "wholeness" in response, employing these very terms to commend Eliot even as, in doing so, he violates his own political allegiances.

This chapter should show that I dissent from the view that Matthiessen is important because he reconciled differences and conflicts in modern criticism. Rather, he is crucially important to think about precisely because, like many literary radicals past and present in the academy, he did not achieve such an act of reconciliation, though he tried to undertake one and may have believed that he did so successfully. Frederick Stern is incorrect when he argues that Matthiessen's ability to "link" various "modes of critical thought" is perhaps his "greatest contribution." Matthiessen attempted but did not manage to "combine literary theories that seemed so totally at odds with one another that it appeared they could not be brought together into a whole" (31, 32; cf. Morris 129–32). At first encounter, Matthiessen does seem to many readers to profess an organic literary/sociopolitical commitment that the New Critics lacked. In 1929, more than a decade before *Understanding Poetry*, Matthiessen warned against the way that "literature has been studied in a vacuum without relation to anything but itself, a genealogy of printed works, one book begetting another" ("New Standards" 181). And there are many similar statements in Matthiessen's later books, essays, and reviews. But his Eliot book shows ample affinities with the position to which he objects. The study of Eliot is not an isolated case: one can detect the same dedication to an intrinsic "literary" method among the very books, essays, and reviews that one would initially cite to affirm Matthiessen's divergence from the New Criticism. Before the Eliot book and after it, Matthiessen repeatedly states that "the critic's primary task is to discern the object as it is" ("In the Tradition from Emerson" 280)—which is exactly what Ransom, Brooks, and other New Critics said (Cain, *Crisis in Criticism* 98–100).

A critic like Matthiessen conceivably could practice "close reading" in the service of politics, *reading as a socialist*. But a critic cannot effectively be two discrete things at once, cannot be a socialist *and* a formalist, a cultural historian *and* a critic of "self-enclosed" literary art. The costs are too high, the ambiguities too serious, the tensions too severe. Matthiessen subscribed to (and sought to keep separate) the loyalties of the political man and the literary critic. He did not work out their competing claims and labor to unify them in his practice, but, instead, tried to live with—perhaps by never really seeing—their contradictions.

Matthiessen's political beliefs never penetrated into the privileged literary zone where he had located Eliot. Nor did they ever emerge with full clarity as part of his analytical procedure in *American Renaissance* and the books that came afterward. But Matthiessen's politics did begin to play a somewhat more active, if ambivalent, role in his writings of the mid-to-late 1940s, particularly in the studies of James (1944) and Dreiser (published posthumously in 1951). Eliot, who in 1918 had celebrated James's "sense of the past" and identified this novelist as "positively a continuator of the New England genius" ("On Henry James" 129, 127), assisted in leading Matthiessen to James. James proved to be a writer whose craft Matthiessen revered but whose antidemocratic vision he found angering and alarming.

THREE

The Making of Henry James

James believed that democracy inevitably levels down.
—*Henry James: The Major Phase* 110

PROBABLY MORE than any other modern critic, F. O. Matthiessen legitimated the study of American literature. Not only did he define and develop the basic analytical method—a "close reading" of texts keyed to the articulation of central "American" myths and symbols—but he also did much to establish the canon of major authors. Matthiessen was not the first person to examine the writings of Eliot, Emerson, Thoreau, Melville, Hawthorne, Whitman, Dreiser, and others now securely a part of American literature as we know it; but in most cases, it was his critical work that proved to be crucial in bringing the author into focus and hence into the midst of scholarly debate. It comes therefore as somewhat of a surprise to discover that the American writer to whom Matthiessen devoted the most prolonged attention, and whose novels and stories he made especially significant for students of American literature, was not, finally, a writer he appears to have greatly prized. Although he published extensively on Henry James and in the process helped to confirm James as a canonical figure, Matthiessen seems to have been, at best, highly ambivalent about him—and ambivalent in ways that testify to his own conflicted attitudes toward the relation between literary criticism and politics.

The revival of critical and scholarly interest in Henry James dates from the mid-1930s. Its central text, which appeared to much acclaim in 1934, was the special issue of the avant-garde little magazine *Hound and Horn*, edited by Lincoln Kirstein and including essays by Edmund Wilson, Stephen Spender, R. P. Blackmur, Francis Fergusson, and others. There had been, of course, a good deal published on James before 1934. Rebecca West (1916), J. W. Beach (1918), Pelham Edgar (1927), and Cornelia Kelley (1930) had written books about his work. More important, in 1918 Ezra Pound and T. S. Eliot had published essays in the *Little Review* which highlighted James's craftsmanship and the lessons that his unstinting devotion to art could bring to the modernist movement.

Not all agreed, however, that James's example was a positive one. The question of his artistic and cultural situation, noted by Pound and Eliot, was explored, skeptically and sometimes disdainfully, by Van Wyck Brooks (1925), V. L. Parrington (1930), and Granville Hicks (1933). Each, dwelling upon James as a case study, stressed the psychological and social limits of his craft. Parrington's indictment was especially severe:

> The spirit of Henry James marks the last refinement of the genteel tradition, the completest embodiment of its vague cultural aspirations. All his life he dwelt wistfully on the outside of the realm he wished to be a free citizen of. Did any other professed realist ever remain so persistently aloof from the homely realities of life? From the external world of action he withdrew to the inner world of questioning and probing; yet even in his subtle psychological inquiries he remained shut up within his own skull-pan. His characters are only projections of his brooding fancy, externalizations of hypothetical subtleties. He was concerned only with *nuances*. He lived in a world of fine gradations and imperceptible shades. Like modern scholarship he came to deal more and more with less and less. It is this absorption in the stream of psychical experience that justifies one in calling Henry James a forerunner of modern expressionism. Yet how unlike he is to Sherwood Anderson, an authentic product of the American consciousness! (*Beginnings of Critical Realism* 240–41)

By the end of the 1930s, much of what Parrington attacked had become grounds for enthusiastic praise. James's psychological inquiries, it was now said, pointed to his sophisticated understanding of consciousness; his "projections" and "shadings" indicated an extraordinary attention to problems of artistic form and to an awareness of myth and symbolism which connected him with Joyce and Kafka. His differences from Anderson and other naturalists dramatized not a failure to conform to main currents in America so much as an invigorating echo of the native strain of Hawthorne's stories,

sketches, and romances. In those studies in which James was judged
to lie outside an American context, he was praised for drawing upon
the richest features of European realism, particularly those evident
in the novels of Balzac, Turgenev, and Flaubert. True, as Brooks
and Parrington had charged, James had withdrawn from the "world
of action." But significantly, this decision now was taken to typify
the inevitable plight of the artist in America. James's expatriation
further emblematized the failure of audiences to support the best
artists and interpreters of not only the American but the international scene as well. James's unpopularity with the mass reader had
been transformed from a liability into a virtue.

This "James revival," as Jay Hubbell aptly notes, "is in some ways
a curious thing":

> During the Great Depression when so many of our writers were
> denouncing the capitalist system and flirting with Russian commu-
> nism, who would have expected a renewed interest in a Victorian
> novelist concerned not with the proletariat but with the lives of well-
> to-do American travelers and British aristocrats living on inherited es-
> tates? Who that had been reading the work of Thorstein Veblen, John
> Dos Passos, or William Faulkner could find the time or the patience
> to wade through James's verbose stories of the manners and minor
> morals of people living in country houses or vacationing in Switzer-
> land? And what reader familiar with the theories of Sigmund Freud,
> the novels of Ernest Hemingway, or the plays of Eugene O'Neill could
> tolerate the voluminous novels of an old bachelor, who seemed both
> ignorant and squeamish in matters pertaining to sex? (131)

As Hubbell goes on to point out, James's expansive concern for artistic "form" made him, whatever his social and political peculiarities,
a writer particularly well suited to the analytical techniques that
the New Critics devised and promoted during the 1930s and 1940s.
Some have even said (not always in the spirit of an accolade) that
the New Criticism "chose Henry James" as its paramount author,
as though he were an invention of New Criticism and a compelling
instance of its power to institutionalize its values.

The New Criticism did play a formative role in heightening and
complicating interest in James. New Critics and their students, writing often about him, produced numerous examinations of formal
structure, imagery, symbolism, and metaphorical patterning. But

what is striking about the James revival is how disparate was the group of critics, inside and outside the academy, which helped to bring it about. Edmund Wilson, Yvor Winters, Philip Rahv, Joseph Warren Beach, Morton Zabel, Leon Edel, W. H. Auden, F. R. Leavis, Lionel Trilling, and many others not closely affiliated, or not affiliated at all, with the New Criticism and its interpretive style made estimable contributions, moving James "from a coterie studio to the hall of the immortals" (Habegger 294). By the late 1940s, extravagant praise like that which Lionel Trilling lavished on *The Princess Casamassima* in 1948 was not at all uncommon: "If we comprehend the complex totality that James has thus conceived, we understand that the novel is an incomparable representation of the circumstances of our civilization" (*"Princess Casamassima"* 100)

Matthiessen was a crucial figure in reshaping the discussion of James. He edited and provided substantial introductory essays for two valuable collections, *Henry James: Stories of Writers and Artists* (1944) and *The American Novels and Stories of Henry James* (1947). He also assembled, in 1947, a fascinating collection of primary materials on "the James family," stitched together with his own biographical and critical commentary, and, in the same year, he co-edited, with his friend and Harvard colleague Kenneth B. Murdock, *The Notebooks of Henry James*.

Henry James: The Major Phase is, however, clearly Matthiessen's most influential work on James. Matthiessen called the book—the bulk of which he presented as the Alexander Lectures at the University of Toronto in the fall of 1944—his "overaged contribution to the war effort," an allusion to the 1940 deal in which the United States sold outdated destroyers to Great Britain (Hyde 283). To readers of the present day, *Henry James* admittedly may seem superficial, a pale contrast to the monumental scope and richness of *American Renaissance* (1941), Matthiessen's masterpiece. But at the time it was published, *Henry James* was extremely significant, shifting critical attention from James's hermeticism to his artistry. Deftly countering the still-lingering influence of Brooks and Parrington, Matthiessen argued that their criticism—"sociological" rather than "literary"—mistakenly applied itself to "content" at the expense of the artist's "form." For Matthiessen, James, the preeminent artist, must be approached formally, as literary art mandates. Seen from this angle, Matthiessen's book has a polemical thrust, as he strives to make leftists and progressives, among whom he numbers himself, more sophisticated about how art works.

This formal approach was always Matthiessen's favored perspective—it suggests his links to the New Criticism—but no doubt it was especially so during the war years. Though a defender of dissidents and pacifists, he was not a pacifist himself, and he had sought unsuccessfully to enlist in the marine corps (he was turned down because he was half an inch too short). Despite this willingness to join the armed struggle against Nazism and Fascism, Matthiessen did not lessen his commitment to the "primary values" (xvi) of sympathy, love, and understanding incarnated in art and transmitted in humanistic education at its best. *Henry James* is thus a statement flung against the war's horrors, a statement both of loss—the war had taken away most opportunities for intellectual and imaginative comradeship—and of hope for the saving remnant of teachers and students who nevertheless labored to sustain true values.

In his book, Matthiessen views James's craftsmanship and fealty to literature as a personal and cultural enterprise. After surveying the artist's career, Matthiessen characterizes the writing of James's last three completed novels—*The Ambassadors, The Wings of the Dove, The Golden Bowl*—as the "major phase," where the art is at its greatest pitch of complexity. In a brief account of James's indebtedness to Hawthorne in *American Renaissance*, Matthiessen had already accented "the amazingly prolific sequence," the "final great series," of novels (292, 294); indeed, he had not even been the first to single out the late works. But it was Matthiessen, speaking as the prestigious author of *American Renaissance*, who gave the claim its potency. Save for a few dissenting voices, notably Leavis' in *The Great Tradition* (1948), Matthiessen's judgment, bolstered by his portrait of the late Jamesian imagination as displayed in the notebooks, has been the accepted one. A measure of its importance is the degree to which pursuing the labyrinths of "the major phase" became a key item on the agenda of postwar criticism and pedagogy.

Henry James was also noteworthy for drawing attention to *The American Scene*, which Pound had celebrated in 1918 as the "triumph of the author's long practice," a "creation of America," a "book no 'serious American' will neglect" but which few other readers had taken seriously ("Henry James" 327). Matthiessen sparked an interest that burst forth in 1946, with the publication of W. H. Auden's edition of *The American Scene*, followed by a number of reviews. Matthiessen also heralded something of a breakthrough when he devoted a detailed chapter to James's revisions of *The Portrait of a Lady* for the New York Edition, a chapter that exhibited the kind of vigilant scrutiny of word choice and phrasing which had first become evident in his 1931 study of Elizabethan translations. Dozens of essays on James's revisions followed Matthiessen's example, and they gave a new dimension to treatments of James. Not everyone, it should be added, has approved of what Matthiessen inaugurated. Hershel Parker, in a tough-minded critique, has rebuked Matthiessen for his naive notions about the process of revision, his lack of a theoretical framework, and his "banal" and "vacuous" tributes to James's "painterly" talent in altering *Portrait*'s style and structure (94–95).

For my interests, however, what is important about *Henry James* is not so much the salutary influence it had upon criticism or the errors it may have embedded in scholarship. The important—and quite curious—fact is that Matthiessen was, at best, ambivalent toward James. Despite the editorial and critical tasks that he devoted to this author, Matthiessen does not appear to have warmed to James or to have sympathized with his preoccupations and standards. Evidence of this can be found not only in the critical book but in nearly everything else he said and wrote about James.

Matthiessen taught his first course on James in the spring semester of 1943, yet he apparently was not wholeheartedly taken with James's writings. In a letter to Russell Cheney early that year (10 February 1943), he confides that "the James course is launched, though I waver back and forth continually in the degree of my interest in him. He certainly is not someone I'm instinctively with all the way like Melville" (Hyde 274). In another letter, a month later, he seems even more dubious about James, at least as a subject for a book-length study:

> I'm up through *The Spoils of Poynton* and on the verge of the three big novels. I continue to alternate between admiration and satiety. I guess it grows even clearer that I don't want to do an extended job on James. One revealing symptom is the joy with which I rush back to Shakespeare on the alternate days. (Hyde 277)

Traces of this divided response show up repeatedly and sometimes attest to a thinly veiled hostility. In *Stories of Writers and Artists*, for instance, Matthiessen cities, and does not dispute, H. G. Wells's reply to James's famous affirmation of the primacy of art over life. "When you say," Wells had observed, that " 'it is art that *makes* life, makes interest, makes importance,' I can only read sense into it by assuming that you are using 'art' for every conscious human activity: I use the word for a research and attainment that is technical and special." Matthiessen's commentary on this exchange is revealing:

> That draws the central issue between them as sharply as possible, since the emptiness or living intricacy of the figure in James's carpet depends on whether he was using "art" as a mystical abracadabra or with verifiable comprehension of the enormous value he imputes to it. (12)

Matthiessen doesn't tender the customary interpretation here—that the lumpish sensibility of Wells was unequipped to rise to James's demands. Not only does Matthiessen refrain from siding openly with James, but he also refuses to credit James forthrightly with actually using "art" in a truly noble and not merely self-deluded and obfuscating sense. One could perhaps argue that Matthiessen is "balanced," intent upon leaving the case open, but it is nonetheless striking that he employs very strong language ("emptiness," "mystical abracadabra") to imply what a limiting judgment of this writer could amount to: James as more of a curiosity than a vital presence. "The value of James's figure in the carpet," Matthiessen states later in *Stories of Writers and Artists*, "may be judged, as he insisted, only if it is sought through his work as a whole. Only thus may be decided whether his scruples and renunciations are a sterile emptiness, or the guides to a peculiarly poignant suffering and inner triumph" (17). The intense phrase "sterile emptiness" once more implies the condition that might be the consequence of James's extraordinary faithfulness to "form."

In *The James Family*, in the midst of much laudatory comment one again finds flashes of disapproval. "Though projecting the drama of consciousness, [James] is not a philosophical novelist. By no definition of the term is he an important thinker" (245). James, Matthiessen avers,

> was often at his flimsiest on the subject of politics. In contrast to the equalitarianism of both his father and his brother, he grew to take

it for granted that democracy must inevitably level down; and on his late return to America he worried about the new aliens in a way that brought him dangerously near to a doctrine of Anglo-Saxon racial superiority. He was consistent within his own terms in that he carried his primary standard, his aesthetic perception of fitness, into all his judgments. (646)

Thus, although Matthiessen often celebrates James's astuteness and sensitivity, he chafes against James's retrograde politics and over-riding passion for form: the artful observer's obsession with form sometimes distorted his view of the world.

In such comments, Matthiessen is, I believe, bearing unintentional witness to his own fissured allegiances. He is, on the one hand, a literary critic committed to examining form, the object as it is; in this respect, he is attracted to James as a paradigmatic instance of the "art of fiction." Yet he is also a socialist and, by the time he was writing on James in the middle and late 1940s, a member of the Citizens Political Action Committee and a budding supporter of Henry Wallace, who would eventually become the Progressive party candidate for president in 1948. What Matthiessen seems to expose, but not really confront, in his work on James are the tensions and contradictions between his own literary and political views. He has progressed since his work on Eliot, and often appears on the verge of major revelations, both about James and about himself; but he does not express them in a sustained fashion, does not rigorously follow through on them. He fails to inquire deeply into the possibility, one he gestures toward himself, that there might be a problematic re-lation between James's conception of his art and his shortcomings both as a writer and a political man. Matthiessen does not con-sider, that is, whether the conception of art which James beautifully defines and celebrates is connected to an acutely discontented sense of the modern world, and a questionable, not to say satirically scorn-ful, attitude toward reformers, socialists, and visionaries laboring to change it. To his credit, Matthiessen is striving to make the left more aware of the complexities of verbal art, yet he then does not proceed forcefully to set out the leftist judgment which James's writing may still amply warrant.

I want to turn shortly to the critical book on James, where the issues I have touched upon are much in evidence, but first I think it is valuable to have some understanding of Matthiessen's own politics in 1944, the year *Henry James: The Major Phase* was published. Matthiessen tells us in *From the Heart of Europe* that he had long searched for a party in America that, while promising some likelihood of success, would base itself upon socialist principles— "economic revolution," hatred of the "concentration of wealth" and the tyranny that accompanies it, and the rights of all "to share in the common wealth."

> In present day America, the one time when I have felt that there was a chance to share in the direct political implementation of such views was during the rise of the Citizens Political Action Committee in the presidential campaign of 1944. Here at last there seemed to be the kind of organization through which middle-class intellectuals and white-collar workers sympathetic with the labor movement could cooperate in forwarding their common aims. I had worked with many liberal groups of good will, but had come to share Lincoln Steffens' doubts of their permanent accomplishments. For without a strong ballast, such as organized labor alone can provide, these groups soon get lost in an idealistic void. By allying ourselves as closely as possible with the progressive membership of the unions, we gain the kind of discipline that has so often been lacking among American reformers —the first-hand discipline of knowing what is actually going on in the minds of the people, and of what, therefore, is feasible. Only after thorough immersion in that knowledge is any intellectual able to offer the kind of help for which his particular gifts have fitted him. (84)

Matthiessen had already sounded these political sentiments in *American Renaissance* when he had chastized "our so-called educated class" for knowing "so little of the country and the people of which it is nominally part" and had lamented the "selfish indifference of our university men to social or political responsibility" (475). These sentiments seep into Matthiessen's criticism on James, as they had not in *The Achievement of T. S. Eliot* in 1935. Matthiessen was more successful, it seems, in cordoning off his politics in his encounters with Eliot. While that restraint keeps Matthiessen's work on Eliot from overt tensions and contradictions, it prevents him from addressing such fundamental matters as the ties between Eliot's poetry and classicist, royalist, and Anglo-Catholic point of view. Because it is not broken and disrupted by political urgencies Matthiessen cannot keep in check, the Eliot book exhibits a greater purity of argument than *Henry James* but is therefore not so cogent about Eliot and is less interesting about Matthiessen. Matthiessen's religious bond and friendship with Eliot doubtless made the difference. He did not agree with Eliot that belief in Christianity went hand in hand with homage to other conservative institutions of the state, but he did assent to Eliot's pained sense of man's radical imperfection and effort to place Christian values at the center of a reconstituted society. With James, Matthiessen does not have such bonds to buffer more frequent, thornier kinds of disagreement. When he was poring over James—"flimsy" on politics and not an "important thinker"—Matthiessen's considerable admiration for the artistry is qualified by his uneasiness about its implications.

If you read *Henry James* closely, you will detect, in the midst of Matthiessen's endorsement of the "major phase," much that intimates his reservations about James. So abundant are these small slighting comments that they constitute a kind of second narrative which turns the book into something other than what it appears to be at first—"Matthiessen's paean to art," the "single most eloquent celebration of the artist as creator and conserver of value for society" (Ruland 264). Sometimes Matthiessen frankly combines commendation and critique, as when he states in the preface that *The Bostonians* and *The Princess Casamassima* reveal "the strange mixture of perception and blindness in [James's] grasp of political issues" (xiv). More often, his appraisals and descriptions veer into wary or estranged phrasing. Here, for example, are sentences from Matthiessen's account of James's notebook entries and letters dealing with his life in London and Paris in the early 1880s:

> For page after page he might well be any fastidious but amiable young American with a sufficient bank account to allow him to give his time to somewhat vague cultural pursuits. . . . Nearly every glimpse of his personal life, in his letters as well, is just as decorous and mild, quite separated from the real concerns of any community. . . . The most usual topics are the marriages, the liaisons, and the divorces of the rich, and as we reconstruct the scene and envisage the dark serious man inclining his head gravely now to the right, then to the left, we can hardly fail to be struck with how far he has drifted from the social world of his inheritance. Both his father and his elder brother were militantly democratic, and both reacted strongly against

such occasions as made Henry's nightly fare, and carried away a sense
of the hideous and overpowering stultification of a society based upon
such class distinctions. (3, 4, 5)

Matthiessen's own sympathies are for the cause of "community"
and "militant democracy," and, as an ally of Henry Senior and
William James, he keeps voicing his discontent with the novelist
son-and-brother's social and political views. At one point associat-
ing James with Henry Adams, Matthiessen observes that "neither
. . . could be said to have remotely understood the American world
of their maturity" (51). Later, in a brief treatment of *The American
Scene*, he notes that

> James looked at the common man with shy friendliness, but believed
> that democracy inevitably levels down. Whenever he started general-
> izing about the America of 1905 and trusted his impressions alone to
> lead him to social truths, he was apt to end up with odd propositions.
> . . . He worried a good deal about what the new aliens from southern
> and central Europe would do to our Anglo-Saxon culture, and drifted
> dangerously close to a doctrine of racism. (109–10)

James could be "even more misled," Matthiessen firmly adds, "when
seizing upon something to praise, for positives to balance his negatives," as in his favorable treatment of "the Country Club," an institution whose "brittle glamour" Sinclair Lewis and Theodore Dreiser
would crack (110).

Such passages about James's limitations as a person and thinker
could be regarded as Matthiessen's inverse measure of the greatness
of the artist. When James's language is reducible to propositions,
one could take Matthiessen to be saying, James is unreliable and
even deplorable; therefore, how beautiful the work and how skilled
a craftsman James must be, to make us see not the meanness but
the art. I am not sure, though, that such a formulation explains
satisfactorily the intensity of Matthiessen's comments. I think he
found it hard, writing as he did during a period when democracy was
endangered, to speak of James only as a supreme artist. "Doctrine of
racism" is a stiff sentence to pass, and it was doubtless even more so
in 1944, given what was happening to the families and descendants
of those "aliens from southern and central Europe" at the hands of
the Nazis.

Perhaps Matthiessen's judgment did not acquire the full impact I have assigned to it until the end of the war and afterward, when Americans began finally to absorb the truth of the Holocaust. It could be argued that Matthiessen's first readers, in 1944, would not have felt the power in his reference to James's "doctrine of racism"; indeed, Matthiessen may have been only vaguely aware of it himself. But the evidence suggests that much about the Nazis' systematic extermination of European Jewry had become widely known in the Allied countries—if not fully comprehended in all its terrifying dimensions—by the fall of 1944, when Matthiessen gave the lectures that formed the basis for his book (M. Gilbert 339; Wyman 19–58). Matthiessen's words about James carry a sting.

Often Matthiessen does speak passionately about James's "art" in the "major phase." He is particularly eloquent about *The Wings of the Dove*, which he stamps James's "masterpiece," "that single work where his characteristic emotional vibration seems deepest and where we may have the sense, therefore, that we have come to 'the very soul'" (43). But even when he addresses the art on its own terms, Matthiessen is often decidedly critical, and not only in obvious places, as in his aside about "the inertness of form" in James's plays (8). In his chapter on *The Ambassadors*, Matthiessen compares the imagery James employs to represent Lambert Strether's "will to live" with that which Thoreau furnishes for his own "will to live" in *Walden*. Thoreau's will was "dynamic," Matthiessen contends, "and he expressed his desire 'to suck out all the marrow of life' in a series of physical images, the energy of which was quite beyond Strether—or James" (27). Matthiessen acknowledges James's fondness for Strether but maintains that the reader inevitably feels a thinness, even a "relative emptiness," in him (39). What saves *The Ambassadors* is James's characterization of Madame de Vionnet: "her positive suffering and loss are far more affecting than Strether's tenuous renunciation" (41). But saving the novel in this manner obliges Matthiessen to discount the depiction of Strether's growth, which for James was the novel's motive force and technical showpiece.

Also dealing severely with *The Golden Bowl*, Matthiessen stresses that James appears "to take Mr. Verver," the American billionaire, "at his own estimate" and sees his actions as springing from a wonderful naiveté. James does not succeed in handling the moral

complexities implicit in a drama of good and evil that has as its pro-
tagonists the fabulously wealthy. He simply did not know what the
American businessman in the late nineteenth century was like: "Mr.
Verver's moral tone is far more like that of a benevolent Sweden-
borgian than it is like that of either John D. Rockefeller or Jay
Gould" (89, 90). Nor does James seem alert to the sexually ambiguous contours of the relationship between Mr. Verver and his
daughter, Maggie. The writer's psychological grasp, Matthiessen
argues, is extremely limited: "What it comes down to, again and
again, is that James's characters tend to live, as has often been objected, merely off the tops of their minds" (93).

It is, above all, the "unsatisfactory nature of the positive values"
in *The Golden Bowl* to which Matthiessen continually returns—Mr.
Verver's wealth, which he innocently acquires; the father/daughter
relationship, which is also innocent, in James's view, but which
strikes the reader as morally and psychologically disturbing; and,
finally, Maggie's own behavior, which, yet again, gives forth the
luster of innocence even as she traffics in evil by immersing herself
in the affair between her husband, Prince Amerigo, and her father's
wife, Charlotte Stant. "James was trying," Matthiessen concludes,
"to invest his triumphant Americans with qualities they could hardly
possess," and, in the process, he demonstrates his lack of sensitivity
to issues of morality, psychology, and the workings of American
society. *The Golden Bowl* is, in a word, a "decadent" book (102)
that

> forces upon our attention too many flagrant lapses in the ways things
> happen both in the personal and in the wider social sphere. With all
> its magnificence, it is almost as hollow of real life as the chateaux that
> had risen along Fifth Avenue and that had also crowded out the old
> Newport world that James remembered. (104)

Even in his chapter on *The Wings of the Dove*, Matthiessen frequently points to James's defects and limitations. He does praise
James's craftsmanship in depicting Kate Croy's machinations, Mer-
ton Densher's discovery of his own complicity in Kate's plot, and
Milly Theale's suffering, but throughout his chapter, and in its concluding pages in particular, Matthiessen remains skeptical about
whether *The Wings of the Dove* ultimately merits the stature ac-

corded the greatest literary works. The problem is that Milly lacks the spiritedness, active faith, and energy that James himself celebrated in her "original," his cousin Minny Temple, who had died of tuberculosis at the age of twenty-four. Milly's character—more akin to Desdemona than to Othello, Matthiessen reflects—falls short of the "substance" that tragedy requires. Her death is not truly "tragic," and her story, taken as a whole, yields only "exquisite pathos" (78, 79). Although closing his chapter positively, Matthiessen lapses into special pleading, as if to counter the adversarial tone of his insights:

> If James has shown again that the chords he could strike were minor, were those of renunciation, of resignation, of inner triumph in the face of outer defeat, he was not out of keeping with the spiritual history of his American epoch. Art often expresses society very obliquely, and it is notable that the most sensitive recorders of James's generation gave voice to themes akin to his. In the face of the overwhelming expansion, the local colorists felt compelled, like Sarah Orne Jewett, to commemorate the old landmarks before they should be entirely swept away and obliterated. Emily Dickinson discovered that the only way she could be a poet in such an age was by withdrawal, by depending, virtually like a Jamesian heroine, upon the richness of her own "crowded consciousness." And the least feminine, most robust talent of the age, Mark Twain, who may seem at the farthest pole from James, did not find his themes in the facile myths of manifest destiny or triumphant democracy. His masterpiece was also an elegy. It gave expression to the loss of the older America of his boyhood, which, no less than the milieu of Henry James and Minny Temple, had been destroyed by the onrush of the industrial revolution. (79–80)

It's one thing to say that Jewett and Dickinson commemorated the past and withdrew into their own artistic consciousnesses. But this differs from what Matthiessen has discovered about James—that he engaged social and economic aspects of life and failed to understand them. When we read James, we apprehend superbly executed forms that are ill suited to the accurate management of their subject matter. This insight, all along, has been Matthiessen's central evaluative point.

Matthiessen also forces the connection between James and Twain. One might perhaps question, first, the degree to which *Huckle-*

berry Finn is, at its core, an elegy rather than a relentlessly satiric novel about the world of Twain's boyhood and the corruptions of life on the shore. Like many who have written about *Huckleberry Finn*, Matthiessen tends to sentimentalize it by seizing upon a relatively small part of the novel—the passages in which Huck expresses the wonder of life on the raft—to stand for the whole. It would have been interesting for Matthiessen's study of James, and especially for his effort to link James and Twain, if he had probed what *Huckleberry Finn* teaches us about "manifest destiny" and "American democracy." Twain obviously did not accept "facile myths" about America; his distinction lies in his complicated strategies for attacking those myths. In *Huckleberry Finn*, and even more in two other disorderly but provocative books, *A Connecticut Yankee in King Arthur's Court* and *Pudd'nhead Wilson*, Twain deals with issues—slavery, miscegenation, colonialism and imperialism, technology, militarism—that help us to grasp American history. These are issues, Matthiessen has been maintaining, that James didn't care about; these are the issues that formed so much of the "world" that James, in Matthiessen's view, did not "remotely" understand.

Another problem emerges in this passage, one that is harder to articulate because it involves speculating about Matthiessen's homosexuality and its effect on his critical judgment. Matthiessen groups James with two women writers, and, at the other extreme, labels Twain as "the least feminine" of America's major authors, thereby resting his literary evaluation upon a sharply stated gender dichotomy. It is not at all clear that such conventional masculine/feminine oppositions can adequately serve to define differences between writers and texts. Nor is it apparent that James himself subscribes in his theory and practice to this kind of gender-bound language for expressing and exploring his artistic identity. One suspects that, on some level, there is a sexual unease in Matthiessen that pushes him to identify writers as either masculine or feminine: his limited employment of these terms and their attributes keeps his own complex, and tormented, sexuality at a distance. His literary distinctions hence possess a polarized clarity that his homosexuality challenged.

The strength of *Henry James* is Matthiessen's critical attitude toward his subject; the book's weakness lies in his inability or unwillingness to push his criticisms even further, to spell out clearly his sense of the social and political complexities of James's art. What is intriguing, especially to someone drawn to Matthiessen, is that he is doing something here that he could not do in his earlier book on Eliot or even, as we shall see, in *American Renaissance*: he is beginning, if not with complete success, to bring together his literary critical skills and his politics. He is not quite "reading as a socialist"; if he were, he would undoubtedly have been even more critical of James. He is a critic in conflict with himself as he seeks and struggles to find his way in *Henry James*. Matthiessen feels the tension between his literary and political values, and at moments tries to voice it, but there remains much that he does not see and cannot verbalize.

In view of his emerging emphasis on a literary criticism that is also social and political, Matthiessen conceivably might have developed his remarks about *The American Scene*. Usually, as is the case with Matthiessen, critics locate *The American Scene* on the margins of the Jamesian canon: it is an anomaly of his oeuvre and a "curiosity" of American literature (107). For purposes more general— and more subversive—one would like to have prompted Matthiessen to consider how perceptions of James might change if we saw *The American Scene* as among his central books. When Matthiessen states that in it James "drifted dangerously close to a doctrine of racism" (110), one wishes that he had focused this judgment in the action of James's language, perhaps in a passage like the following on life in "the Yiddish quarter":

> It was the sense, after all, of a great swarming, a swarming that had begun to thicken, infinitely, as soon as we had crossed to the East side and long before we had got to Rutgers Street. There is no swarming like that of Israel when once Israel has got a start, and the scene here bristled, at every step, with the signs and sounds, immitigable, unmistakable, of a Jewry that had burst all bounds. That it has burst all bounds in New York, almost any combination of figures or of objects taken at hazard sufficiently proclaims; but I remember how the rising waters, on this summer night, rose, to the imagination, even above the housetops and seemed to sound their murmur to the pale distant stars. It was as if we had been thus, in the crowded, hustled roadway, where multiplication, multiplication of everything, was the dominant note, at the bottom of some vast sallow aquarium in which innumerable fish, of over-developed proboscis, were to bump together, for ever, amid heaped spoils of the sea. (131)

In the face of such a passage, one's moral judgment seems obvious. James proffers a fantasia of self-pleasing images that depict Jews as racially odd, rapacious creatures. The good feature of these people, it seems, is the marvelous opportunity they afford for working the metaphorical transformations that James generates so readily. In a sense, then, this language is transparently racist and calls for our condemnation of it. But the extravagancies of the language make such a judgment appear at once both appropriate and simplistic, even simpleminded. James's verbal inventiveness, in all its brilliance, invites moral disapproval while mocking and threatening to disarm it. The capacity for simultaneously evoking and disengaging himself from moral discourse is what makes the James of *The American Scene* so difficult, and perhaps Matthiessen might have spotted this if he had toiled with the text's language: the morally right response is essential to register, but it finally does not characterize the stunning (and taxing) experience of reading *The American Scene*.

James continually calls attention to the plight of the English language in America as it strains to be heard above the immigrants' foreign voices. The reader cannot but be conscious, page by page, of the incredible thickness of James's own language, which is his way of being faithful to his multiplying impressions as he registers for us what a sustained and unnervingly total fidelity to language entails. James judges that the immigrants endanger his own delight in, and painstaking service to, language. The East Side cafés that he visits show themselves,

> beneath their bedizenment, as torture-rooms of the living idiom; the piteous gasp of which at the portent of lacerations to come could reach me in any drop of the surrounding Accent of the Future. The accent of the very ultimate future, in the States, may be destined to become the most beautiful on the globe and the very music of humanity (here the "ethnic" synthesis shrouds itself thicker than ever); but whatever we shall know it for, certainly, we shall not know it for English—in any sense for which there is an existing literary measure. (139)

James assumes that the immigrants' languages—apparently containing no "living idiom" of their own—torture the truly idiomatic speech that is the essence of the English he cherishes and has sought to consecrate in his novels. Here, indeed, one might be inclined once more to invoke the charge of racism that Matthiessen levels. But again such a moral response does not feel entirely appropriate to a reading of *The American Scene*. While it is correct to say that James dislikes the immigrants and fears the incursion of their languages, this bare statement does not, for me, get to the heart of what makes this passage, and a great many others in the book, both repugnant and disconcertingly affecting. However much James may loathe the immigrants—and he is ironic toward and contemptuous of them—he is nevertheless capable of envisioning some future epoch when their languages blend into a beautiful harmony quite beyond his own powers of appreciation. I like to believe, in fact, that when James refers to the "very music of humanity," he is echoing language like that which Shakespeare uses in the fifth act of *The Merchant of Venice*, where Lorenzo describes the "sweet harmony" of the "sounds of music." If the allusion is intended, the passage becomes resonant, even self-ironical, as James celebrates the immigrants by referring to a play written by the authoritative source for, and guardian of, the English idiom. *The Merchant of Venice* is a suggestive point of reference for James, for it displays the Jew, tainted with the money passion, as alien and outcast, fated, like James, never to speak like others or hear the music that they take such pleasure in.

The American Scene and the journey it records are, after all, financial as well as literary acts. Even before James sailed to America, he had contracted with George Harvey of Harper and Brothers "for the serialization of his American experiences" in The *North American Review* and "the collection of them in book form upon his return to England" (Hewitt 179). Writing about the trip, James realized, would be necessary to help finance it in the first place. He also hoped to make money by delivering lectures in America; as Leon Edel points out, "James became interested" in lecturing "from the moment he learned that he could command substantial fees" (229). James further planned to attend to copyright matters while in America and, above all, to undertake business arrangements for the collected edition of his works.

James's terror at seeing the immigrants becomes, in part, a kind of self-horror and self-amazement as he recognizes his bonds with the foreigners who have displaced him. He feels deep antipathy for the exotic people he encounters, yet he himself, he knows, resembles them in striving for the best deal and in cultivating his own well-traveled, highly mannered exoticism. In returning to an America very different from the one he left twenty years earlier, he too is an outsider, an immigrant and stranger. As Ross Posnock has incisively remarked, James was both distressed by and entangled with the immigrants' situation and fate. This complex attitude explains James's immense curiosity about and fascination with the scenes enacted at Ellis Island, over which he lingers for several pages (84–86). He stresses, on the one hand, his immense distance from the immigrants, each of whom epitomizes for him the changes being remorselessly driven into America's language, national identity, and cultural consciousness; yet he is also intimately in touch with the immigrants as he senses the disorientation and disturbance that the shock of "the new" creates in them.

James's sympathy does not necessarily soften his disdain for the immigrants. His response is extremely complicated, maybe confused, and the reach of his language may touch sympathetic feelings whose full implications James did not comprehend himself and would not have accepted. Possibly the central problem is that he cannot convert whatever sympathy he feels into an acceptance of the ideal of American democracy: he cannot *accept* the conditions that he senses bond him to the immigrants. Matthiessen's term "racism" finally seems not quite to fit the strange case of *The American Scene* because while the issue at the center of the problem involves race, it is as much political as racial in its character. Democracy is what bothers James. It is "monstrous" to him (54), for its full realization requires the eradication of familiar kinds of privilege, distinction, difference. The aliens speak many different languages, and this, for James, is tantamount to saying that they speak one language massively different from English or, perhaps more accurately still, that they speak in a "hum" or "noise" that is not really language at all.

The "babel" of immigrant "tongues" forestalls communication, James emphasizes, but it is evident that his notion of "communication" obliges the communicators to perform traditional roles. To cite but one instance from *The American Scene*: in a surprisingly unguarded and unironical moment, James recounts his dismay at a thwarted communication between himself and some Italian workmen he meets one day on the New Jersey shore.

> To pause before them, for interest in their labour, was, and would have been everywhere, instinctive; but what came home to me on the

spot was that whatever *more* would have been anywhere else involved had here inevitably to lapse.

What lapsed, on the spot, was the element of communication with the workers, as I may call it for want of a better name; that element which, in a European country, would have operated, from side to side, as the play of mutual recognition, founded on old familiarities and heredities, and involving, for the moment, some impalpable exchange. The men, in the case I speak of, were Italians, of superlatively southern type, and any impalpable exchange struck me as absent from the air to positive intensity, to mere unthinkability. It was as if contact were out of the question and the sterility of the passage between us recorded, with due dryness, in our staring silence. The impression was for one of the party a shock—a member of the party for whom, on the other side of the world, the imagination of the main furniture, as it might be called, of any rural excursion, of *the* rural in particular, had been, during years, the easy sense, for the excursionist, of a social relation with any encountered type, from whichever end of the scale proceeding. Had that not ever been, exactly, a part of the vague warmth, the intrinsic colour, of any honest man's rural walk in his England or his Italy, his Germany or his France, and was not the effect of its so suddenly dropping out, in the land of universal brotherhood—for I was to find it drop out again and again—rather a chill, straightway, for the heart, and rather a puzzle, not less, for the head? (118–19)

Such a passage exhibits the anxious and jeopardized but finally complacent dimension of *The American Scene* (Cox 237). Democracy cuts short the communication that a class-bound society treasures, communication that would allow James to enjoy the types he greets during pastoral interludes even while resting assured that any "exchange" will be momentary, on his terms, and, in the final analysis, "impalpable," intangible, insubstantial. His encounter with the Italian immigrant workers distresses him precisely because he cannot establish and meet these men on familiar—that is, on his own known and recognized—terms.

One wonders how Matthiessen responded at heart to James's descriptions of immigrant language and behavior, especially when one remembers how committed he was himself to "universal brotherhood" in politics and education. As a point of contrast with *The American Scene*, one can cite a memorable passage in *From the*

Heart of Europe, taken from the chapter in which Matthiessen sketches his life as a Yale undergraduate:

> I had volunteered to teach English to a group at the New Haven Hungarian Club who wanted to qualify for their citizenship papers. These men had a serious awe before the possibility of the education which I had grown up taking for granted. Most of them were double my age, but by the end of the lessons we had achieved something close to friendship. After the last session, one of the men suggested, with a sly wink, that I might like to see the rest of their building. They took me down cellar where each one had been fermenting his own cask of prohibition wine. We sampled several, with a good deal of ceremony, and the stars seemed unusually bright as I walked back to the Yale campus. I had felt in the natural and hearty comradeship of these men a quality that I was just beginning to suspect might be bleached out of middle-class college graduates. It was a kind of comradeship I wanted never to lose. (73)

Like Kenneth Lynn, I think there is something forced in Matthiessen's desire to line up with working people, as though he were determined, in a mix of moral fervor and sentimentality, to overcome the discomfort of alienation ("F. O. Matthiessen" 113). Matthiessen's embrace of democracy, moreover, seems to depend on principles overly generalized and insufficiently examined. The celebratory rhetoric he frequently employs reveals that in his view democracy in America means bringing to fulfillment the opportunities for freedom and equality that the Revolution bestowed; it means capitalizing at last upon our nation's "undiminished resources" (*American Renaissance* xv). Nowhere does Matthiessen make clear how this rhetoric could translate into particular kinds of social, political, and economic change. It may be unfair to demand such precision from Matthiessen on these matters, but it is important to see that he never grappled in his books with the nonliterary subjects toward which his literary rhetoric about democracy often gestured. Though officially a socialist, Matthiessen often seems, judging from his writings, more of an American democrat in the tradition of Whitman. He characteristically defines and extols democracy in overwhelmingly literary language, citing texts from Whitman, Emerson, Louis Sullivan, and others. Their language empowers and enriches his own, but it may also have diverted Matthiessen from addressing the political and economic consequences of a democracy truly geared toward socialism and prevented an inquiry into what a full commitment to democratic socialism might ordain for his own scholarly and professional life.

This limitation to Matthiessen's understanding of democracy is important to register, but we should take care that it not cause us to miss the difference between Matthiessen, who tries to "teach English" to immigrants seeking to become citizens, and Henry James, who defends English against the barbaric attack of foreign tongues and insinuates that English is the exclusive property of men of letters like himself. Matthiessen aspired—fiercely, unrelentingly, and at great emotional and psychological cost—toward an ideal of democratic solidarity that might bridge the differences which Henry James hankered to preserve even as he ruefully articulated the blunt truth of their disappearance.

Matthiessen reveals in *Henry James* that his socialism had begun to infiltrate his criticism. And when one looks closely at *The American Scene* and observes the social and political implications of James's language, one readily sees why writing about this novelist had to be, for Matthiessen, more than a purely literary critical undertaking. A related way of making this point is to state that Matthiessen increasingly found his concern for America and the world prompting him to assess James in the light cast by Theodore Dreiser. Reading, teaching, and writing about Dreiser drew Matthiessen to put an edge on his appraisal of writers like James, and, as he expanded his sense of the relation between form and content, to alter his attitude toward criticism in general.

FOUR

Criticism and the Cold War

> Only a perfectionist would define a radical as one who has been consistently radical throughout his lifetime.
> —Alinsky, *Reveille for Radicals* 23

MATTHIESSEN FIRST referred to Theodore Dreiser in his 1929 book on Sarah Orne Jewett, remarking in passing that this novelist lacked true "style":

> Style means that the author has fused his material and his technique with the distinctive quality of his personality. No art lasts without this fusion. If the material is important and the technique crude, the work will continue to have historical value, such as even the clumsiest Dreiser novels will have in throwing light upon their time, but they are not works of art. (145)

At this point in his career, Matthiessen subscribed to the classical dicta of Hulme, Pound, and, especially, Eliot, and unsurprisingly, he viewed Dreiser as more of a historian than an artist. Even Dreiser's defenders, after all, had spoken of him in terms that seemed in keeping with those one would use about a superb journalist. Randolph Bourne and H. L. Mencken, for example, had noted the failings of Dreiser's art even as they supported him for challenging social pieties and conventions, for, in Bourne's words, "flouting the American canons of optimism and redemption" (466). Dreiser flustered the spokesmen for the genteel tradition, dared to introduce scandalous subject matter and ideas, and risked the hostility of a "mass opinion" too timid to accept the truth about things. To Bourne and others, then, Dreiser was not necessarily a great artist, yet somehow he was still a great novelist with historical sense and an extraordinary eye for detail.

Mencken's description of Dreiser's virtues, given in the context of an exuberant account of *A Hoosier Holiday*, Dreiser's 1916 travel book, is a memorable one:

> One sees in the man all the special marks of the novelist: his capacity for photographic and relentless observation, his insatiable curiosity, his keen zest in life as a spectacle, his comprehension of and sympathy for the poor striving of humble folks, his endless mulling of insoluble problems, his recurrent Philistinism, his impatience of restraints, his fascinated suspicion of messiahs, his passion for physical beauty, his relish for the gaudy drama of big cities, his incurable Americanism. The panorama that he unrolls runs the whole scale of the colors; it is a series of extraordinarily vivid pictures. (145)

These are the talents and the tendencies of mind which, says Mencken, enabled Dreiser to write *Sister Carrie* and *The Financier* and to achieve even greater successes with similar themes and materials in *Jennie Gerhardt* and *The Titan*. But, Mencken repeatedly concedes, Dreiser's "manner," though powerful, is at bottom uninspired and clumsy:

> He blasts his way through his interminable stories by something not unlike main strength; his writing, one feels, often takes on the character of an actual siege operation, with tunnelings, drum fire, assaults in close order and hand-to-hand fighting. . . . I often wonder if Dreiser gets anything properly describable as pleasure out of this dogged accumulation of threadbare, undistinguished, uninspiring nouns, adjectives, verbs, adverbs, pronouns, participles, and conjunctions. . . . What joy can there be in rolling up sentences that have no more life and beauty in them, intrinsically, than so many election bulletins? (118, 121)

Early on, Matthiessen believed that no writer who warranted this kind of characterization could be a legitimate artist—though he might be something else. As, above all, a *literary* critic, Matthiessen judged himself loyal, at this stage of his career, to style and form, to mastery of technique. Dreiser's language was a scandal; his boisterous, uncaring, apparently even unmindful violation of the truly literary and artistic offended Matthiessen's sensibility.

This traditional image of Dreiser as an effective and moving writer but an ungifted stylist has always been potent, and it remains so to this day. In order to praise Dreiser, it seems incumbent upon the critic first to bemoan the novelist's inadequacies. "Graceless, lumbering under passages of cliché, flat exposition, guidebook description, and portentous authorial meditation and intervention," one recent commentator has observed, "Dreiser's prose nevertheless gets its job done" (Kaplan B126). This isn't, to say the least, the best foundation for praise: how much bad writing will a reader tolerate before he begins to query whether "the job" is truly well done or even worth undertaking in the first place? Not only Dreiser's detractors, but also his friends and supporters, have erected barriers to readers' ability to respond appreciatively to this writer's work as "art."

It is therefore all the more a sign of Matthiessen's imaginative and intellectual growth, and testimony to the new flexibility of approach he achieved in the 1940s, that he overcame this tradition (and his own reservations) and turned much more favorably to the ungainly Dreiser. The reasons for this were many. Matthiessen perceived, first, that Dreiser's own literary interests were similar to those of other writers that he had studied and written about. Dreiser was an avid reader of Emerson, admiring in particular the *Essays* and *Representative Men*. He also had devoted intensive study to Thoreau, editing a selection of Thoreau's "Living Thoughts" for publication in 1939 (two years before the appearance of *American Renaissance*) and highlighting in the introduction that "underlying all" of Thoreau's direct observations is a belief in "a universal, artistic, constructive genius" (*Living Thoughts* 23)—a belief that bears close affinities with Dreiser's own faith, in the latter part of his life, in "the creative force" informing the universe. Dreiser's strange brew of mysticism and science, religion and concrete fact, connected him, for Matthiessen, not only with Thoreau but with Poe, Whitman, Henry Adams, and other American searchers for cosmic unity.

In addition, Matthiessen came increasingly to respect Dreiser's truth-telling power, the aspect of his novels that Mencken and Bourne had celebrated, and that Parrington, Hicks, Alfred Kazin, and others had underscored in the 1930s and 1940s. Dreiser, according to Parrington, "does not seek refuge in the ideal. He will confront things as they are" (*Beginnings of Critical Realism* 355); "one feels his honesty," states Hicks, "his determination to present life exactly as he sees it" (*Great Tradition* 228); no other writer, contends Kazin, "has affirmed so doggedly that life as America has symbolized it is what life really is" (*On Native Grounds* 90). These were, in fact, Dreiser's own terms for his art, especially in the first decades of his career. The function of the artist, he stated, is "to put things down as they are, not as they ought to be," and he once praised Maugham's *Of Human Bondage* in a review for being "a social transcript of the utmost importance" (quoted in Elias, *Theodore Dreiser* 182). More and more in the late 1930s and 1940s this mattered to Matthiessen—the writer's ability to perceive, record, and understand the American scene, to respond to the spectacle of modern industrialism, to stand united with the working class, and to feel compassion for the lowly and oppressed. He may also have identified with Dreiser's religious and political odyssey, though he was not unmindful of its excesses and obscurities. Matthiessen admired and respected James, but possibly his real emotional kinship, by the 1940s, was with Dreiser, the convert to Quakerism and Communist/socialist sympathizer.

In suggesting that *Theodore Dreiser* represents a kind of breakthrough for Matthiessen and new breadth in his literary sensibility, I am going against the grain of opinion. Usually critics have seen the book as a disappointment, as the final scholarly enterprise of a man whose insights either had abandoned him or else had been deliberately kept in abeyance so that Matthiessen could praise a novelist he must really have known to be a very clumsy writer. Giles Gunn, for example, suggests that "because of his intense concern to demonstrate Dreiser's relevance, Matthiessen was willing to dull the edge of his own critical instrument in order to make Dreiser's virtues stand out more boldly and unambiguously" (170–71). But Matthiessen did not surrender his devotion to form and style when he worked on Dreiser: he did not altogether exchange the critical tenets of Eliot for those of Parrington. He makes many negative judgments, as when he points out that Dreiser is unfortunately always "hurrying beyond the words to develop the idea that was mastering him" (32) and emphasizes that "he was never to display much invention, which indicates a severe limitation to his imaginative resources" (112). He makes abundantly clear his reservations about *The Financier, The Titan,* and especially *The Genius,* and also speci- fies the shortcomings that weaken Dreiser's best novels, *Sister Carrie* and *An American Tragedy.*

Matthiessen knows where Dreiser falls short in comparison with James. But beyond diagnosing Dreiser's artistic defects, he wants more positively to celebrate this novelist's distinctive power and achievement, and to describe similarities and differences between Dreiser and other important American and European realists and naturalists. *Theodore Dreiser* is, for the most part, an effective mix of biography, criticism, and literary history. Appreciative but bal- anced, it is a solid introduction to Dreiser, a life-and-works volume of a sort that Matthiessen had attempted only once before, in his impressionistic monograph on Jewett.

Like *The Achievement of T. S. Eliot,* Matthiessen's book on Drei- ser is very important historically. As Robert Elias observed in a review, *Theodore Dreiser* was the first study to treat "all Dreiser's major writings" and "to mete out full justice to Dreiser the man of letters" ("Review" 506). Matthiessen himself was not wholly pleased with the manuscript, which was completed, but not wholly revised, at the time of his death in April 1950. There was doubtless something intensely willed and desperate in Matthiessen's effort, at an enormously difficult period of his life, to fight his way through the writing of this book. The signs of this struggle are occasion- ally evident in strained prose. Yet I will risk saying that *Theodore Dreiser* is a better book than Matthiessen thought; it still provides rewards to readers, especially those coming to Dreiser for the first time. Though not always deep and probing in its level of percep- tion, its literary critical sections are adequately contextualized, and there is good, if basic, analysis of *Sister Carrie* and *An American Tragedy* in particular. Matthiessen comments well on the manner in which the characters of *Sister Carrie* reflect versions of Dreiser himself (66–68), demonstrates effectively the thematic and stylistic rhythms of the novel, and stresses Dreiser's mastery of "the plain style" in the scenes of Hurstwood's decline and death (87). He also deals sensitively with Dreiser's methods in *An American Tragedy,* and offers a stimulating inquiry into the ways in which it is both "tragic" and "American" (201–11).

The literary criticism in *Theodore Dreiser* is, however, finally more suggestive than fully satisfying. Frederick Stern, in his excellent treatment of the book, outlines the intriguing, but finally equivocal and evasive, nature of Matthiessen's account of *An American Tragedy*. Stern shrewdly details how Matthiessen's argument never quite manages to sustain a view of the novel as either "particularly American" or "tragic" (207–17). For all this, even the section on *An American Tragedy* is still valuable. It is possible to work productively *with* Matthiessen's commentary, as Stern does himself, which involves taking seriously the terms Dreiser invoked for his title. The chapter on *Sister Carrie*, on the other hand, is marred by a more disabling limitation. Matthiessen responds to the novel for its depiction of social forces, the city, and Hurstwood; he does not seem to grasp the significance of Carrie herself or possess a vocabulary for exploring how Dreiser portrays sexual desire. Here again Stern is helpful, in indicating the tentativeness with which Matthiessen approaches sexuality in texts and his lack of knowledge about Freudian psychology (202–7).

Matthiessen's remarks about Carrie warrant further consideration, however, for rarely in his criticism does he seem so imperceptive as he does here.

> We have a hard time believing in her "emotional greatness" as she works her way up from chorus girl to star, largely because from the moment Dreiser introduces her as "a half-equipped little knight" he has tinged his conception with banality and sentimentality. Dreiser's realm of "the spirit," in rejecting conventional standards, is so loosely defined and moreover so cluttered with clichés that it is hard to respond any longer to his sense of liberation in it. His most serious inadequacy in presenting his heroine is not what Mrs. Doubleday thought—that Carrie is too unconventional—but that she is not unconventional enough. The only way we could sense what Dreiser calls her "feeling mind" would be to see her deeply stirred, and this she never is. Her affairs with Drouet and Hurstwood are so slurred over, in instinctive accordance with what was then demanded of fiction, that they are robbed of any warmth. She is never a woman in love. (73)

Matthiessen seems not to see that Dreiser is interested in sentimental language and banal attitudes as formative elements of his characters' selves. Drouet, Hurstwood, and Carrie break moral conventions in order to satisfy desires that are very conventional but, at the same time, extremely formidable, and especially so in Carrie's case. These desires are no less vehement, in Dreiser's view, for being typical and expressed through commonplace, unoriginal terms. Matthiessen misses the curiosity and complexity of Dreiser's approach to conventional and unconventional behavior. He is too quick to assume that Dreiser's echoes of sentimental language are unselfconscious and that the novelist retails clichés simply because his verbal inventiveness is restricted.

More important, Matthiessen is simply wrong to contend that Dreiser fails to show Carrie "deeply stirred" and that he "slurs over" Carrie's love affairs. In part this mistake may have derived from the fact that Matthiessen relied on the 1900 edition of the novel and apparently did not consult the original manuscript (which Arthur Henry, Dreiser's wife, and Dreiser himself edited in order to make the book acceptable for publication). The recently published "unexpurgated edition," which returns to Dreiser's original manuscript, is very frank in its depiction of sexuality, and is particularly explicit about the nature of Carrie's attraction to Hurstwood. But even a close reading of the 1900 edition should have made evident to Matthiessen that Dreiser is candid about sexual desire and shows Carrie in a variety of situations, sexual and otherwise, "deeply stirred." This feature of the novel is much in the foreground, and it is puzzling that Matthiessen ignores it.

Dreiser makes plain that Carrie "craves pleasure" and "followed whither her craving led": "her craving for pleasure was so strong that it was the one stay of her nature. She would speak for it when silent on all else" (Norton Critical Edition 24, 57; this text is the same as that used by Matthiessen). Carrie is a desiring self, simple in what she wants yet extraordinarily powerful in making certain that she gets it. Dreiser magnifies her sexual desire even as he also indicates its continuities with other desires. Sexuality and conspicuous consumption at a department store, for example, are seen as part of the same network of needs and interests. Soon after Carrie receives her gift of twenty dollars from Drouet, she takes a shopping tour:

> There is nothing in this world more delightful than that middle state in which we mentally balance at times, possessed of the means, lured by desire, and yet deterred by conscience or want of decision.

When Carrie began wandering around the store amid the fine displays she was in this mood. Her original experience in this same place had given her a high opinion of its merits. Now she paused at each individual bit of finery, where before she had hurried on. Her woman's heart was warm with desire for them. How would she look in this, how charming that would make her! She came upon the corset counter and paused in rich reverie as she noted the dainty concoctions of colour and lace there displayed. If she would only make up her mind, she could have one of those now. She lingered in the jewelry department. She saw the earrings, the bracelets, the pins, the chains. What would she not have given if she could have had them all! She would look fine too, if only she had some of these things. (51)

Dreiser's language ("warm with desire") focuses the sensual thrill that Carrie's desire for possessions gives her. It brings out, too, the eroticized *absoluteness* with which Carrie craves alluring things: "What would she not have given if she could have had them all!" She views herself as significant only when she displays herself effectively through nice clothing and jewelry—only then will others look at her. From this perspective, it is not really accurate to maintain, as Dreiser's critics, including Matthiessen, frequently do, that he depends too heavily on "externals" in his characterizations (Frohock 17). "Externals" are the relevant means by which Dreiser's characters represent and define themselves.

If Carrie secures what she desires, then she believes she will be present to the eyes of the world and to herself. Carrie's strength is also her ironic limitation: once she acquires these or any other fine things, she invariably hungers for more and shows, when necessary, a plucky persistence in moving herself to catch hold of that next desirable object. She constantly judges herself diminished when she senses that there is more beyond what she has managed to acquire. Her restless desire is never satisfied, and always leaps ahead to something or someone else as the guarantee, at last, of fulfillment and happiness. One day, while taking a drive along Chicago's fashionable North Side Drive with her friend Mrs. Hale, Carrie pauses to gaze longingly at the "elegant mansions":

Across the broad lawns, now first freshening into green, she saw lamps faintly glowing upon rich interiors. Now it was but a chair, now a table, now an ornate corner, which met her eye, but it appealed to her as almost nothing else could. Such childish fancies as she had had of fairy palaces and kingly quarters now came back. She imagined that across these richly carved entrance-ways, where the globed and crystalled lamps shone upon panelled doors set with stained and designed panes of glass, was neither care nor unsatisfied desire. She was perfectly certain that here was happiness. If she could but stroll up yon broad walk, cross that rich entrance-way, which to her was of the beauty of a jewel, and sweep in grace and luxury to possession and command—oh! how quickly would sadness flee; how, in an instant, would the heartache end. She gazed and gazed, wondering, delighting, longing, and all the while the siren voice of the unrestful was whispering in her ear. (86)

Dreiser often observes that Carrie is not a "thinker." Yet she is nevertheless capable of making discriminations and distinctions by comparing what she has now with what she intensely wants to have and regards, in her childish and very determined way, as the embodiment of perfection and happiness. Drouet and, later, Hurstwood are desirable to Carrie only so long as they offer to satisfy the "craving" and "longing" that she feels at a particular stage in her career. Whatever she "has" always pales in contrast with what she might possess if she were involved with another person, adorned with richer clothing, living in more luxurious surroundings.

The logic of desire plays itself out forcefully in Carrie's relationships, and in the love affairs whose meanings Matthiessen does not sharply see. Hurstwood's polished manner reduces Carrie's esteem for Drouet; Hurstwood is "the man of money and affairs" (96). But Dreiser's very phrase, "the man of money and affairs," forecasts Hurstwood's downfall. Carrie values not persons but rather what persons represent for her. During one of their early encounters, Carrie hears not Hurstwood's "words" but "the voices of the things which he represented. How suave was the counsel of his appearance! How feelingly did his superior state speak for itself!" (88). Hurstwood is superior to Drouet, in Carrie's vision, because he is superior as a representation: he stands for better things than Drouet does, and this is why, to adopt Matthiessen's phrase, he so "deeply stirs" her. What is interestingly radical in Dreiser's presentation is his understanding of "who" Drouet and Hurstwood are. They are

99

not persons as much as they are things, one group or assortment of things standing higher on the scale than the other. As a momentary representation of the "more" that Carrie seeks, Hurstwood is compelling enough to push Drouet into the background. Yet he, in turn, will eventually fade from view as well, once Carrie comes into contact with still "more" and perceives that he cannot help her any longer to attain it.

Carrie dwells in an "anticipatory world" that "has as its consequence a state of the self preoccupied with what it is not" (Fisher 263; cf. Michaels 382, 387; See 151–59). She always lives in the future, since she constantly is drawn toward it to remedy the dissatisfaction she experiences in the present. One could refer to Carrie's "enlargement of being" (Markels 529) and chart a kind of progress in Carrie's life as she advances from her initial poverty to Drouet to Hurstwood to—after she leaves him—success on the stage in New York City. But while Dreiser does provide language that gestures in this expansive, spiritualized direction, he also intimates that Carrie's course is random: the key factor is not progress, but is merely movement, change, difference. Soon after her relationship with Hurstwood begins, Carrie receives this revealing "summing up" from Dreiser's narrator:

> There was nothing bold in her manner. Life had not taught her domination—superciliousness of grace, which is the lordly power of some women. Her longing for consideration was not sufficiently powerful to move her to demand it. Even now she lacked self-assurance, but there was that in what she had already experienced which left her a little less than timid. She wanted pleasure, she wanted position, and yet she was confused as to what these things might be. Every hour the kaleidoscope of human affairs threw a new lustre upon something, and therewith it became for her the desired—the all. Another shift of the box, and some other had become the beautiful, the perfect. (107)

Life, for Carrie, is a series of brightly colored images, like those the "kaleidoscope" produces through its play of mirrors and tiny bits of junky glass and plastic. One illusion follows another; as the box "shifts," the previously all-desirable is replaced by something else that itself represents the beautiful and perfect. Hurstwood comes along, and Drouet, like the formerly glimpsed image, simply dissolves into insignificance. Here again, as in Carrie's fairy-tale reverie before the glamorous mansions, Dreiser's language is eloquently suggestive. Sometimes it is simply awkward, and warrants a verdict upon its author like the one that Malcolm Cowley has rendered—Dreiser's "genius [is] almost completely unfortified and refined by talent" ("Dreiser" 305). But often Dreiser's language is appropriate and purposeful, and when it is examined carefully, it offers much that is of local and immediate interest. His verbal resources are a good deal more supple, especially in *Sister Carrie*, than the many disparaging remarks about his cumbersome manner would indicate.

I have commented on the novel in some detail in order to bring out a crucial feature of it that Matthiessen neglects: he does not grasp Dreiser's interplay of desire, selfhood, and representation. Either he fails altogether to perceive this dimension of *Sister Carrie*, or else, perhaps responding on some level to its radical meaning and intensity, he invokes a surprisingly conventional catchphrase about fiction (we need to see the heroine "in love") that blocks him from having to confront and investigate it. This weakness in the section on *Sister Carrie* may mark, as Stern implies, a characteristic limitation in Matthiessen as a critic: he cannot, for personal or intellectual reasons, address sexuality in literary texts. But the weakness here may also be the result of a lack of critical depth in *Theodore Dreiser* as a whole. The book is, as I have said, a good, workmanlike introduction that extends Matthiessen's critical and historical range. But it might have been a better book if Matthiessen could have given it further revision, developing in greater detail some of the specific insights and working his way through some of the superficial commentary.

This is easy to say: it was obviously not something Matthiessen was able to do. His final years were hard. He suffered the desolating blow of Russell Cheney's death in 1945, a blow made all the worse by the antagonistic feelings which the Cheney family directed toward Matthiessen during the funeral (Hyde 355–56). Matthiessen later lost two other close friends, the poet Phelps Putnam, who died in 1948, and the poet and Harvard scholar Theodore Spencer, who died in 1949. He continued to work feverishly on his research and teaching, but he was often bitter and depressed, and he felt himself out of phase with his colleagues and the postwar generation of students at Harvard. Matthiessen's death occurred when he was on leave from teaching during the 1949–50 academic year; as several of his friends have pointed out, the absence of frequent human contact, coupled with protracted study of Dreiser's grim scenarios of misery and loneliness, undoubtedly made Matthiessen's sense of isolation all the more severe (Marx, "The Teacher" 37–39).

We can also learn about Matthiessen's final years from May Sarton's 1955 novel *Faithful Are the Wounds*, whose central character, Edward Cavan, is modeled upon Matthiessen. Several of Matthiessen's friends and former students have complained about the portrait of Cavan, which, they insist, makes Matthiessen seem narrow in his range of feelings, simply perverse in his unyielding politics, and less generous and loving than he was. In characterizing Cavan, Sarton does distort the original; and it is, clearly, hazardous to extrapolate from a literary character based on Matthiessen to Matthiessen himself. But Sarton effectively dramatizes aspects of Cavan that accord with the Matthiessen one knows from his books and essays, and from the abundant descriptions of him written by others. Cavan is anguished, demanding, capable of rudeness and belligerency even to close friends, isolated (233) and self-isolating (131), tense, vulnerable, always on guard (37). Ravaged emotionally and physically by the failure of the Wallace campaign and the Communist take-over in Czechoslovakia (44, 197), he is all exposed feeling; as one of his students, George Hastings, observes of him, Cavan "must have felt that nobody really cared, you know. Lately it must have been lonely to be himself, terribly lonely. The things he believed in aren't working out, you see" (253). Before the war, reflects one of Cavan's colleagues, things had been different: "Eight, ten years ago? [Cavan] had not been so angry, so difficult, so untouchable then. Then the various parts of his life had been harnessed together —the big book on the American roots in literature, the Teachers' Union, just then being founded, the Radical Club of students where Edward felt so at home and at ease, the New Deal which seemed the very proof that at last the intellectual was to be assimilated into the political scene, used instead of isolated" (64–65).

Sarton shows Cavan to be imprisoned by his absolute sense of political commitment and responsibility. "The trouble with Edward," says Damon Phillips, a friend and former political ally, "is that he's too passionate about these things. It isn't his real self—

because when it comes to the things he really cares about—Wallace Stevens' poetry, say—he can be judicial and balanced. Why is it? It's like some illness he has, and it's much worse now than it used to be" (56–57). But the passion that eats away at Cavan until it destroys him is also the source of his magnificence and heroism. This is what distinguishes Cavan from everyone else in the novel, and what makes him the inspiring teacher that Hastings and other students revere and the scholar that even his departmental enemies profoundly respect. He embodies an ideal, and serves as the intellectual conscience for the Harvard community. His life, and the memories of him that painfully linger after his death, burden his friends, but also enrich and inspire them, as becomes movingly evident in the "Epilogue: November 1954" in which Phillips speaks out in defense of Cavan's reputation before a committee investigating Communist subversives. "Although Edward Cavan may have been wrong in his belief that Communists and Socialists could and should work together," Phillips declares, "in the sense of his belief he was right and many of us were wrong. . . . That belief was that the intellectual must stand on the frontier of freedom of thought, especially in such times as these when that frontier is being narrowed down every day" (278–79). In its emphasis upon Cavan's "sheer passionate intensity" (166), his capacity for "comprehensive tenderness" (63), and his deep longing for intimacy and communion (181), Sarton's novel helps suggest why Matthiessen was such an extraordinary (and complex) teacher and friend, and why the institutional and political changes that followed the war so wounded him.

Some sense of Matthiessen's strengths and limits can also be gleaned from Truman Nelson's fiery historical novel about abolitionism in the 1850s, *The Sin of the Prophet*. Though rarely read today, Nelson's novel was highly acclaimed when it was published in 1952 for its artistic intensity and relevance to the social and political scene. Its depiction of the crisis caused by the evil of slavery, its attack on state power and repression, and its rendering of the personal and cultural effects of the Fugitive Slave Law, with the accompanying betrayals and acts of treachery, were meant by Nelson to connect with the emerging Civil Rights movement of the 1940s and early 1950s and, more important, to assail McCarthyism. A radical activist himself, Nelson dedicated *The Sin of the Prophet* "To the memory of a friend to man, F. O. Matthiessen," and telescoped many of Matthiessen's traits in his characterization of Theodore Parker, the novel's protagonist.

Parker is a powerful, admirable figure, one through whom Nelson seeks to explain and vindicate Matthiessen, who had died in 1950 and who had himself once referred to Parker as "the principal transcendentalist in action, the very epitome of the movement's social and economic convictions" ("Flowering of New England" 203). Others depicted in the novel, particularly Wendell Phillips, are impressive in their moral firmness and eloquence, but it is Parker who stands out among them. He has a concentrated faith in God and man that propels his own conduct and makes him impatient and angry with those who temporize or backslide. Parker "did not expect people to run at his bidding, but he figured other people should work as hard and tenaciously as himself in a cause that was common to both of them" (17–18). Nelson brings out very effectively Parker's determination to make the right prevail, and he pays frequent tribute to the majestic persistence of the man who drives himself, despite exhaustion, illness, and social ostracism, on behalf of the good cause. In a fine sentence, Nelson notes that "people whose characteristics are set in a firm and unchanging mold are exceptional and even the rude and ignorant pay deference to the clarity of their effect upon the world" (183). Parker says that "the sentence of life" has been passed upon him (367)—he has moral obligations he cannot shirk—and this is his great distinction.

Yet his acutely felt moral commitments also bring Parker pain and alienate him from many of his fellow men. Exemplary in his fervor and idealism, he is also frightening. He is the conscience of the community, yet perhaps enjoys too much the moral wounding he administers to others when he records their defects. His rightness is simultaneously necessary and overbearing—it threatens to overmaster and overwhelm even Parker's own friends and allies. Parker, it seems, takes some real pleasure in rebuking others, including those closest to him, and then suffers from the alienation that his judgments of them trigger. Nelson suggests that Parker knows what he is doing to himself—what price he pays for heatedly staying true to his convictions—but that he cannot, or will not, adjust his behavior. Parker is hard, unyielding, a passionate crusader for fellowship and "faith in man" (450). Yet he is, on some level, closed in his nature, cut off from fully sharing in the lives of other people, however much he is drawn to them in moral and emotional terms.

Wallace Stevens, in a letter commenting on Matthiessen's death, remarked that "at the bottom of the whole thing there was something terribly personal," but acknowledged that those on the outside could never identify what feelings drove Matthiessen to suicide: "when a man's trouble comes down to the final intimacy he just doesn't give anyone access to it" (679). A thoughtful point, in its respect for privacy and recognition of the limits to our knowledge of other persons. But one can at least try to draw together some of the private and public facts of Matthiessen's final years to furnish a more exact context for *Theodore Dreiser*. These years were not only lonely for him, but also indeed arduous and upsetting in political terms, as Sarton's novel indicates. One way of registering this is to reflect that Matthiessen killed himself less than two months after Senator Joseph McCarthy's notorious February 1950 speech before the Women's Club in Wheeling, West Virginia, in which he announced that Communists had crept into the State Department and "thoroughly infested" it (66). Many of America's best and brightest had betrayed their country, McCarthy declared. The guilty were "those who had all the benefits that the wealthiest nation on earth has had to offer—the finest homes, the finest college education, and the finest jobs in government we can give" (65–66).

Some have concluded that Matthiessen was one of McCarthy's first victims; "when Professor Matthiessen died, the cold war made its first martyr among scholars," one friend has said (Dunham 102). The frenzy that followed McCarthy's disclosures of Communists and fellow travelers—the betrayals, the public cruelty and humiliation of innocent men and women, the mindless jettisoning of basic rights and freedoms—doubtless contributed to Matthiessen's despair and suicide. All of this, of course, did not begin with McCarthy. It was President Truman, acting in March 1947, who ordered "loyalty" investigations of three million government employees (homosexuals were one of the groups targeted as "suspect"). In the same month, Truman also articulated the containment "doctrine" designed to halt the spread of Communism in Europe. It was not, in other words, simply the renegade behavior of McCarthy that spurred the cold war in America. It was the executive branch, aided by the Congress and an easily aroused public, that sounded the alarm of internal subversion and assaults on American interests abroad.

Nineteen forty-nine had been especially bad. This was the year of the Alger Hiss case (after a lengthy trial, he was convicted of perjury in 1950), and the accompanying furor about the passing of intelligence secrets to the Russians by members of the liberal intelligentsia. In another key court case, eleven members of the Communist party were found guilty of sedition under the terms of the Smith Act, which Congress had passed in 1940 and which outlawed any attempt, in speech, writing, or action, to overthrow the government of the United States. On the foreign policy front, the Soviet Union exploded its first A-bomb, and in the fall, Mao Zedong and his Communist army defeated Jiang Jie-shi's Nationalist forces and established the People's Republic of China. Both events deepened fears of the red menace, and made liberal and leftist positions dangerous to advocate. As one scholar has observed, by the late 1940s "everyone to the left of Atila the Hun was considered Communist or Communist influenced" (Cantor 167).

The postwar years also witnessed the arrival of a fierce anti-Communism on college and university campuses (Bloom 244–50; Caute 403–30; Schrecker). Like other radicals, Communists and former Communists, and fellow travelers, Matthiessen found his own "loyalty" to America called into question. As George Abbott White will show in his illuminating biography, a number of government agencies spied on Matthiessen, and maintained extensive files on his "suspicious" conduct and speech. Matthiessen was greatly pained by the degradation of intellect and the assaults on academic freedom which the loyalty oath requirements occasioned and that many administrative and congressional hearings propelled. Everything to which Matthiessen had dedicated his intellectual life, everything that had made him believe in the university as one of America's best hopes for a revitalized democracy, seemed in danger of being lost forever amid the rush to purge the nation of its political enemies.

For two decades, Matthiessen had written about and taught a group of American writers—including Emerson, Thoreau, Melville, James, and Dreiser—who, he maintained, could enable common readers to envision "the possibilities of democracy" (*American Re-*

naissance ix). He must have been shocked by the sight of a country doing its utmost to disserve the aspirations and ideals of its most fervent spokesmen. Even more, he must have suffered as he realized that his own acts of "translating" the masterpieces of American literature had not been successful. Things were getting worse in a postwar period marked by "a resurgence of conservative and rightist forces" (Lipset and Raab 215), and Matthiessen—proud, intense, moody—likely judged that he had failed in his ambitions of service to the nation. He had fallen lamentably short of the achievements of the Elizabethan patriot-translators whom he had treated so positively in the dissertation that inaugurated his scholarly career. These men had been organically in tune with their native audiences; Matthiessen had not.

Matthiessen self-punishingly recognized during his final years that he was speaking in a voice that his countrymen could not hear. In 1948, he had avidly supported Henry Wallace, the former Democratic vice-president and now Progressive party candidate for president. For Matthiessen and other Wallace backers, the election results were dismaying. They had not expected their man to win, but they had hoped for a much greater display of support, perhaps as much as 10 percent of the vote. Wallace tallied barely more than a million votes (roughly 2 percent of the total) and failed to carry a single state; in the two states where the Progressive party forces had been especially optimistic, New York and California, he received just 8.1 and 4.7 percent of the vote. Some have even suggested that numbers of Wallace's own workers voted for Truman, either because they feared the election of the Republican, Thomas Dewey, or because they were disturbed by the influence of the Communist party on the Wallace campaign (Walton 245). The Progressive coalition had initially looked formidable, mobilizing ranks of farmers, intellectuals, blacks, segments of organized labor. It also had aroused many teachers and students in colleges and universities, in this regard "pioneering the campus as a political arena" (Buhle 196). But while it was "outwardly rather impressive as a popular front, the Wallace movement was inwardly beset with disharmony, suspicion, recrimination, and a conflict of conceptions" (Starobin 182). Its actual base of support turned out to be both fractious and alarmingly thin.

Matthiessen's friends tried to cite the results—"by any standard

. . . a complete disaster" (Walton 295)—as evidence for his folly in persisting in the Progressive party's cause. Here are Paul Sweezy's words:

> I developed the argument that the small Wallace vote meant that the PP had failed to do what it set out to do—to establish itself as a genuine contender for political power—and that for this reason alone it could not be an effective political vehicle for the future. The American people would never again take it seriously as an alternative to the old parties, and it lacked a philosophy and a long-run objective (such as real socialist parties have) which might enable it to live and grow as a small minority party. My conclusion was that the PP should be liquidated as a national party, and that the various state and local bodies should decide their course—whether to retain party status or transform themselves into non-partisan political action groups—in accordance with specific local conditions. (71)

A man on the left himself, Sweezy was respectfully but firmly telling Matthiessen that it would be self-defeating to stay with the Progressive party. Matthiessen agreed, Sweezy goes on to report, with the thrust of the analysis yet nevertheless continued to fasten on the Progressive party as the only movement to which he could belong. There is something admirable about this kind of tenacity—a determination to keep one's political faith despite the current situation. But, knowing Matthiessen, we cannot help but find something severely willful here—a lonely, grieving, but terribly resolute demand to be allowed to go his own way.

Matthiessen's support of the Progressive party in 1948 remains difficult to understand. In certain respects, Wallace stood for admirable goals; he sought to secure postwar cooperation and coexistence in foreign affairs, and, on the domestic front, he assailed and sought to correct shortcomings in American democracy. These, he said, were all too numerous, and were egregiously evident in the poll tax disenfranchisement of Negro voters and in job discrimination on the basis of race, religion, or sex. But Wallace was more a Jeffersonian liberal and New Dealer than a leftist: he did not favor the kind of socialist equality that Matthiessen himself often espoused. In addition, Wallace did not seem able to acknowledge the reality of Soviet aggression; as early as 1946, he had embraced the view that "the Soviet Government and its leaders disdain aggressive intentions and any desire for world dominion" (Schapsmeier 149). In 1948, in an act he later regretted as one of his worst failures of judgment, he blamed the takeover of Czechoslovakia and the apparent murder of Foreign Minister Jan Masaryk (whom Matthiessen had met and admired) on the consequences of American policies: "the Czech crisis is clearly another fruit of the utterly stupid and possibly suicidal Truman Doctrine" (Walker 187; Markowitz 273–74; Pells, *Liberal Mind* 110). Ironically, while Wallace felt himself to be steadfastly fighting against militarism and corporate power, "big brass and big gold," and thereby resisting the rise of an "American fascism," his soft tones about the Soviet Union made him seem, to many observers, to be the kind of politician who made Fascism possible—the *New York Times* even compared him in an editorial to Neville Chamberlain (Walker 184).

Nor did Wallace fully acknowledge the impact on his own campaign of the Communist Party of America, whose statements (and actions) on his and the Progressive party's behalf were explicit. The CPA, though not wholly enthusiastic about Wallace himself, had nevertheless declared that "in 1948 we Communists join with millions of other Americans to support the Progressive Party ticket to help win the peace. . . . The new Progressive Party is an inescapable historic necessity" (quoted in Schapsmeier 182). As John Morton Blum has noted, "in his determination to resist redbaiting," Wallace became "indifferent to the debilitating tactics of Communists within his Progressive Party" (*Price of Vision* 48), and this made him appear impractical, utopian, dangerous.

Wallace did direct some accurate criticism at the Truman administration for its cold war provocations—its anti-Russian statements, high defense budgets, atomic bomb testing and construction of U.S. air bases around the world, military aid to foreign governments. For all his confusions about the Communist party in America, he was also noteworthy for having defended the right of the party to be heard and to be protected under the Constitution: "in this he stood almost alone in American life" (Starobin 183). Anticipating Eisenhower's warnings about the "military-industrial complex" in his 1961 farewell address, Wallace counseled against the growing linkage between big business and national defense policy. Citing examples of this kind, Blum and Walton, among others, have gone so far as to describe Wallace as a prophet who foresaw where cold war mentality and behavior would lead. The late 1940s were not a period when most Americans brooked much difference of opinion on the matter of the Soviet Union; and Wallace's own statements grew more shrill and defensive as he was subjected to increasingly furious attacks in the press, was sometimes prevented from delivering speeches, and was heckled and pelted with garbage while campaigning. After one such incident in North Carolina in September 1948, he wondered aloud, "Am I in the United States?" (Walker 202). But the fact remains that Wallace did not speak forthrightly about the Soviet Union's failure to honor agreements made at Yalta and Potsdam, and he failed to label the Berlin blockade and the Czech takeover for what they were. He thus appeared to be anti-American and pro-Soviet; if he was not that, he was certainly a man whose dreams of mutual coexistence had imprisoned him and skewed his judgment.

Wallace's limitations are clear in his frequently platitudinous writings. Despite his deep interest in language, Matthiessen did not notice this, doubtless because he was so drawn to Wallace's professed commitment to Christianity, democracy, and education. The most striking thing about Wallace's writings today is their thinness; his moral and liberal sentiments are simultaneously admirable and contentless. His idealism is sometimes stirring, as when he announced "the century of the common man" in a speech in May 1942 (*Democracy Reborn* 190–96). Toward the end of the war and afterward, in *Sixty Million Jobs* (1945) and other books, he again sounded this note effectively. His language reverberated well for many liberals and leftists eager to realize "a fuller life for all" and anxious to distance themselves from the conflict-ridden, polarizing rhetoric of the cold war. But his writing in general does not hold up. One turns hopefully to pieces such as "The Power of Books" (1937) and "Lincoln" (1944), both included in *Democracy Reborn* (130–34, 255–56), yet these consist mostly of a succession of lame sentences. It is here, in its close analysis of Wallace's books, speeches, public statements, and interviews, that Dwight MacDonald's 1948 book *Henry Wallace: The Man and the Myth*, is so devastating. MacDonald is occasionally unfair and abusive in harping on Wallace's "Stalinoid connections" (100), but he brings out compellingly Wallace's marriage of moral idealism and amorphous, fuzzy, confused language.

One wonders how Matthiessen, who believed that the "use of language is the most sensitive index to cultural history" (*American Renaissance* xv), could ever have rebutted MacDonald's blistering critique.

Other liberals and leftists were far more harsh than Sweezy in their response to Matthiessen's politics, and their public attacks on him became especially virulent after the publication of his travel memoir, *From the Heart of Europe*, in 1948, the year of the Wallace campaign. In this book Matthiessen described his experiences at the first Salzburg Seminar in Austria and at Charles University in Prague in the summer and fall of 1947. Just before its publication, the Communists seized power in Czechoslovakia, and their brutal destruction of any hope for democratic rule in that country made Matthiessen's celebrations of comradeship and community look pathetically foolish and misguided. In a hard-hitting review of *From the Heart of Europe*—titled "The Sentimental Fellow-Travelling of F. O. Matthiessen"—Irving Howe attacked Matthiessen as a dupe of Stalinism and as a befuddled enthusiast of the Wallace movement, that "completely contrived creature of Stalinism" (1128):

> Here, then, is the political portrait of our outstanding literary fellow-traveller: a literary critic succumbing to the most abominable totalitarian movement of our time; a man of literary refinement insensitive to half a continent of victims and charmed by the pseudosocialist rhetoric of those who grind these victims; an American intellectual who would join the French Communist Party because it is large but not the American Communist Party which is small, even though their aims are identical; a writer who calls himself a democratic socialist while apologizing for the regimes that have jailed, exiled, and murdered democratic socialists.
>
> Is this too harsh, too fractious? Will some judicious souls cry "Stalinophobia"? Does it offend genteel sensibilities ready to become violently partisan about questions relating to the structure of poetry but indifferent to Stalinism as a bogey that frightens only New York intellectuals?
>
> I would only record the fact that as I read Matthiessen's book an uncontrolled fear arose within me, of a sort I had never known while reading outright Stalinists. For I could not help thinking of

the thousands of European Matthiessens who, with the best will in the world, had helped bring about their own downfall; I could not help thinking that if some of us ever end our days in a "corrective labor camp" it might well be because of the equally good intentions of intellectuals like F. O. Matthiessen. (1129)

Matthiessen's weak rebuttal to this piece in November 1948 drew further fire from Howe, who again lambasted Matthiessen's "Stalinized thinking" and labeled him "an apologist for a brutal totalitarian state and its agents" ("Reply" 1256).

Matthiessen's political reputation among liberal and leftist intellectuals, already precarious at best, never recovered from this blast at his apparent fondness for Stalinism. Whereas the right had assaulted Matthiessen for sidling up to the Communists, polemicists on the left, led by Howe, now assaulted him for what they branded as an act of intellectual and political betrayal. In reviews of *From the Heart of Europe*, and, later, of *Theodore Dreiser*, the left argued that by refusing to denounce the totalitarian evils of Stalinist Russia, Matthiessen had dirtied the very cause of democratic socialism he took himself to be supporting. It is Matthiessen and others like him to whom Philip Rahv referred, in 1949, when he identified Orwell's *Nineteen Eighty-four* as giving readers "an extension into the near future of the present structure and policy of Stalinism" and showing the "double-think" consciousness "practiced by the Communists and their liberal collaborators, dupes, and apologists" who bolstered the Stalinist state ("Unfuture of Utopia" 333, 334).

Decades later, Matthiessen remains unforgiven. In his autobiography, published in 1982, Howe refers to Matthiessen as a "gifted, tragic figure" who "seemed perversely intent at putting his cultivation to the service of the commissars" (*Margin of Hope* 157). In *New York Jew*, Alfred Kazin, who had taught with Matthiessen at Salzburg, calls *From the Heart of Europe* "a book of total political innocence," adding that Matthiessen grew "steadily more defensive of Stalinism" and carried "various students with him" (260). Liberals and leftists, their memories of *From the Heart of Europe* still, it seems, quite fresh, have effectively banished Matthiessen from their midst. Like his candidate Henry Wallace—recently described by a leftist critic as merely "a disillusioned member of the ruling elite" (Lipsitz 149)—he has had no political impact and left no political legacy. It is striking to realize that, with very few exceptions, the New Left factions of the 1960s and early 1970s paid little attention to Matthiessen. In some ways one might think that he would have been manifestly relevant as a model and hero—a socialist and radical activist, an internationalist, a humanist and passionate scholar/ teacher, a fighter against institutional authority, a martyr who died at the outset of the McCarthyite frenzy. Yet he is not cited even once in representative New Left volumes such as *The Dissenting Academy* (1968) and *The Politics of Literature: Dissenting Essays on the Teaching of English* (1972). Matthiessen is remembered not for his politics but for his scholarship. And today, his scholarship is itself often invoked to signify the type of literary conservatism and cultural elitism that regularly has omitted women and Afro-Americans from the canon: he is seen as a progenitor of cold war criticism (Pease). Most people who know about, and who usually dispute, the influence of Matthiessen's books probably are unaware of his leftist politics. The amusingly incorrect sentence in the National Cyclopaedia entry for Matthiessen—"politically he was a Republican" (397)—would likely be accepted by them as fact.

We cannot recuperate Matthiessen's politics, any more than we can ignore the limits to his choice of canonical authors. But without giving up a critical perspective on his final years, one can still see strength and innovation in *Theodore Dreiser* and even in *From the Heart of Europe*. In the Dreiser study, whatever its analytical shortcomings, he extended his power and range as a literary critic, and in the book about his European experiences, he attempted a type of cultural criticism he had not performed so explicitly before. Matthiessen was not stringent in his assessment of Stalinism, speaking of it in *From the Heart of Europe* in muted and fairly generalized terms, as when he remarks that "the Soviet state takes the position, which states have tended to do throughout history, that thought can be dangerous" (48). He was not a Dwight MacDonald. Nor was he a George Orwell, whose *Animal Farm* appeared in 1945 and whose *Nineteen Eighty-Four* was published in 1949, a year after *From the Heart of Europe*. But within his personal and political limits, he did move forward in his critical work in *Theodore Dreiser* and *From the Heart of Europe*. This was, for him, a modest and limited, but real, victory.

In the final reckoning, these books may show potential rather than fully realized achievement, indicating where Matthiessen was heading, unevenly but importantly, in his conception of the tasks of criticism. Inevitably one wants to think here, as elsewhere, about the Matthiessen who might have seized on the discoveries of his later life and applied them well if death had not intervened. When surveying his work in the 1930s, one feels inclined to criticize Matthiessen for divorcing his politics from his literary studies; when looking at what he did in the 1940s, one still has to be critical but also more generous toward him, commending his effort—uneven and unclear though it was—to realize his organic ideal more fully and develop somehow an integrated vision of literature and life, criticism and politics.

I intend shortly to turn once again to the study of Dreiser, but need first to consider *From the Heart of Europe*, since Matthiessen's critics have often said that the two books belong together as exhibits of Matthiessen's decline. Irving Howe and others have stressed that "sentimental" passages abound in *From the Heart of Europe*, as Matthiessen strives in a "slightly ridiculous," "pulpy" manner to affirm his solidarity with "the people" ("Sentimental Fellow-Travelling" 1125; see also O'Neill 175–83). There is some of this, without question, but it is less silly and disabling than Matthiessen's critics claim. It is also necessary to see what in Matthiessen motivates these various scenes of festivity and comradeship. Repeatedly, Matthiessen stresses the value of "communication" between men and women of different nationalities and cultures, revealing something that not only matters greatly to him in emotional terms but also bears witness to the influence on his values of Eliot, Pound, and Henry James. Each of these writers was concerned to establish lines of communication between America and Europe, and each, Pound in particular, emphasized the role that language, when sensitively used, plays in securing cross-cultural communication and understanding. This, among other things, is what Pound has in mind when he refers in "How to Read" to the connections between language and "the health of the matter of thought itself" (21), and when, in his essay on James, he celebrates James's efforts to preserve the "American idiom" and pursue "the great labour, this labour of translation, of making America intelligible, of making it possible for individuals to meet across national borders" (296).

This appreciation of language helps to account for why Matthiessen, as all observers report, read and explicated Melville, James, Whitman, and other American writers with special passion when he taught European students from sixteen countries at the Salzburg Seminar and at Charles University. He wanted to communicate the authenticity of his desire for fellowship, and did so, as would be natural for him, through literature and criticism. Reading great texts and commenting upon them gave him a means of expressing feelings and aspirations that were hard for him to express in other ways, and that imaged for him a world built on brotherhood. I suspect he felt a freedom during these seminars in Europe that was, especially after the war and after Cheney's death, very rare for him—an opportunity to be really in contact with himself and with others.

The hope and need for "communication" is everywhere in *From the Heart of Europe,* and it is openly voiced again and again:

> We have come [to Salzburg] to enact anew the chief function of culture and humanism, to bring man again into communication with man. (13)

> The role of a Hemingway or an Eliot . . . is to keep alive the vital, delicate, and always menaced accuracy of communication, without which there can be no renewed discovery of man by man. (59)

> Hardly more than a hundred men and women, some already worn beyond their years, we were nevertheless going back to our many countries with a renewed belief in the possibility of communication. We were carrying with us too the belief that there was much we could still do, by our speaking and writing, to cut through prejudice, to destroy the barriers of ignorance and hate that otherwise will destroy us all. (66)

"Communication" means "community," and here, for Matthiessen, Whitman is crucial:

> Whitman knew, through the heartiness of his temperament, as Emerson did not, that the deepest freedom does not come from isolation. It comes instead through taking part in the common life, mingling in its hopes and failures, and helping to reach a more adequate realization of its aims, not for one alone, but for the community. Something like this was what Whitman had in mind when he said that his "great word," the one that moved him most, was "solidarity." (90)

Matthiessen maintains that it is precisely this yearning for "communication" and "community" which the postwar American university system, run by administrators and not by teachers, no longer respects. "If you want to be a teacher in a large university in America, you are working against the grain," he reflects:

> Most of our big institutions seem as lacking in a sense of intellectual community as Henry Adams and William James found Harvard to be. One should not underestimate the freedom provided at Harvard, once you have a job, to do that job in your own way, without interference. Indeed, defenders of free enterprise in other fields might well find that state the *Summum Bonum*. But I doubt that the results are as good as American society has a right to expect. . . . The individual teacher is scarcely more than a hired hand. (67, 68)

Matthiessen does not condemn Stalinism with the ferocity that Howe would like to see displayed; and Matthiessen's absorption in "community" tells us something about his own longing for intimacy. But one can accept these two points and still find honest, sincere utterance in *From the Heart of Europe*. Matthiessen's internationalist vision, his appeal for cross-cultural understanding, his dedication to teaching and criticism as enactments of community, his critique of the impersonality and anti-intellectualism of the American educational system—all of this and more in the book remain valuable. Four decades after the book's publication, the reviewers of *From the Heart of Europe* now sometimes seem rigid, not Matthiessen.

Such a judgment may not be entirely fair to Howe, but it nonetheless carries a measure of validity. In *A Margin of Hope*, Howe has emphasized that "the fear of Communist power in the ten or fifteen years after the Second World War was real," a "warranted fear," and he has thus sought to defend himself against the accusation that in attacking Stalinism in the 1940s and 1950s he "succumbed to Cold War propaganda" (206). In his view, it was incumbent upon the left to declare resoundingly the truth that "wherever Stalinism conquered, freedom vanished" (206). But one can credit Howe's intention without necessarily approving of the consequences that followed from it. What Howe does not clearly see is the ideological function of his own anti-Stalinism. In denouncing Matthiessen, Howe was not only exposing what he deemed a glaring instance of fellow-traveling. He was also unwittingly helping to amplify ideological vocabularies and charges that limited the cold war left. Though certainly not wrong to criticize Stalinism, Howe, through his vituperative tone, abetted others for whom anti-Stalinism became, as Philip Rahv later characterized it, "almost a professional stance" ("Our Country and Our Culture" 307)—a totalizing, inflexible vision that basically disallowed any socialist/progressive ideas.

To say this is not to deny the inadequacies of *From the Heart of Europe*. These are political, but they also are intellectual, and involve Matthiessen's attempts to make his socialism and Christianity cohere. In a very general sense, Matthiessen is able to bring together the two worldviews. Christianity urges that we should love our neighbor, and, for Matthiessen, such an injunction impels us to labor for a society based on equality and tolerance and fraternity. This, he counsels, is the society that socialists, too, seek. But Christianity teaches the additional lesson that men are imperfect. No society, socialist or otherwise, can be perfect, because its members are not perfectible. Men must look to God to fulfill the needs that human society alone cannot meet.

This conjunction of Christianity and socialism, however, starts to come apart whenever Matthiessen tries to explain it in detail. In *From the Heart of Europe*, Matthiessen argues courageously—given the political climate at that time—for the significance of Marxist insights but presses home that he is "not a Marxist in any sense" (82).

> I am a Christian, not through upbringing but by conviction, and I find any materialism inadequate. I make no pretense of being a theologian, but I have been influenced by the same Protestant revival that has been voiced most forcefully by Reinhold Niebuhr. That is to say, I have rejected the nineteenth-century belief in every man as his own Messiah, along with the other aberrations of that century's individualism; and I have accepted the doctrine of original sin, in the sense that man is fallible and limited, no matter what his social system, and is capable of finding completion only through humility before the love of God. (82)

One odd feature of this passage is the reference to Niebuhr. Matthiessen does not probe the consequences for his own position of Niebuhr's postwar writings, which are militantly anti-Communist, and which, for this reason, appealed to a sizable number of cold war establishment intellectuals. Nor does he deal with the fact that

Niebuhr was resolutely opposed to Matthiessen's candidate, Henry Wallace, and disdained socialism. Niebuhr at one time had been a socialist, though his origins were in the Social Gospel movement rather than in the Marxist tradition; in 1930, he founded the Fellowship of Socialist Christians and even ran as a Socialist party candidate for Congress in New York City. Furthermore, in the 1930s he did draw upon Marx to reinforce his critique of capitalism and bourgeois liberalism. But by the mid-to-late 1940s (he had resigned from the Socialist party in 1940), Niebuhr was regularly spotlighting Russia as America's great foe. He was a very influential critic of Communism, often writing articles for popular magazines as well as for journals of opinion. A notable case in point is his 20 September 1948 piece in *Life*, "For Peace, We Must Risk War," in which he calls for adamant resistance to the Communist threat. Ironically, in its previous issue, *Life* had run a three-page story, "The South Gets Rough with Wallace," that depicted the heckling and abuse Henry Wallace had experienced during a campaign swing into the deep South; *Life* showed some sympathy for his plight, but stressed, as usual, that he had naively allowed himself to be steered into trouble by his Communist backers. Niebuhr would have agreed with this; just before the November election, he editorialized in *Christianity and Crisis* that Wallace was an incompetent leader and the front man for "a party in which Communists and their sympathizers hold all the levers of power" ("Presidential Campaign" 137).

All of us read selectively and do not take whole the writers who influence us: it was undoubtedly the Niebuhr who authored *Moral Man and Immoral Society* (1932) and *Beyond Tragedy* (1937), with their evocations of the tragic limits of human life and the plight of the sensitive conscience, who mattered most to Matthiessen. But one still feels an absence of intellectual depth in Matthiessen's bonding of his Christian mission to Niebuhr's. Matthiessen does not perceive (or does not wish to perceive) the pressure that the authority he cites applies to his own position. One thinks, too, of the vigorously anti-Soviet line taken in Niebuhr's *The Irony of American History*, a provocative, influential book that assailed American complacency and denounced Communism as a "demonic religion" (Fox 247). It was published in 1952, but given in part as lectures in the spring of 1949—about the same time, in other words, as Matthiessen's May 1949 lecture "The Responsibilities of the Critic," where he bravely contended that "the principles of Marxism remain at the base of much of the best social and cultural thought of our century" (11). Matthiessen does not inquire into the way in which the Protestant revival that counters Emersonian individualism may also challenge Marxist tenets that he endorses. He is engaging issues at a level of generality that allows him to believe that a quite varied, competitive group of thinkers and ideas flows together harmoniously. The lucid movement of Matthiessen's prose in fact glosses over the potential— if the thinkers and ideas were deeply pondered—for grave disorder.

Matthiessen emphasizes that "the Russian Revolution [is] the most progressive event of our century, the necessary successor to the French Revolution and the American Revolution and to England's seventeenth-century Civil War" (*From the Heart of Europe* 83). But how does he connect this judgment with his Christianity and invocation of Niebuhr? The degree of intellectual discord heightens when Matthiessen approvingly refers to Lenin on the next page:

> Owing to the vast developments in industrialization, political revolution now can and must be completed by an economic revolution. It must be so completed because we have now learned that otherwise the immense concentration of wealth in a few hands makes for a renewed form of tyranny. This is the truth we grasped through the theory and practice of Lenin. It would be the worst folly to lose sight of it, no matter what aberrations from or distortions of it have occurred in the special circumstances of current Russia. And the Russians, whatever their failures in practice so far, however short they may have fallen of some of Lenin's aims through the grim pressures of dictatorship, have not been deflected from the right of all to share in the common wealth. (83)

An obvious problem with this is the soft sentence that Matthiessen writes about Stalinist Russia. But there is another difficulty as well. If Matthiessen had grappled with the theory and practice of Lenin in a rigorous way, he would have experienced considerable shock to his educational and literary values. Lenin's 1905 article, "Party Organization and Party Literature" is just one of many relevant examples that could be cited to challenge the very beliefs Matthiessen cherishes:

> In contradistinction to bourgeois customs, to the profit-making commercialized bourgeois press, to bourgeois literary careerism and individualism, "aristocratic anarchism," and drive for profit, the socialist proletariat must put forward the principle of *party literature,* must develop this principle and put it into practice as fully and completely as possible.
>
> What is the principle of party literature? It is not simply that, for the socialist proletariat, literature cannot be a means of enriching individuals or groups; it cannot, in fact, be an individual undertaking, independent of the common cause of the proletariat. Down with non-partisan writers! Down with literary supermen! Literature must become *part* of the common cause of the proletariat, "a cog and a screw" of the one single great Social-Democratic mechanism set in motion by the entire politically conscious vanguard of the entire working class. Literature must become a component of organized, planned and integrated Social-Democratic Party work. (23)

"Freedom of speech," says Lenin, is a bourgeois myth: it amounts to allowing the rich "the freedom" to purchase the literature and journals of opinion that will benefit and solidify the existing class structure. For Matthiessen to commend the "theory and practice" of Lenin, and not deal with their bearing on his own critical and literary views, is a political failure, but it is an intellectual failure, too—a failure of mind, a failure in knowledge.

One is tempted at this point to cite part two of Lionel Trilling's famous essay "Reality in America," with its pointed critique of Matthiessen's commentary on Dreiser's last novel, *The Bulwark.* His case is often convincing, and I am inclined to echo it in outlining the inadequacies of *From the Heart of Europe.* Yet Trilling's argument is also misleading. Like Howe's review and other polemical attacks on Matthiessen in the 1940s, it has hampered critical discussion of Matthiessen's politics. Trilling's piece also provided reviewers of the Dreiser book, as well as later commentators upon it, with authoritative backing for their complaints about Matthiessen's approach to this writer. It stands behind Brom Weber's reference to Matthiessen's "tongue-tied consideration" of Dreiser's last years (Stern 175), Richard Hofstadter's claim that Matthiessen "declass[ed] himself intellectually" in writing about Dreiser" ("Native Sons"), and other, equally stringent (and sometimes smug) observations.

Trilling published this essay in the *Nation* in April 1946, eventually including it in *The Liberal Imagination* (1950). In it he mounts an attack not only on Matthiessen and Dreiser but also on the entire spectrum of liberal, progressive, and radical criticism. In polemical form, "Reality in America" reflects the story of intellectual betrayal and tragic innocence that Trilling presents in his only novel, *The Middle of the Journey*, which he was writing in 1946 and which was published in 1947. Naively drawn toward Communism and socialism, many writers, critics, and professors had, in Trilling's view, defaulted upon their obligations to "mind." If a novelist like Dreiser mirrored the huge, ugly, chaotic facts of American experience, then he was presumed to be commendable; if, on the other hand, a novelist like Henry James concerned himself with mind, morals, and the creative imagination, he was guilty of a flight from politics and society. Liberals and their ilk, Trilling argues, are hostile toward James, yet are grotesquely tolerant of Dreiser, whom they treat with "doctrinaire indulgence" (24). The treason of liberal intellectuals as a class—this is the burden of Trilling's essay, an essay that is as much about Communism and Stalinism as it is about James and Dreiser. It is also about an act such as Dreiser's decision to join the Communist party in August 1945, and Trilling's indictment of the misguidedly generous "liberal" response to it.

The issues, though, are more complex than Trilling suggests, and there is a certain manipulativeness in his handling of his argument. Here, for example, is his first reference to Matthiessen; it begins with a quotation from Matthiessen's March 1946 review of *The Bulwark*:

> "The liability in what Santayana called the genteel tradition was due to its being the product of mind apart from experience. Dreiser gave us the stuff of our common experience, not as it was hoped to be by any idealizing theorist, but as it actually was in its crudity."

The author of this statement certainly cannot be accused of any lack of feeling for mind as Henry James represents it; nor can Mr. Matthiessen be thought of as a follower of Parrington—indeed, in the preface to *American Renaissance* he has framed one of the sharpest and most cogent criticisms of Parrington's method. Yet, Mr. Matthiessen, writing in *The New York Times Book Review* about Dreiser's posthumous novel, *The Bulwark*, accepts the liberal cliché which

opposes crude experience to mind and establishes Dreiser's value
by implying that the mind which Dreiser's crude experience is presumed to confront and refute is the mind of gentility. ("Reality in
America" 28)

Whatever his other faults, Matthiessen is not doing quite what Trilling says he is doing. Matthiessen affirms that Dreiser resists the authority of the genteel tradition by presenting experience that is both
"crude" and "common" (Trilling drops out the word "common").
This has some historical particularity for Matthiessen. Dreiser, he
believes, is impatient with the idealizations and theories about life
represented by Howells and, even more, by James Russell Lowell.
He aims in his novels to face aspects of experience that the social
conventions of his day regularly masked or shunned. Trilling translates this into something much more grandly ignoble: Matthiessen
extols Dreiser because he, like other "liberals," instinctively opposes
"mind" and prefers "crude experience." In order to secure his argument, Trilling also rapidly glides over the fact that, by 1946, Matthiessen had already written much about Henry James, and had
explicitly celebrated James's art even as he indicated the limitations
of the novels. Trilling concedes that Matthiessen has fine feeling for
James's "mind," but nevertheless stamps Matthiessen as basically an
apologist for "crude experience."

In his eagerness to prosecute Dreiser and liberal criticism, Trilling
himself becomes an apologist for Henry James and ends up seeming less flexible in his critical categories than Matthiessen. Contrary
to what Trilling says, Matthiessen does not fundamentally privilege
"reality" over "mind," whatever fleeting gestures he might make
in this direction. The general truth is that Matthiessen wanted, if
he could, to integrate reality and mind—to accept both James *and*
Dreiser, and thereby preserve the very "dialectical" tension in cultural criticism for which Trilling appeals (23).

Seen in the context of Trilling's essay, Matthiessen's study of
James is striking in that he does address the kind and caliber of
the ideas displayed in *The Golden Bowl*, *The American Scene*, and
other books. He tries, not always with complete success, to make
distinctions. Which is something that Trilling himself, in "Reality
in America," revealingly neglects to do. Writing just a few months

after the war's end and as the extent of the Holocaust was increasingly coming to light, Trilling is very quick to condemn liberals for "brushing aside" Dreiser's anti-Semitism (26, 31). But this is not strictly accurate—a number of liberals and radicals, in the *Nation* and the *New Masses*, had in fact criticized Dreiser for his anti-Semitism. Michael Gold, in particular, condemned Dreiser for his anti-Semitic and fascist words (Casciato 42). Nor is it correct to identify Dreiser's intemperate remarks about Jews in the 1930s and early 1940s as signs of "doctrinaire" anti-Semitism ("Reality in America" 26). Anti-Semitism, I think, wasn't an "idea" for Dreiser (31), but was, instead, to his discredit, a callous, fumblingly expressed prejudice that he sometimes lunged at. This does not make his anti-Semitism less culpable, but it does distance it from the status of a doctrine. Dreiser is not Ezra Pound.

More important still, one is curious about how Trilling might have responded to Matthiessen's very harsh reference—one that I quoted in Chapter 3, and one that admirers of "the Master" dislike—to James's "racist" passages about the Jews and the other immigrants in *The American Scene*. It is all well and good to profess, as Trilling does, that James manifests in his writings "the electrical qualities of mind," a "complex and rapid imagination," and an "authoritative immediacy" (27). But it is not enough to observe that we are in contact with a powerful mind: one wants also to know and to assess *what* that mind is thinking. Trilling values the Jamesian mind, yet oddly does not insist in his essay on investigating the actual work that this mind undertakes. He objects to critics who praise Dreiser for simply confronting "reality"; in turn, one feels impelled to object to him for praising James simply because he possesses a finely grained intelligence. Trilling's language about James, which fails to address the nature of the novelist's mind and the content of his ideas, exhibits the very fault Trilling tells us mars the criticism on Dreiser produced by Matthiessen and the liberals.

Though hardly a perfect book, *Theodore Dreiser* is not uncritical in the manner Trilling describes. Matthiessen sympathetically examines Dreiser's politics and philosophy—the writer's "ideas"—but, when necessary, treats them critically. He obviously shares Dreiser's compassionate feeling for the poor and downtrodden, and anger at the sight of social misery in America. Yet Matthiessen's main concern is not to give general approval himself to Dreiser's attack on capitalism in his social and political writings, nearly all of which appeared after the publication of *An American Tragedy* in 1925. Rather, as Matthiessen states clearly, he seeks to trace the movement of this writer's thought, in order to see the changes that occurred between *Sister Carrie* (1900) and the two books that Dreiser left in roughly finished form at the time of his death in 1945, *The Bulwark* and *The Stoic*.

Matthiessen does, of course, feel personally pulled toward Dreiser for various reasons. This provides *Theodore Dreiser* at moments with a tone that seems autobiographically slanted, as when he examines Dreiser's joining the Communist party:

> In judging his act we must remember the temper of the period in which it was made. His major concern was the prevention of further wars, which he was convinced would destroy civilization. He had slowly learned the lesson that there could be no humane life in the United States until the inequities should be removed that had thwarted or destroyed so many of the characters in his fiction. He now believed that the next step was to do everything he could to break down the destructive barriers of nationalism, and to work for equity among all the peoples of the world. Otherwise there would be no world in which to live. (233)

To say that Matthiessen felt kinship with Dreiser is not the same as saying he was altogether uncritical, however. In becoming a Communist, Dreiser had, after all, taken a step that Matthiessen himself adamantly refused to take; and Dreiser's religious sources rested more in the *Bhagavad Gita* and in radical Quaker texts such as John Woolman's *Journal* than in the Sermon on the Mount and the other Gospel passages to which Matthiessen, like Henry Wallace, keenly responded. Matthiessen could readily see differences between his and Dreiser's understanding of politics and religion, and there is plenty of evidence in his book that he recognized the deficiencies of Dreiser's views. Matthiessen attends to the shortcomings of *Dreiser Looks at Russia*, the book the novelist wrote about his visit to the Soviet Union in 1927; he stresses Dreiser's lack of talent as a political pamphleteer in *Tragic America*, a survey of America in the midst of the Depression; he emphasizes the controversy surrounding Dreiser's lamentable anti-Semitic remarks, adding that Dreiser had to learn to fight his way past this, "the most destructive prejudice of our time" (224–25); he states that, especially before the war, Dreiser was sometimes too quick to parrot Communist positions without bothering to investigate them; and he speaks in a measured voice about Dreiser's flawed, if intriguing, effort to embody in *The Bulwark* and the final chapters of *The Stoic* the religious mysticism that came to mean so much to him.

The problem, then, with *Theodore Dreiser* is not that Matthiessen fails to criticize this writer's politics, but that he does not press his criticisms further. This is not so much a flagrant betrayal of mind as a failure of mind to do its work fully. In this respect, Matthiessen suffers here from a fault similar to the one that marred his book on Henry James—an inability or unwillingness to follow through on local insights and perceptions, and to risk major reorientations of his judgments and attitudes. But *Theodore Dreiser* may also fall short because Matthiessen does not devote the same kind of analytical attention to the nonliterary social and political books as he does to the novels. We cannot expect these books to figure as centrally to him as do *Sister Carrie* and *An American Tragedy*. But in order to get a real grasp on Dreiser's thought, one has to accord his nonliterary books a careful reading. By briefly considering them, we can learn lessons about Matthiessen, Dreiser, and the predicaments of the American left.

Dreiser Looks at Russia (1928), *Tragic America* (1931), and *America Is Worth Saving* (1941) are quite interesting in their disaffected, disorderly way. All three books are dominated by a single theme—the tragic paradox of poverty in the midst of plenty in America. Dreiser observes in *Dreiser Looks at Russia*, for example, that the Soviet system promises a means to close the gap between rich and poor:

> Still another fact that I harvested in Russia, and which I will never forget is this—that via Communism, or this collective or paternalistic care of everybody—it is possible to remove the dreadful sense of social misery in one direction and another which has so afflicted me in my own life in America and ever since I have been old enough to know what social misery was. The rich districts as opposed to the poor ones in all our great cities and our poorer and smaller towns and villages. The fine houses as opposed to the wretched ones. And the

slums, strikes, unemployed. So late as 1907 in America, how common it was to see crowds of men in the poor sections of our cities, idling about and brooding, or, if they had any money left, drinking. The old Bowery in New York, with its hundreds and thousands of "down and outs." South State and Clark Streets in Chicago, with their shambling, bleary-eyed, hopeless hordes. And then Fifth Avenue, Michigan Avenue, Schenley Drive, a-clank and a-glitter with the trappings and vanities and gauds and follies of those with endless means. The gulf was too wide, the comparisons cruel and unnecessary. (252)

He returns to the same point in *Tragic America*, though this time stressing even more vividly his outrage at the capitalistic exploitation of the masses:

The great quarrel today in America is between wealth and poverty—whether an individual, however small or poor, shall retain his self-respect and his life, or whether a commercial oligarchy shall at last and finally take charge and tell all the others—some 125,000,000 strong now—how they shall do and what they shall think and how little (not how much) they may live on, the while a few others (the strong and cunning) exercise their will and their pleasure as they choose. That is the war that is coming! (16)

America Is Worth Saving insists on this as well:

Poverty in the midst of plenty—the great paradox of our day. How many hundreds of times in the past decade have we read and heard those words? They have been recited so often, and with so little visible effect on the allegedly "free" actions of *homo sapiens,* that they have become just another catch-phrase, like "Yes, We Have No Bananas. . . ." We seem incapable of doing anything about such an obvious absurdity as this poverty amid plenty. . . . We have become so used to living in a gigantic paradox that paradox is already accepted as the normal state of affairs. (16)

Dreiser is not saying anything remarkably new in focusing on the unequal distribution of wealth in America. Many similar statements were made throughout the 1930s (as well as before and after) that not only emphasize the bitter truth of American poverty but also connect it to a general crisis in human history—Norman Thomas called it "the ancient division of men and nations into the House of Have and Have-Not" (233)—which men and women of the left have sought to rectify. But the nature of the proper next step to take has always been the vexing question for intellectuals and writers like Dreiser. American social critics, legitimately angered by inequities everywhere, have never had anywhere to go to anchor this perception in a vital, long-lasting social movement and party (Lasch 56, 58). The socialists under Debs and, later, under Thomas did have an impact, and leftist and left-leaning liberal factions, ranging from the Communists to the Progressives led by Wallace, rallied supporters among some branches of labor and intellectuals from the time of the Depression to the outbreak of the cold war. But during the Depression years and since, the more that a particular writer aligns feelings of indignation at the American scene with Marxism, socialism, or Communism, the more he or she appears to be dangerous and subversive and, therefore, the feared enemy of the poor and oppressed that he or she is seeking to help. The more ideologically geared toward Marxism the language of protest becomes, the more it frequently threatens and alienates its intended audiences, including the poor themselves.

Dreiser's own experiences, as narrated in his autobiographies, and his observations, as recounted in the sketches collected in *The Color of a Great City* (1923) and other books, made clear to him that American society is based on a fundamental division between rich and poor. America's rhetoric of upward mobility translates in reality, Dreiser suggests, into a pattern of "giant and rapacious individualism" that benefits the few and debases the many ("Introduction to *Harlan Miners Speak*" 271). When he tries, however, to develop arguments for ending this entrenched state of affairs, he appears naive and wrongheaded, and, particularly in *Tragic America* and in *America Is Worth Saving*, he is frequently out of control. He suffers from the absence of a generally applicable and acceptable language of protest and, given that fact, broods in a dim if fearfully impassioned way that Americans will indeed increasingly assume that "poverty in the midst of plenty" is inevitable and unchangeable: there is nothing that can be done about it.

To be sure, Dreiser's social and political commentary in his three books is often perverse and shrill simply because he was an eccentric, sometimes bigoted, unsystematic writer and thinker. Here I have in mind the attacks on religion in *Tragic America*, and the foolishly mild remarks about Hitler (46, 47) and tortured linkages between Nazi Germany and "aristocratic," "imperialist" England (125 ff.) in *America Is Worth Saving*. Much of this stems from Dreiser's own gruff, stubborn determination to preach what his own instincts, if not the facts, instruct him is right. Yet much of the stunted thinking in these books derives, too, from Dreiser's self-deluded, desperate attempt, like that of many other writers and intellectuals during the 1930s and 1940s, to clutch at Communism in order to supply his position with ideological coinage and buoy his hope that America might at last be able to generate a broad, long-lasting leftist movement.

Communism is the only answer that Dreiser can perceive, the only social organization that can, he believes, defend men and women from greedy individuals and predatory corporations: only Communism can curb the kind of Nietzschean will and Machiavellian ingenuity of the Frank Cowperwoods of the world (Pizer 296–97). Dreiser regularly does acknowledge in letters and elsewhere the factional in-fighting that weakens the American Communist party, recognizes that the party is too dependent upon Moscow for its interpretation of events, and maintains on more than one occasion that Communism appears less suited to conditions in America than to conditions in Russia (Lehan 194–95). His truculent, abrasive views so disturbed the head of the party in America, Earl Browder, that he repeatedly denied Dreiser's request for membership. Yet Dreiser nevertheless leaned toward Communism from the time of his journey to the Soviet Union in 1927, and he finally did become a party member when his friend William Z. Foster replaced Browder in July 1945.

The confusions and blindnesses that afflict Dreiser are especially evident in *Dreiser Looks at Russia*. Dreiser, it should be said, is not a mouthpiece for Communist ideology. He praises the dedicated leadership of the party officials, commends the improvements being made in education, highlights the new freedoms granted to women, and so forth. But he states throughout his book that he cannot agree with the "philosophy" or "technique" of the Soviet form of government, which strikes him as "too much like replacing one kind of dogmatic tyranny with another" (10). He comments on numerous ways in which the Soviets undermine individual freedoms; and during the trip itself, as one can discover from reading the chronicle written by his secretary, Ruth Epperson Kennell, Dreiser persistently registered his complaints to the authorities (*Theodore Dreiser and the Soviet Union*). Less than a year after his trip, in a letter to Michael Gold, he called himself a philosophical pessimist who views "the human race" as a "predatory organism," and adds that "in Russia" there is "the ruthless suppression of individualism by communism . . .—peace and prosperity under a gun" (*Letters* 2:474–75). But Dreiser's gapingly obvious failure in his book is his inability really to absorb how such a loss of individual freedom would affect a writer like himself.

Dreiser intensely dislikes the "endless outpour and downpour of propaganda" (*Dreiser Looks at Russia* 89), the ruthlessly ideological underpinnings of schooling, the controls on the press, the refusal to tolerate criticism of the party and state (95–96). He admits to being troubled by the failure of the social and economic changes he records in Russia to produce anything of literary or artistic interest (202–4). Above all, he objects to the repressive attitude toward creative work that pervades the Soviet system:

> The Communists' restless concern for the welfare of the future mind of Russia, their determination to reeducate all of the citizens of the land, young and old, to their way of thinking causes them to insist upon coloring and twisting all art, where possible, to their way of thinking. The result thus far is that there is neither art for art's sake nor knowledge for its own sake in Russia. . . . My own two plays, "The Hand of the Potter" and "An American Tragedy," were entirely agreeable to Stanislavsky, who would have liked to produce them, but the Communist censors would have none of them. They were, as I heard, too grim. (97–98)

Since Dreiser sees how his own writing fares at the hands of the Russian censors, it is startling that his tone remains so blandly accommodating. Perhaps Dreiser felt that the Russians were no worse than the American publishers and guardians of virtue who restricted sales of *Sister Carrie*, and that they were in fact more admirably principled than those in America who had served as the "wasp-like censors" (Dreiser's words) of *The Genius* (Elias, *Theodore Dreiser* 198). Dreiser's hosts made plain that they approved of the picture of social conditions he had drawn in his novels; and Dreiser rapidly became, along with Twain, Hemingway, and Jack London, one of the most widely read novelists in the Soviet Union. Yet Dreiser did not ask himself whether he could have written his novels under the Soviet system, a system, he reflects, that places no credence in art or knowledge for its own sake. The Soviets respected Dreiser and welcomed him in Russia because his writings, kept under control, ministered to the interests of the state. If Dreiser's literary practice had taken different directions, his works would have been banned.

To spell this out may seem rather tedious. Dreiser is often an easy target, a man who did good work in the 1930s for particular causes —among them, the Scottsboro boys trial, the Harlan County miners' strike, and the Tom Mooney case (Lehan 179–89; Elias, *Theodore Dreiser* 242–68)—but who committed gross errors of judgment and theorized about politics and society badly. Yet Dreiser may be more typical than we would like to believe. In his fond regard for Communism, he shows a drifting away from democracy and freedom that makes him—for all his huge peculiarities—a brother to many Americans on the left in this century. These men and women have not been wholly uncritical of Marxism and Communism, yet they nevertheless fix upon ideological solutions that would deny space for free intellectual and creative work. If they took with full seriousness what they claim to believe, they would destroy the intellectual and artistic values to which their own careers testify—and they would also default on the ideals of democracy and freedom that have distinguished America at its best.

Both Dreiser and Matthiessen, one might say, too often "write against themselves" politically, write, that is, in political terms that are at odds with the terms they employ as critics and intellectuals. Dreiser refers to the rigid limits that the Soviets set on art without weighing what this would mean for himself and other literary pioneers he esteems. Matthiessen celebrates Lenin's theory and practice while failing to absorb the relentless challenge that Lenin poses for literature, criticism, and pedagogy. Matthiessen did not subject his own political terms, values, and authorities to intellectual scrutiny, though he gave them his emotional allegiance, and he exempted from criticism the politics that he claimed to foster in his literary work.

Matthiessen, then, is a difficult case. He was not adequately critical of Stalinism, but he was not a Stalinist ideologue, either. He held certain progressive convictions passionately, and he strove to practice them in his own political work in the community and nation. Braced by the words of Whitman, Louis Sullivan, and other classic American writers, he sought furthermore to place his criticism in democratic service to the American people. His problem was not that he made local mistakes or poor specific judgments but, more generally, that he did not really see and engage the major contradictions in the political work and scholarly writing he was earnestly executing. Matthiessen's positions, one might say, were heartfelt, yet could not bear close inspection. If looked at too intently, they would begin to crack apart.

Perhaps for this reason, Matthiessen often appears anxious to avoid questions that his arguments inevitably raise. In *American Renaissance*, as my final chapters will show, he tries to exhibit the social and political meanings of his five major authors, in order to demonstrate the ways in which they might vitally renew the present. Yet even as he encourages us to recognize how these authors could revivify our history, he refrains from inquiring in any significant detail into the historical contexts of the authors themselves. Emerson, Hawthorne, and the others matter crucially for our political life, Matthiessen affirms, but their own politics, it seems, do not merit scrutiny.

Nor did Matthiessen calculate, except in fairly vague terms, the relation between his choice of American texts—and the values they expressed—and the European situation in socialist and Communist dominated countries with which he wished to feel himself in league. He knew what he wanted politically, and he hoped to overcome obstacles to it through the sheer force of his hope, steadfastly reiterated, and his sincere invocations of what American writers had seen and celebrated.

FIVE

Reading American Renaissance, *Part 1*

> *American Renaissance* reset the terms for the study of American literary history; it gave us a new canon of classic texts; and it inspired the growth of American Studies in the United States and abroad. It is not too much to say that Matthiessen, *American Renaissance*, and the Salzburg Seminar brought American literature to postwar Europe.
>
> —Bercovitch, "Problem of Ideology" 631

F. O. MATTHIESSEN is so inescapably for us the author of *American Renaissance* that it seems perverse to wonder what his career would look like without that remarkable book. But it was not inevitable that Matthiessen would come to the texts of Emerson, Thoreau, Hawthorne, Melville, and Whitman for his masterpiece. Despite the efforts of Vernon Louis Parrington, Van Wyck Brooks, Lewis Mumford, Newton Arvin, and others, American literature in the 1920s and 1930s did not enjoy the prestige and distinction attached to English literature. Critics had begun to study and think highly of *Walden*, *Moby Dick*, and *Song of Myself*, but these texts and others from the period we now know as the "American renaissance" had only recently begun to secure their place in the literary canon. American literature, the subject as we understand it, was in the process of being formed and articulated (Vanderbilt).

Prior to 1914, American literature was generally perceived to be "a branch of English letters, a subordinate, if locally interesting, expression of the Anglo-Saxon spirit" (Jones 79–80). When critics and teachers paid attention to American writers, they asked how these writers contributed to English culture and letters: a specifically "American" literature, a body of texts different in some crucial way from English literature, was not a recognized category for the most part. New England provincialism and Protestant moral emphasis, combining with the Anglo-Saxon bias of philology, solidified the place of English literature in the academy, and, in addition, accented those American writers who seemed idealistic in their tone and morally beneficial in their values. The turn-of-the-century canon of American literature included more poetry than prose, focused on New England worthies such as Whittier, Longfellow, and Lowell, and simplified Emerson, Thoreau, and Hawthorne when it included them. Writing in 1932, Carl Van Doren described the early-twentieth-century canon in the following terms:

> Bearded and benevolent, the faces of Bryant, Longfellow, Whittier, Lowell, Holmes, and sometimes (rather oddly) Whitman, looked down unchallenged from the walls of schoolrooms. Emerson was the American philosopher, Irving the American essayist, Cooper the American romancer, Hawthorne the American explorer of the soul, Poe the American unhappy poet (unhappy on account of his bad habits), Thoreau the American hermit, Mark Twain the American humorist (barely a man of letters), Henry James the American expatriate, and Howells the American academy. Here were fifteen apostles set in a rigid eminence, braced by minor figures grouped more randomly about them. (429; see Brodhead 3)

Even to use the term "canon," however, is somewhat misleading, since it assigns to American literature a stature it did not enjoy. American literature, in the early 1900s, basically existed as "a mere footnote" to the study of English literature (Jones 97), and this was particularly true within high schools, colleges, and universities. Most of the school textbooks in use during this period appended to the selections of American literature a short history of English literature, as though to remind students of the main stream of texts to which America was a tributary (Dunmire 248). In fact, as late as 1930, American literary history appeared under the heading of "English XI" or "English XII" at the annual meeting of the Modern Language Association.

There had been some significant work on American literature during the late nineteenth and early twentieth centuries, especially the American historian Moses Coit Tyler's impressive volumes *A History of American Literature, 1607–1765* (1878) and *The Literary History of the American Revolution* (1897). The New Humanists

Irving Babbitt and Paul Elmer More also published a number of interesting essays. Babbitt, for example, examined the ethical implications of Emerson's philosophy, and More, also ethically slanted but showing greater critical sensitivity and tolerance, treated Hawthorne, Thoreau, Poe, Whitman, and other American writers in his *Shelburne Essays*. W. C. Brownell, in *American Prose Masters* (1909), also commented scrupulously, from an Arnoldian perspective, on the style of nineteenth-century authors ranging from Cooper to Henry James. But the formal histories by Katherine Lee Bates, Barrett Wendell, and others were limited by Saxon assumptions and New England parochialism. Wendell's *Literary History of America* (1900), according to one of his contemporaries, should have been titled "A Literary History of Harvard University, with Incidental Glimpses of the Minor Writers of America." The New England historians, concludes Jay Hubbell, "made room for Irving and Cooper, but they could not see Poe, Melville, or Whitman as worthy of a place in the canon of great American writers. . . . [They] were unaware of the real significance of the Yankee rebel, Henry David Thoreau; and they failed to see how far superior Emerson and Hawthorne were to Whittier and the three Cambridge poets" (103–4).

It was not until 1908, with the publication of Van Wyck Brooks's *The Wine of the Puritans*, followed in 1913 by the appearance of John Macy's *The Spirit of American Literature*, that critics truly began to assault the New England canon and initiate the reassessment of American writing. Brooks, who worked in the genre of cultural polemic and critique, and Macy, who assembled a more familiar kind of appreciative overview, stressed in their different ways that it was time to break with cultural timidity and to highlight native traditions. It was also time, said Macy, Brooks, and others, to free American writers and readers from the grip of the genteel tradition and Puritan morality. The nationalistic fervor sparked by America's entry into World War I in 1917 reinforced the exploration of a "usable past" and deepened anxious inquiry into America's identity as a distinctive society and culture. Brooks's *America's Coming of Age* (1915) and Mencken's marvelous essays "Theodore Dreiser" (1917) and "The National Letters" (1920) were especially potent forays in this national debate about the condition of American culture, the literary heritage, and the power that an art liberated from religious and social constraint might exercise. The New Humanist critic Norman

Foerster, whose books *The Reinterpretation of American Literature* and *American Criticism* Matthiessen reviewed in 1929, also made an effective case for American literature throughout the 1920s. Stuart Sherman's criticism has not aged well, but he, too, was influential as a critic of American literature during the teens and twenties, both as an editor of and contributor to the Cambridge History of American Literature (1917–21) and as an essayist on Emerson, Hawthorne, James, and Twain.

Macy was a socialist as well as a literary critic—his *Socialism in America* appeared in 1916—and this fact points to the impact of American radicalism on the study of American literature during the first four decades of this century. Brooks, also a socialist, and, later, Granville Hicks, V. F. Calverton, and Bernard Smith, all of whom wrote Marxist histories of American literature and criticism in the 1930s, insisted on a literature in intimate relation to the contemporary scene. Their essays and books were often judged then (and are often judged now) to be distortions of aesthetic truth, belonging more to the annals of the class struggle than to the history of literature. But these men brought an urgency to their criticism that made the fate of American literature seem momentous. Even their excesses and mistakes generated spirited responses and hence expanded debate and discussion about what American literature was and why it counted.

American literature drew strength and legitimacy from other sources. Neither Pound nor Eliot found much value in an "American" literary tradition, but their essays, especially on Henry James, kindled renewed interest in American writers and prompted other critics, who were more concerned about and sympathetic to the cause of cultural nationalism, to investigate the nature of tradition in American art and culture. Though this is harder to demonstrate, the prose and poetry of American writers such as Hart Crane and William Carlos Williams likely also played a role in the literary and cultural awakening I am seeking to describe. I have in mind, for instance, Crane's fertile encounters with Melville and Whitman in *White Buildings* (1926) and *The Bridge* (1930) and Williams' suggestively impressionistic pieces on Columbus, Cotton Mather, George Washington, and Poe in *In the American Grain* (1925). But probably the key text in this modernist recasting of American literary history is D. H. Lawrence's *Studies in Classic American Literature*

(1923). With exotic eloquence, Lawrence emphasized the "double meaning," "symbolism," and "subterfuge" of American writing at its most supreme and in effect argued that Americans had to rediscover and rechart the literary landscape they thought they already knew (viii). Lawrence made extraordinary claims, claims that proposed "the old people"—Poe, Melville, Hawthorne, Whitman—as not only the pioneers of American literature but also the most experimental and disquieting of modernists: "The furthest frenzies of French modernism or futurism have not yet reached the pitch of extreme consciousness that Poe, Melville, Hawthorne, Whitman reached. The European moderns are all *trying* to be extreme" (viii).

Lawrence's book dramatically assisted in the collaborative modernist effort to reinvent American literature. Lawrence furnished a language freighted with dark mythic overtones and symbolic majesty, and the New Criticism, emerging in the late 1920s and gaining in influence through the 1930s, supplied the exacting analytical techniques. At least in part, American literature as we know it today is a masterly achievement of modernism, an imaginative enterprise on a grand scale that was undertaken by writers and critics inside and outside the university. This is the development to which Malcolm Cowley alluded when, looking backward from the vantage point of the mid-1950s, he observed that "perhaps the principal creative work of the last three decades in this country has not been any novel or poem or drama of our time, not even Faulkner's Yoknapatawpha saga or Hemingway's *For Whom the Bell Tolls* or Hart Crane's *The Bridge*; perhaps it has been the critical rediscovery and reinterpretation of Melville's *Moby-Dick* and its promotion, step by step, to the position of national epic" (*Literary Situation* 14–15).

Within the academy, the emergence of American literature was also, quite simply and a good deal less dramatically, perhaps just a matter of time. As the profession of literary studies grew, so did the numbers of fields and specialties. For American academics teaching American students, American literature was an obvious subject. It is testimony to the prestige of English literature that it took so long for Melville and Whitman to seem serious and challenging enough to be frequently treated in courses. (Matthiessen himself once ruefully remarked that until 1930, the library at Yale listed *Moby Dick* in the "cetology" section of its card catalogue.) Members of history departments, after all, had always highlighted American history in their curricula and research; as John Higham has noted in his book on the "profession of history" in America, "the earliest efforts of professional scholars were concentrated overwhelmingly in American history, for which original sources were most accessible and patriotic motives strong" (*History* 37). By the 1930s, professors of English were finally learning from the example of their colleagues in history even as the history professors themselves were, in turn, becoming increasingly alert to the undue "American" orientation of their discipline and shifting in greater numbers in their scholarship toward European topics.

Matthiessen began to teach and write at a fortuitous juncture: English literature was still (and would remain) ascendant, but American literature was coming resolutely into its own. All of the forces I have mentioned were accelerating general critical interest (and national pride) in American writers, and the meager attention paid to American literature in colleges and universities was on the verge of a dramatic reversal. Thanks to an essay by Ferner Nuhn on the teaching of American literature that appeared in the *American Mercury* in March 1928, we can draw a good picture of what the situation looked like in the late 1920s, when Matthiessen was getting his career under way as an instructor first at Yale and, beginning in 1929, at Harvard. Nuhn noted that while the number of dissertations on American literature and the number of scholars expert in the field had increased somewhat during the 1920s, colleges and universities persisted in failing to respect "the native culture of the Republic" (331). Nearly all the institutions Nuhn examined offered just a single survey course on American literature; it was not a requirement, often was only a half year in length, and was sometimes given (as was the case at Princeton) only every other year. On the undergraduate level, one out of eleven courses in the English department concentrated on American literature; on the graduate level, the figure was even worse —one in thirteen. To judge from the various emphases in college and university courses, American literature stood, Nuhn concluded,

About equal in importance to Scandinavian literature.
One-half as important as Italian literature.
One-third as important as Spanish literature.
One-third as important as German literature.
One-fourth as important as French literature.

One-fifth as important as Latin literature.
One-fifth as important as Greek literature.
One-tenth as important as English literature. (328)

When would colleges and universities wake up to the need to ad-dress American culture? Nuhn wanted to know. Why was American literature being accorded so little dignity? Painful as these questions were to Nuhn and others, it would not take long for conditions in higher education to alter. When one reflects on the pressures on so many sides *for* American literature, one is again surprised only that the change within the academy did not occur sooner.

Nuhn's complaints may matter less as a sign of what was wrong than as a final protest against a situation undergoing a dramatic change. The new canon of American literature had, in fact, already begun to clarify itself by the early 1930s, as Carl Van Doren indi-cates in the same article I quoted earlier. The turn-of-the-century masters had lost much of their charm and luster, and new names were replacing them:

> Emerson and Hawthorne and Thoreau, risen dramatically above Bryant, Longfellow, Whittier, Holmes, and Lowell, stand in the rarer company of Poe and Whitman. Irving and Howells have shrunk and faded. Cooper has scarcely held his own. Mark Twain seems a great man of letters as well as a great man. Henry James seems a brilliant artist whatever nation he belongs to. Herman Melville has thrust him-self by main strength, and Emily Dickinson has gently slipped, into the canon. (429)

American literature didn't exactly triumph in colleges and univer-sities between the late 1920s and the early 1940s, but within this period of time, which reaches from the publication of Parrington's work to the publication of *American Renaissance* in 1941, American literature secured its very considerable status within the academy. Profiting from the example of Matthiessen as much as from that of anyone else, it acquired legitimacy and prestige as a subject for scholarly study.

Matthiessen himself was not trained as an Americanist, of course; and his own early experience of American writers seems to have been a homemade affair. He concentrated on Greek and Latin and the great books of English literature during his years at Yale and Oxford;

as a graduate student at Harvard, he surveyed English literature, and, except for a single seminar on early American historiography, taken with Kenneth Murdock, he did not pursue any course work in the American field. Once he started teaching at Harvard in 1929–30, he was responsible for a course on American literature, but, interestingly enough, it excluded most of the writers with whom we now associate Matthiessen's name. The course was initially titled "American Writers of the South and West," a title Matthiessen later changed to "American Writers outside New England" so that, as he remarked to Russell Cheney in a 20 April 1930 letter, he could include Melville without any feeling of "absurdity" (Hyde 215).

Matthiessen's career would, I think, possess a certain logic even if *American Renaissance* were absent from it. One could view him as the author of a book produced in sentimental homage to a distant relative of his mother's, Sarah Orne Jewett, and, in a more typically professorial vein, as the scholarly author of a rigorous appraisal of Elizabethan translation. This second book, informed and vitalized by Matthiessen's response to T. S. Eliot, could be seen to lead naturally to a full-length treatment of Eliot. And that book could be taken to prefigure the detailed scrutiny of Henry James, to whom Eliot devoted critical essays and whose impact on Eliot's verse is evident in the temporizing consciousness of J. Alfred Prufrock and in the language and rhythm of "Portrait of a Lady" and other poems. The next and final stage, for Matthiessen, would then arrive with his book on Dreiser, his attempt to complicate and counter his absorption in the "formal," "technical" enterprise of Eliot and James.

If, however, Matthiessen's career had followed this shape, we would know him as an interesting minor critic. It was, and it remains, *American Renaissance* that established Matthiessen's reputation as the foremost scholar/critic of American literature. For most people, this book keeps alive interest in the books that preceded and followed it: the other books largely still matter because they were composed by the author of *American Renaissance*.

Matthiessen perceived himself as a revisionist historian of American literature at least as early as 1929, when, in his review of Foerster's books, he announced that it was "time for the history of American literature to be rewritten" ("New Standards" 181). The example of Eliot, who had rediscovered the English Renaissance as a source (and poetic analogy) for modernist practice, and the example of the Elizabethan translators, who had approached their scholar-ship as a patriotic mission, contributed to Matthiessen's sense of vocation. Matthiessen was also a very ambitious man: he set a chal-lenge for himself that would be enormously difficult, but that would clinch his own status as a critic of American letters. The publisher W. W. Norton's December 1930 proposal that Matthiessen craft a history of American literature "from the new social and historical angle" (Hyde 225–26) prodded his ambitions still further. He had an enthusiastic publisher—though Oxford would eventually pub-lish the book, Norton having rejected the 1006-page typescript (and Houghton Mifflin rejected it too) as too long and expensive to pro-duce—and he had an excitingly original topic, a topic that others, including Brooks and Mumford, had started to explore, but that awaited examination on the massive scale that it merited.

In its size and scope, *American Renaissance* must be judged an astonishing achievement. Writing it was a heroic act that required painstaking research, steady commitment of time and energy, and dogged determination to see the daunting job to its end. Matthiessen somehow managed to complete the book despite the obligations he faced as a teacher, tutor, and administrator at Harvard, and despite the pressures of his labor as a political and social activist involved in the Harvard Teachers' Union. He also succeeded in finishing the book while doing a great deal of other writing; throughout the 1930s, he maintained an impressively productive pace as an essayist and reviewer. Even as he wrote and then published his monograph on Eliot in 1934, he was underway in planning and reading for his big book, a book that Eliot himself reported to Matthiessen "sound[ed] extremely promising" (Hyde 226).

The writing of *American Renaissance* almost killed Matthiessen. Not only did he often doubt his own ability to complete the manu-script, but he also recognized (and was aggrieved by) the severe strain that the project was creating for his relationship with Russell Cheney. Toward the end of 1938, while Matthiessen was on leave from teaching and focusing his full energies on the book, he suf-fered an emotional breakdown, and he soon committed himself to McLean's Hospital where he remained for a three-week period from late December to mid-January. His letters and journal entries from this period show him extremely tense and exhausted, self-loathing and suicidal. Matthiessen fears losing Cheney and is obsessed by the thought of Cheney's death (Cheney's own health was often poor, and he drank excessively). He reflects anxiously on the disappearance of his own capacities as a critic, brooding in particular that he might simply be cheerleading for American writing and surrendering the analytical standards that serious literary criticism mandates.

The following 8 January 1939 entry from Matthiessen's journal describes the demons that haunted him:

> What are some of the things that have shaken me most? The first days were a nightmare that had to be constantly fought back to keep it from becoming me. I had never before been surrounded by the mentally deranged, young men quite out of touch with reality, old men with softened wits, the vacant faces much less horrible than the suffering ones. I had to wrestle with the dread that having gotten in here I wouldn't be able to get out, that I too would be faced with years of soothing baths, shuffling feet and disintegration. I knew that death would be better than being kept alive on those terms. If I could convey the full intensity of the horror of those days, it would take me deep into misery.
>
> Step after step of humiliation has brought me a new understanding of humility. I have hated imaginary illnesses in tweed coats and costly sanitariums, and here I am. I have prided myself most on clarity and control, and have been confused, without self-understanding or any mastery. My great resource, books, has become meaningless. I have tried to read and though I recognize the individual words, the debate with myself obtrudes between me and them, the paragraph slides away and seems not worth pursuing. And even words that I know suddenly look strange,—what is *ramify*?—and I have no resilience to pursue them. My steel-trap memory is blurred. I have had a distressing time with the names of the attendants. (I can recognize that I am better, however, for I am considerably clearer now.) I who was sure have become unsure, unable to make decisions, unable to see my way from *a* to *b*, most agonizingly unable to get out of the sterile round of my own miserable thoughts, to see the shapes and colors of the world, to feel the values of society or any meaning to God. (Hyde 253–54)

It is ironically in keeping with Matthiessen's fidelity to language that the nightmare assumes the form of words becoming laughable and meaningless. Reading is not "worth pursuing," the reader drifting into indifference. These sentences from the journal become all the more revealing in light of Matthiessen's frequent emphasis in *Ameri-*

can Renaissance on "reading" as necessarily serving for the man of "instinctive wholeness" as an answer to "immediate questions"; it is not a "polite refinement," but a formative, self-defining aspect of experience (125; see also 395). For Matthiessen in his breakdown, reading is irrelevant, a distraction; he cannot turn to it because the questions that burden him are too unnervingly immediate to be re- solved by books.

"The death wish," he continues,

> took agonizingly vivid images of jumping out of a window during those first tortured days. But that image is much less insistent now. By living with it I may have built up an anti-toxin. But I am living with it: that is the fact I face. I have every reason to live that can be enumerated: work that I believe to be important, an interest, no a zest for understanding and participating in shaping the society of which I am part, more generous and devoted friends than ordinarily fall to the lot of any man. And none of the more usual pressures: I have money in the bank, a good job, no physical illness. Where has this fear come from to engulf one who has never even been bothered by anxiety or worry before? If I dread life without Russell, the fact is that he is alive, buoyant, rich, and I am merely hastening by my melancholy the event that might lie far in the future, for this strain is very hard for him. It hasn't heretofore been my habit, has it, to leap across bridges long before they were in sight? The nub of the problem is here. When you give yourself entirely to love, you cannot demand that it last forever. For then fear intrudes, and there I am.
>
> This obviously doesn't state the whole problem. Much of the ice- berg lies hidden. Barrett [a doctor at McLean's] talks of the aggression that I am now turning against myself, and God knows I have been knifing my confidence, rubbing salt into the wounds of my self-esteem.
>
> What I know is that I am living with the phantom of death, and I have resolved to fight it. I cannot die because it would kill Russell. And to keep from jumping I must cast out this fear of Russell's death. Many times in these past weeks I have felt possessed with a devil. I pray now for strength of nerve and courage to resist the temptation of violent unreason. (Hyde 254)

This is writing that is self-punishing in its rhythm and violent in its imagery ("knifing my confidence"). Yet it is also fairly orga- nized writing that indicates Matthiessen's resolve and movement toward recovery. His carefully controlled phrasing, which at moments echoes the Bible, Melville, and Poe, exposes his psychological afflictions but also functions to grasp and appraise them. Matthiessen is engaging here in an effort at self-understanding and emotional clarification, drawing upon his reading as a resource after all, and he produces something that is admirably eloquent, especially as it reaches its guarded conclusion. This journal entry depicts for us the cost to Matthiessen of writing *American Renaissance*, the torment and deep insecurity he had to overcome to master himself and his subject.

The product of perseverance and courage, *American Renaissance* is a "critical monument" that has few if any rivals in this century. Its only real competitor in American literary scholarship is Perry Miller's two-volume study of "the New England mind," *The Seventeenth Century* (1939) and *From Colony to Province* (1953). By "critical monument," I mean to suggest not only the significance of the book—its formative impact on its audiences—but also its sheer bulk and its ties to an academic setting that amplified its influence. There are, unquestionably, a good many other critical and scholarly books that have exercised a particularly invigorating and often usefully contested kind of authority. Eliot's *The Sacred Wood* (1920) comes immediately to mind, a book that tossed off a bounty of compressed insights and ideas about poetry and tradition that Eliot left to others to pursue and unpack. Leavis' *The Great Tradition* (1948)—passionate, irresponsible in places, always provocative—is another intriguing example. But while these books are undeniably important for their rechanneling of literary criticism and history, neither Eliot nor Leavis enjoyed the stable institutional base that is probably essential to a critical work of truly monumental stature. Though profoundly academic in his training and manner (more so than we usually admit), Eliot did not make his living as a teacher and academic scholar and did not train students to carry on his legacy. Leavis did win many student-converts to his cause, and he prided himself upon his teacherly allegiances. But his relation to the university at Cambridge was tragically problematic at best—it took decades for him to receive even a modestly secure position.   .

Matthiessen is different in this respect. Though his own relation to Harvard was sometimes highly disputatious, he was nevertheless very much an honored (and tenured) Harvard professor, teacher, tutor, administrator of the history and literature program, and adviser to graduate students. This gets at a pivotal part of Matthiessen's identity, and indicates the powerful institutional foundation that ensured and multiplied the success of *American Renaissance* through several generations of students.

Are there other examples? Parrington's *Main Currents in American Thought* (1927–30), Van Wyck Brooks's Makers and Finders series (1936–52), and Edmund Wilson's *Patriotic Gore: Studies in the Literature of the American Civil War* (1962)—all of these books, one could propose, are also critical monuments. But neither Brooks nor Wilson was an academic, and while this freed them from the numbing pedantry of much scholarship, it also limited their influence and kept many of their critical discoveries from entering into common academic and pedagogical circulation. Nor were Brooks and Wilson given to the explication of texts, and their critical practice was therefore out of phase with the close reading approach that grew and gained popularity during the 1930s and 1940s.

Both the Makers and Finders series and *Patriotic Gore* have their independent intelligence and somewhat eccentric sensibility as their virtue and vice. Brooks presents an engaging, but finally hazy, tour of American literature and culture. Wilson, though clearly a superior critic, is nevertheless at his best in *Patriotic Gore* when he concentrates on underrated or minor writers, politicians, and generals. His portraits and summaries of the writings of Stowe, Lincoln, Grant, Sherman, and Alexander Stephens are wonderful, but his pages on Melville and Whitman are hurried and superficial.

Though rarely read today, the first two volumes of Parrington's *Main Currents* remain an often lively Jeffersonian survey of American writing from its beginnings to the mid-nineteenth century. At the time of their publication, these books were greeted with tremendous enthusiasm; "readers in 1927 felt the same quality of excitement," Howard Mumford Jones has said, "as Jeffrey experienced when in 1825 young Macaulay sent his dazzling essay on Milton to the *Edinburgh Review*" (141–42). When historians were polled in 1950 to select the best book in "American history and biography" published between 1920 and 1935, Parrington's *Main Currents* was the easy winner (Caughey). But Parrington never achieved the influence within the institutional networks of literary criticism that Matthiessen did. In addition, the fact that it was a group of historians who saluted Parrington as the author of the best book of 1920–35 says something about his approach. Literary critics, including Matthiessen very explicitly, stamped *Main Currents* as economic and political rather than literary, and hence they judged it finally as suffering from a defect that aesthetic criticism would have to remedy. Matthiessen himself emphasizes literature, not liberalism.

Parrington never claimed in his books to be conducting a literary critical analysis, so in a sense Matthiessen's and others' cavils about the aesthetic failures of *Main Currents* may appear unfair. In his first volume, Parrington observed in the introduction that he had chosen to "follow the broad path of our political, economic, and social development, rather than the narrower belletristic; and the main divisions of the study have been fixed by forces that are anterior to literary schools and movements, creating the body of ideas from which literary culture eventually springs" (*Colonial Mind* ix). He reaffirmed this intention in the second volume, noting there that "with aesthetic judgments I have not been greatly concerned. I have not wished to evaluate reputations or weigh literary merits, but rather to understand what our fathers thought, and why they wrote as they did" (*Romantic Revolution* v). But this was not finally an adequate explanation for Parrington's lame chapters on Melville, Thoreau, and other writers. It doubtless seemed to Matthiessen— and with good reason—that Parrington was engaging rich, complicated literary texts in a shallow and ultimately misguided way. To Matthiessen, one could not legitimately refer to *Moby Dick* and *Walden*, as Parrington did, without addressing their aesthetic properties. This struck Matthiessen as a crucial failure of judgment, a failure to see central truths about important writers and texts in the "main currents" of American tradition.

One could go further with contrasts and comparisons, measuring *American Renaissance* against such distinguished books about English and European literature as Frye's *Anatomy of Criticism* (1957), Abrams' *The Mirror and the Lamp* (1953), and Auerbach's *Mimesis* (1953). One could conclude that these are, in some intrinsic fashion, "better" books, and could estimate, too, that their influence was more pervasive in certain directions than that of *American Renaissance*. But I am not convinced that any of these books (or others one might name) exhibit the same combination of originality, research, scale, and institutional authority that Matthiessen's book does. *American Renaissance*, as Sacvan Bercovitch states, "reset the terms" for the study of American literature; it posited and substantiated claims for a revised canon; and it provided the impetus and rationale for a new discipline, American Studies. In its mapping of a "new mythography of American experience" (Gunn 69; see also Arac 90–91), it inspired and equipped innumerable teachers and critics, in the United States and abroad, for the task of analyzing and celebrating American literature and life. So extensive has its impact been that one scholar has defined the era that followed *American Renaissance* as "post-Matthiessenian" (Pearce 55). How many other critical books have achieved this renown and have done so much decisive work?

"American Renaissance" is such a fitting title for Matthiessen's book that one is surprised that Matthiessen himself did not come up with it. Borrowing a phrase from Whitman, he favored "Man in the Open Air," but was asked by the publisher to find something "more descriptively categorical." It was Harry Levin, one of Matthiessen's students, who suggested "American renaissance," and he has said that this title likely appealed to Matthiessen for the way it caught his "liberal idealism, his warm feeling for the creative potentialities of American life" (*Power of Blackness* vii–viii).

Matthiessen also liked the title, I would hazard, because it signaled his effort to extend (and correct) what Parrington and Brooks had done in their books. Parrington had referred in his second volume of *Main Currents* to "the New England renaissance," a period which, in his view, embraced "the twilight of Federalism" and "the rise of Liberalism" as well as the transcendentalist movement (*Romantic Revolution* 263). Matthiessen, on the one hand, greatly reduced Parrington's cast of characters, omitting Garrison, Stowe, Theodore Parker, Margaret Fuller, and others who had written and spoken as abolitionists, social reformers, and polemicists rather than as literary artists. Yet even as he reduced the number, he heightened the significance of those writers who remained, translating the "renaissance" of New England (and New York) into a "renaissance" of "America" in general. Matthiessen nationalized and amplified the more local, regional emphasis that Parrington had favored: his approach made *fewer* writers *more* important.

In *The Flowering of New England*, Brooks had also accented the antebellum period as a time of rebirth:

> In later years, when people spoke of the "renaissance" in New
> England, they spoke with a measure of reason; for in Boston, as in
> Florence, four hundred years before, there was a morning freshness
> and a thrill of conscious activity. The New England imagination had
> been roused by the tales of travellers and the gains of commerce,
> the revival of ancient learning, the introduction of modern learn-
> ing, the excitements of religious controversy. After the long winter of
> Puritanism, spring had come at last, and the earth reappeared in its
> beauty. (111)

Matthiessen respected Brooks's range of reference and vivid evocation of life in Boston and Cambridge, but not his distinctly uncritical
methodology. In Brooks's portrait of "the New England renaissance," Matthiessen stated in a review published in 1936, there is
no direct engagement with ideas and—even more disabling for a
literary critic—no inquiry into texts, "no analysis of *The Week* or of
Walden as works of art" ("*Flowering of New England*" 203).

Matthiessen corrected *The Flowering of New England*, then, as
he corrected *Main Currents*. He expanded Brooks's geographical
frame (New England again became equivalent to "America"), pared
down Brooks's canon to five writers of unusually compelling stature, and disputed Brooks's approach to texts in order to dramatize
his own return to the true "works of art." "Renaissance" was still
the proper rubric, but Matthiessen had reorganized its content and
the means by which to examine it. In doing so, he drew, I think,
from Mumford's 1926 book *The Golden Day*. Matthiessen spoke
gruffly in *American Renaissance* about Mumford's errors and defective judgments, particularly his distortion of the Hawthorne/Mel-
ville friendship (488–90). Yet Mumford had said some important
things from which Matthiessen likely learned. He had, for example,
highlighted the "imaginative New World [that] came to birth" in the
pre–Civil War period; he had concentrated on Emerson, Thoreau,
Whitman, Hawthorne, and Melville as the five writers who counted
most; he had emphasized Hawthorne and Melville as writers of great
tragedy, noting their affinities with Elizabethan and Jacobean dra-
matists and with seventeenth-century prose stylists such as Thomas
Browne; and he had nominated *Moby Dick* as America's "epic
poem" (91, 92, 142, 146, 145).

But T. S. Eliot was more Matthiessen's presiding spirit than any
of these other critics. No doubt Matthiessen also responded to the

title "American Renaissance" because it implied that he was undertaking to do for America what Eliot had done for England in his
celebration of the poets of the late sixteenth and early seventeenth
centuries. In his preface, Matthiessen contends that "in reading the
lyric, heroic, and tragic expression of our first great age, we can
feel the challenge of our still undiminished resources" (xv). The language of this affirmation is later echoed in Matthiessen's claim that
Eliot's essay on "the metaphysical poets" powerfully expresses "our
contemporary awareness of the still unspent resources of the seventeenth century" (131). Continually one feels the centrality of Eliot
for Matthiessen: he seeks to recover and revitalize the past just as
Eliot had done, gathering up unspent resources, articulating tradition, and finding the means through literature by which we might at
least momentarily restore the unified sensibility we have lost.

Matthiessen's Eliotic enterprise is paradoxical, however. Matthiessen is making a solid historical argument in connecting the literary/
cultural accomplishments of late-sixteenth- and seventeenth-century
England with that of mid-nineteenth-century America. Melville, for
one, regarded Shakespeare as his great precursor, and, as Matthiessen shows in detail, he mined Shakespeare's texts for images and
allusions throughout *Moby Dick*. "Without the precipitant of Shakespeare, *Moby Dick* might have been a superior *White Jacket*. With
it, Melville entered into another realm, of different properties and
proportions" (416). More generally, as Matthiessen illustrates in his
chapter on "the metaphysical strain" (100–32), nearly all of the
writers of the American renaissance studied, invoked, and measured
themselves against seventeenth-century writers, notably George Herbert and Thomas Browne.

Yet, in another sense, Matthiessen's argument is not centrally historical. In defining the "American renaissance," he seeks to voice and
defend universal values like those we can find not only in the masterpieces of Shakespeare but also in the *Divine Comedy* and in the best
poetry of Eliot and Yeats. Through the "renaissance" they produced
in the 1850s, America's writers affirmed their "rightful heritage in
the whole expanse of art and culture" (vii). All of the writers he
studies, Matthiessen reflected in a 1941 letter to Oxford University Press, "except Hawthorne, thought of themselves as belonging
to an age of reaffirmation of the great timeless values" (quoted in
White, "Ideology and Literature" 497). In this respect, *American*

Renaissance, through enriched by the particulars of American cultural history, is meant to situate its authors and their texts within the "simultaneous order"—"timeless and temporal"—that Eliot describes in "Tradition and the Individual Talent" (*Sacred Wood* 49).

One can additionally see Matthiessen's book as part of the modernist project that Hugh Kenner has termed "Renaissance II," the sustained and minutely detailed return to the classics, "a body of wisdom all men shared," that Pound and Joyce advocated and practiced (41; see also Perl). Matthiessen, however, nominates a new grouping of works as classic, recommending that our nation learn not from Homer but from Melville, not from the warrior Achilles but from the "common men" aboard the Pequod. Put another way: Matthiessen seeks to locate America's best books among the great books of the Western tradition and to demonstrate their international valence even as he also contends that they warrant scrupulous attention and respect from Americans for what they teach about American uniqueness. These American classics, like other such texts, impose exegetical demands upon readers and critics. They require the kind of prolonged study and analysis that one would unhesitatingly devote to the *Iliad*, the Bible, the plays of Shakespeare—and to the *Cantos*, *Ulysses*, *The Waste Land*, and other masterpieces of the twentieth century's artistic rebirth and renewal. Matthiessen always elevated the artist above the critic, but I suspect that he hoped his own book, in all its density, length, abundant citations (it sometimes feels like an anthology), and range of reference, would become a classic too—a classic of criticism that would direct readers to texts greater (and more original) than itself, but that would exact a total commitment and response from its readers and would embody its own truths.

Historical and transhistorical, *American Renaissance* is also both political and nonpolitical. Matthiessen specifically refers to his writers as providing us with a "literature for our democracy" (xv), and he had at one time considered "Literature for Democracy" as a title. This attests to his kinship with other critics, scholars, and intellectuals of the 1930s who were similarly dedicated to a broad, national, "complex effort to seek and define America as a culture and to create the patterns of a way of life worth understanding" (Susman 157; Pells, *Radical Visions* 151–93). Newton Arvin, to name just one of them, maintained in a 1937 speech at the Second American Writers'

Congress that "the real meaning of the American social and cultural adventure has been its democratic meaning. . . . One of the truest things to be said about American literature is that it has reflected, over a period of three centuries, the gradual maturing, rationalization, and deepening of the democratic idea" ("Democratic Tradition" 38). Many wrote in favor of "democracy": the difficulty came when it had to be decided which figures in American literary history were good enough as writers really to advance the democratic cause. Or, as others would have phrased the challenge: when it had to be decided which figures were so uplifting in their democratic sentiments that it made their writing good, whatever its intrinsic aesthetic quality. Like Matthiessen, though for different reasons, Arvin admired Emerson, Thoreau, and Whitman, but, as his 1937 speech testified, he also viewed such poets and politicians as Channing, Lincoln, Whittier, and Longfellow as essential members of the American procession. Matthiessen could not accept this extension of "literary" categories.

Like Arvin, Hicks, Cowley, Joseph Freeman, and others, Matthiessen sought in his own way to assemble a secular scripture that would, first, compensate for the deprivations and cruelties of the Depression in America, and, second, shore up men and women where, as was becoming increasingly clear by the late 1930s, doctrinaire Communism, if not socialism, had failed them. *American Renaissance* is, among other things, an extraordinary "turn" (or, better, "return") to enlightening and consolatory texts that will enable readers to make sense of, and to live beyond, such bad "investments of spiritual capital" as "the Agrarian program for the South" and, even more, "the revolutionary program for the industrial proletariat" (Hollinger 89).

From this point of view, "democracy" has, for Matthiessen, a concretely "American" political resonance, but it also transcends politics. Democracy means freedom from narrow and inevitably disappointing sects, factions, orthodoxies. It signals a resistance to the cult of ideology; it is the vital element, the breath of "open air," that prevents ideology from deadening and dehumanizing us. Democracy is organic, leading to an art that expresses (and gives evocative form to) the aspirations of the common man, whereas ideology is alien and artificial, mechanically imposed from the outside. Another of Matthiessen's key terms, "tragedy," expresses the same insight, but in a more ominously instructive chord. The "tragic" fate of a Macbeth or an Ahab illuminates the limits of human power and potential. Evil shadows mankind, and essential human frailty burdens all aspirations and attempts to make a better world: all earthly orders are doomed to imperfection. Democracy thus frees us from the death grip of ideology—it is vitalizing and empowering. Tragedy, in complex partnership with democracy, makes us aware that human limitation must check the fervent attachment to ideology and rule at last the soaring spirit of democracy itself. Yet it simultaneously still routes us toward the need for democracy, fraternity, and brotherhood, as when it exhibits for us, in the case of Ahab, the terrible destruction wrought by the isolated and overreaching human will and the horror of a spurned common humanity.

Matthiessen invokes "democracy" often in *American Renaissance* (it may be his presiding term), yet he leaves the meaning of this "democracy" oddly unparticularized. As Frederick Stern notes, "just exactly what Matthiessen meant by democracy is a little difficult to ascertain" (156; see also Ruland 216). Matthiessen's ardent tone calls attention to an immediate American scene that, he claims, Emerson, Melville, and the others can equip us to reconstruct; but Matthiessen is concerned, it seems, to keep the political message of his book a general one. This helps to suggest why *American Renaissance* succeeded in inspiring and rallying readers of different temperaments and beliefs to its cause. Though he read Marx and Tawney, Matthiessen finally takes his terms from Emerson and, especially, from Whitman, not from political theorists. He gains vigor and rhetorical power from their texts, but he avoids or lacks an accompanying political specificity that would actually demand changes in behavior. More capacious but less militantly specific than someone like Granville Hicks in *The Great Tradition*, Matthiessen speaks to many readers because he does not insist that they commit themselves to exacting political choices. The cause he champions is imprecise enough to be filled up by varying conceptions of what democracy entails.

Democracy, for Matthiessen, is connected to duty, work, and craftsmanship. In this fashion it perhaps developed as a value for him not only through his reading of Emerson and Whitman but also through his reading (and attention to the art) of Horatio Greenough, Louis Sullivan, and Frank Lloyd Wright—all of whom Matthiessen cites in *American Renaissance.* For each of these men, in contrasting but powerfully interrelated ways, the search for new kinds of artistic, specifically "organic" form goes hand in hand with a faith in American democratic potential and possibility. Greenough (1805–52) absorbs himself in theoretical studies of form and function, structure, and organization in order to conceive of an art truly suited to the status of America's people as "the advanced guard of humanity" (111). Sullivan, in *The Autobiography of an Idea* (1926) and elsewhere, returns continually and passionately to the theme of democratic people engaged in earnest work that a rekindled vision of America's national promise inspires. His language, which expressly adapts and amplifies Whitman's poetry and prose, particularly *Democratic Vistas*, has an exhilaration like that which Matthiessen's language of democracy sometimes displays. It also suffers from the same fate of overgenerality when inspected closely:

> Our dream shall be of a civilization founded upon ideas thrillingly sane, a civilization, a social fabric squarely resting on man's quality of virtue as a human being; created by man, the real, in the image of his fruitful powers of beneficence; created in the likeness of his aspirant emotions, in response to the power and glory of his true imagination, the power of his intelligence, his ability to inquire, to do, to make new situations befitting his needs. A civilization that shall reflect man sound to the core and kindly in the exercise of his will to choose aright. A civilization that shall be the living voice, the spring song, the saga of the power of his Ego to banish fear and fate, and in the courage of adventure and of mastership to shape his destiny. (273)

Matthiessen would not have endorsed the piling up of clauses or the high pitch of this, but he did warm to the conviction that motivates it: the determination to bring American culture into harmonious relation with the democratic energy and character of the American people.

Wright's language often seems more openly Emersonian in its individualism (and this would have troubled Matthiessen); but Wright's vision, like Sullivan's, is also steadfastly and confidently organic, as in this passage from a 1930 lecture at Princeton University:

> This new American liberty is of the sort that declares man free only when he has found his work and effective means to achieve a

life of his own. The means once found, he will find his due place. The man of our country will thus make his own way, and *grow* to the natural place thus due him, promised—yes, promised by our charter, the Declaration of Independence. But this place of his is not to be made over to fit him by reform, nor shall it be brought down to him by concession, but will become his by his own use of the means at hand. He must *himself* build a new world. The day of the individual is not over—instead, it is just about to begin. (101)

Such language is wonderful in its own way, but not so much for what it is in its own right as for what it led Wright to conceive and build. It is not a political language but a vibrant, sometimes sentimental, sometimes mystical language of artistic self-empowerment and prophecy. This same point applies to Matthiessen's language in *American Renaissance*, which conveys the ardor we associate with political awakening without identifying itself concretely. It is uplifting—a "tonic sentiment" (Marx, "Harvard Retrospect" 34)— precisely because it sounds the clarion call to action and reflection without necessarily forcing hard choices. Open to all, this language is powerful, invigorating, and reassuring, as another, more calibrated language would not be. We need to see this aspect of *American Renaissance* if we want to understand how it managed so quickly to gain acceptance from so many people for its canon and its literary arguments.

Matthiessen in fact concludes his preface by citing some stirring sentences from Sullivan's celebration of the "true scholar" as a "citizen" and "exponent of democracy":

> "In a democracy there can be but one fundamental test of citizenship, namely: Are you using such gifts as you possess for or against the people?" These standards are the inevitable and right extension of Emerson's demands in "The American Scholar." The ensuing volume has value only to the extent that it comes anywhere near measuring up to them. (xv–xvi)

Matthiessen tuned his criticism to the strains of American democracy at its most idealistic and self-ennobling. His act of "consensus-formation" (Pease 118) spoke to everybody, including many who would never have shared the socialism that Matthiessen himself clung to and acted upon in his own public political life.

Of course this "everybody" was not really everybody. It mostly consisted of white male academics, students, literary critics, and intellectuals, and as such did not reflect the composition of "the people" as a whole. By the 1930s, when Matthiessen was researching and writing *American Renaissance*, the nature of the population had radically changed.

> In 1930, when the episode of the New Immigration had stabilized, some 14 million persons living in the United States had been born elsewhere, very largely in southern and eastern Europe, and another 25-million-plus persons were first-generation native born. Another 12 million persons, it might be added, were black, so that between 40 and 50 percent of the entire population of the United States consisted of persons who had at best an ambivalent relationship to any such essentialized, mainstream American tradition as anybody might propose. . . . Civilization in the United States was located in the cities, and the cities were ghetto conglomerates. By 1930 the "great cities," those with a total population of a million or more, were made up of persons *two-thirds* of whom were either foreign born or first-generation native born. (Klein 13–14)

Neither Matthiessen nor the members of the fairly select group he represented perceived the awkward failure of fit between the general claim to be of democratic service to "the people"—by the 1930s a very diverse people indeed—and the restricted nature of the canon, limited to five white male authors, that *American Renaissance* announced.

In a suggestive essay, Jonathan Arac has remarked upon affinities between Matthiessen's rhetoric and the language of democratic alliance building favored by the Popular Front in the 1930s (96–97). This "Popular" or "People's" Front, launched in 1935, was the Communist party's response to Fascism and Nazism; no longer was the party to stress its differences from other socialist groups, but rather it would now band together with all left and liberal organizations to stop the advance of the common enemy (Casciato 24–25; 119–20). The Popular Front, Malcolm Cowley recalls, based itself upon "the feeling of present danger represented by Hitler. In the face of that danger, people were willing not to pursue their ideas to the last point. They would glide over, smooth over, ideological differences if they could get cooperation in action" ("Thirty Years Later" 499). As Arac indicates, the Popular Front's relative openness to its former middle-class foes included an advocacy of the "cultural heritage" of each nation. Before 1935, the party had highlighted the riches of proletarian culture, but it now saw the expanded force it could muster by endorsing the humanistic tradition—and the progressive intellectuals who aligned themselves with this tradition. As one commentator has put it, the Popular Front strategy led the Communists to sound more like Woodrow Wilson than like Karl Marx, in their eagerness "to float in the 'main currents' of American life" (Pells, *Radical Visions* 297). In *American Renaissance*, Matthiessen sought to stand with "all the people"—which is different from standing with "the workers" in their class struggle—and to employ the respected texts of Emerson, Thoreau, Hawthorne, Melville, and Whitman as linchpins for his "democratic" arguments on behalf of the "common man."

Arac describes *American Renaissance* as a book that grew within a particular historical moment, and his observations about the Popular Front deepen the meanings of Matthiessen's vocabulary of wholeness and union. There are indeed signs in *American Renaissance* of Matthiessen's concern for how best to come to terms with, and to resist, life "liv[ed] in the age of Hitler" (*American Renaissance* 307, 546). But Arac's good insight also needs qualification. How far, finally, can we go with the Popular Front connection? How much strength could Matthiessen really accrue from it? One irony worth noting is that the rise of the Popular Front itself helped to generate oppositional anti-Communist and antitotalitarian movements which competed with it (Klehr 349–64). Even as many writers and intellectuals supported such Front groups as the League of American Writers and the American Artists' Congress, other writers and intellectuals strove to differentiate themselves from them—the Committee for Cultural Freedom and the League for Cultural Freedom (which revolved around the revamped *Partisan Review*) being two cases in point. The Popular Front's popularity was real, but limited; Matthiessen spoke not only to and for the Popular Front, but to many who disputed it as well.

The Moscow trials of 1936–38 also cut into the confidence and strength of the Popular Front; and it was effectively destroyed in August 1939, when the Soviet and German foreign ministers signed a nonaggression pact between their two countries. American Communists were "shocked, stunned, unprepared, and uncoached" when the news of this pact hit (Klehr 387). As Granville Hicks later noted, it "knock[ed] the bottom out of everything" (*Where We Came Out* 80). Germany attacked Poland in September 1939; and the Soviet Union, hardly the pure alternative to Nazism and Fascism it once seemed, invaded Finland in November 1939. Matthiessen hence was completing his book, and preparing it for publication, during the period when the Popular Front's strategy was being exposed as grotesquely naive and when the Popular Front itself suffered "sudden death" (Howe, *Socialism and America* 92). Alliance building returned to style for the Communist party in June 1941, when Hitler ordered the invasion of the Soviet Union—Roosevelt and Churchill now became "good democrats"—but by then, the party was something that neither the mind nor the conscience of most intellectuals could endure.

The most curious feature of Matthiessen's rhetoric is its free-floating quality. It may indeed have drawn in some manner from the Popular Front, yet it was not dependent upon it, and it did not suffer from the Popular Front's decline. The course of events during the late 1930s and early 1940s is important to our sense of how and why *American Renaissance* took form as it did; one could add here, in fact, as yet another source of power for Matthiessen's title, that spokesmen for the Popular Front often tried to define the writings of their group as "a continuation of the renaissance and revolution" in American culture and letters before World War I (J. B. Gilbert 163). But these events had little effect on the actual reception and impact of the book: Matthiessen's language of "the people" held good and won adherents throughout the 1940s and afterward, appealing to many critics who differed sharply with Matthiessen's politics or who would probably have loathed Matthiessen's politics if they had known what these were. Events *did* badly shake *From the Heart of Europe* when it appeared in 1948, because this book made highly explicit linkages between its social/democratic vision and the politics of postwar Eastern Europe. But there was nothing concrete enough in *American Renaissance* for critics to attack. Its political vocabulary, keyed very much to the tone and timbre of Whitman, Wright, and Sullivan, was too generalized to be objectionable.

Readers of *American Renaissance* in the 1940s and 1950s experienced an exciting sense of discovery. I vividly recall the late Laurence Holland's testimony to the book's impact. *American Renaissance*,

Holland said, was a book "we read everywhere and read constantly." It wasn't simply that *American Renaissance* opened up a rich body of texts for assessment and explanation, that it bonded them to full-toned patterns in American culture and society, and that it revealed a critical intelligence that surpassed Brooks's and Parrington's. It was also, just as much, a book that counted immeasurably for young critics and graduate students at Harvard, where so many professors of literature were trained, because it was the fullest statement by their beloved teacher of the reasons why American literature and criticism were significant: it was a book that was at one with the man who wrote it. Holland's words would have pleased Matthiessen, for they gave prominence to the "integrity" that he so admired in Eliot and sought so adamantly to realize in his own life.

Holland emphasized to me that he read *American Renaissance*, in whole or in part, "many times." But the truth is that most readers today find the book difficult to read even once. Even as one acknowledges the magnificence of *American Renaissance*, one also has to agree with Richard Ruland that "by far the dominant impression today's reader must receive from Matthiessen's discussion of Emerson, Thoreau, Hawthorne, Melville, and Whitman is the familiarity of it all" (231). Much of the time, Matthiessen appears not so much to be presenting ideas and insights as stating commonplaces, saying basic things that everybody already knows and tracing affinities between writers—Hawthorne and James, Melville and Shakespeare—that other critics have probed in deeper, more complicated fashion.

At the risk of seeming to have it both ways, I will say that this response both does and does not point to a flaw in *American Renaissance*. The book does lack a really strong, clearly expressed principle of evaluation like that manifested, for better and worse, in critics such as Leavis and Winters. These critics are frequently intolerant and provincial, but they are challenging because they are dedicated to making judgments and distinctions that subvert standard views and critical pieties. A reader can turn to their books today and still regard them as productively disarming and disorienting. This also reflects the fact, of course, that Leavis and Winters were less successful than Matthiessen in winning institutional accreditation for their views. Matthiessen is more thorough and responsible; his prose does not show the nasty edge and bluff disdain for moderation and common sense which can, in Leavis in particular, incite an adversarial response that alienates some readers but that also defines the perceptions of other readers more accurately and energizes them.

Granville Hicks, a maker, like Leavis, of "a great tradition," was less skillful as a critic than Matthiessen, but his Marxism supplied him with an evaluative firmness and daring that are generally missing from *American Renaissance*. Hicks viewed himself as, above all, a political man with a concrete literary mission. He wanted, in the 1930s, to be the critic who, he maintains, had regrettably not existed during the first two decades of this century:

> If there had been someone to say, "This is the situation of society today; these are the forces that have shaped that situation; here is the power that can bring change," novelists might not have stumbled quite so blindly or taken quite such precipitate flight. If someone had said, "Though this civilization is dying, a new civilization is in the process of building," poets might not so quickly have lost their hope. If someone had said, "You need not stand alone in your fight against the corruption in and about you, for here are your allies," artists of every kind might have faced with new confidence the tasks of creation. Not every artist could have responded to such words, but some would have. The words, alas, were not spoken! (*Great Tradition* 252–53)

Matthiessen would have labeled this passage as presumptuous and dangerously prescriptive, and he would probably have been correct. But a militantly political or aesthetically extreme vision does not have to cripple or date a critical book; it can also give the book a briskness and impatience—even, perhaps, an outrageousness —that enable it to survive past the period when it first appeared. Matthiessen respected this trait in Hicks. Indeed, when Hicks's *Great Tradition* was published in 1933, Matthiessen noted in his review of it that Hicks "reveals the power and clarity that the critic gains by consistently held principles of evaluation. Each individual work is seen in some perspective; instead of the general inconclusive blurring by which most literary history reduces the recent period in particular to a formless mass, the achievement of each author is measured against a defined standard" ("*Great Tradition*" 191). But Matthiessen judged the results of such an approach as all too frequently a distortion of literary truth. If, as he remarked of Hicks, criticism leads to a scanty, dismissive treatment of Dickinson, Twain, and James, then something is askew (192).

Matthiessen distinguishes his approach from Hicks's by arguing that "the greatest art performs its most characteristic action in more subtle ways; it 'does something,' in the novels of Fielding or Proust, by bringing the reader a new understanding or a fresh insight into the full meaning of existence. It thus acts on life by giving it release and fulfillment" (193). This, obviously, is generously appreciative and tolerant. Matthiessen does not insist that art should compel political action, serve the class struggle, or overtly protest against a social problem. His notion of what literature, as an art, "is" and "does" outfits him to respond to and learn from writers with whose politics he might not be in sympathy; whatever their political values, artists may still display an understanding of, and insight into, "the full meaning of existence." Matthiessen is more catholic in his tastes than Hicks, and, in the final analysis, this is perhaps all to the good. But as his own fairly vague phrasing of "fresh insights" and "full meaning of existence" implies, Matthiessen can also sometimes seem too inclusive, flat, and overgeneralizing in his tone. He can be dull and somewhat obscure, and irritatingly so, in the way that Matthew Arnold—another propounder of big generalities and an early enthusiasm of Matthiessen's—can also be.

To refer to the familiarity or dullness that sometimes mars *American Renaissance* still tells only another partial truth, however. Statements that strike us as commonplace were not commonplace to the book's first readers: they became such because of the massive authority of Matthiessen's book. Even the notoriously anti-academic Ernest Hemingway was impressed, observing in a letter to Maxwell Geismar that he "would hate to have to write about the early characters after Matthiessen" (625). Matthiessen established the discursive framework for criticism of American literature, "a substantial platform for the reconsideration of the complete story of American letters" (Spiller 435). And he has especially influenced critical commentary on Emerson, Thoreau, Hawthorne, Melville, and Whitman. His terms have become the terms that we naturally employ when we get our bearings on America's classics. This is what Ruland was referring to when he stated, in 1967, that "there probably has not been a university course in American literature offered in the last twenty years which has failed to echo [*American Renaissance's*] terms or move outward from their implications" (231). The familiarity of *American Renaissance* is also the most impressive evidence of its success.

There is nevertheless no denying that American literature has greatly expanded as a subject since *American Renaissance* appeared in 1941. Studies of American literature and culture before the Civil War abound, and these cannot but make us aware of topics and issues that Matthiessen, for all his massive coverage, treated too briefly or failed to investigate. Michael T. Gilmore, for example, in *American Romanticism and the Marketplace* (1985), has explored the impact of the expanding "market economy" on Emerson, Thoreau, Hawthorne, and Melville, fastening upon their contradictory attitudes toward the commercialization of culture and literary "popularity." Focused as he was on "art and expression," and intent upon showing how his major figures rebelled against mass taste, Matthiessen never delved into the ways in which the pressures of the marketplace affected the writing of texts in "high" as well as in "popular" culture. In *New England Literary Culture: From Revolution through Renaissance* (1986), Lawrence Buell also scrutinizes marketplace conditions, and provides extensive empirical evidence for his assessment of the rise of professional authorship in New England. Matthiessen likely would not have looked favorably upon Buell's quantitative methods, and he might well also have objected to the degree of biographical and historical detail that Buell supplies, detail that would have struck him as impinging upon our ability to appreciate the literary works themselves. Buell also highlights topics —gothic conventions, historiography, Scripture used as a thematic and structural model for narrative—that Matthiessen skirts or only touches upon. His book is not necessarily better than Matthiessen's, but it is a book, along with Gilmore's and others', that alerts us to the limits of what Matthiessen did.

There have also been a number of interesting recent forays, a good many of them produced by feminist critics, in what one could term the "reading" of American culture. The aim here is less to explore specific texts than to survey and map—in a word, to interpret—the general cultural text. Critics have consequently been led to examine the connections between literature and law, noting the discursive patterns that both bond and distinguish them (Ferguson; Brook Thomas), or have built up an understanding of the central organizing metaphors and paradigms that empowered the language and defined the values of North and South before the Civil War (Norton). Such critics work comfortably and fluidly with writings that might have seemed to Matthiessen to belong in very different textual kingdoms, and they foreground social and political issues in ways which he would likely have seen as raising havoc with artistic categories.

Another means of measuring the limits of *American Renaissance* for readers today is to observe that as one reads it, one is regularly aware of specific texts that Matthiessen, like others of his generation, omitted—omitted either through deliberate choice or through a critical unconsciousness about their value. One kind of immediate objection along these lines might be to say, along with William Spengemann, that Matthiessen was mistaken to isolate an "American" renaissance, a body of literary texts that are peculiarly American and thus "different" in essential ways from other texts written in English. Spengemann's central point, which reaffirms and updates the view that prevailed at the turn of the century, is that "the history of what we call American literature" is "inseparable from the history of literature in English as a whole" ("American Things" 477). From this angle, Matthiessen can be seen as giving powerful impetus to a misguided effort to define American texts outside the general Anglo-American currents of literary production. "Anglophone America and England have always constituted a single, complex English-speaking culture," Spengemann maintains in opposition to Matthiessen ("American Writers" 215). We can appropriately speak of *Leaves of Grass* as signaling an important moment in "American culture," but, he adds, this is different from saying that it is a landmark event in "*American* literature." "For the literary scholar, it is a significant event in the development of English literature, and neither that work nor that development can be literarily understood apart from each other" ("American Writers" 216).

In certain respects Spengemann's argument is compelling. It does remind us of the dangers of a literary nationalism that overlooks literary and historical truth. Many British and American writers saw themselves as inhabitants of "the same literary country" ("American Writers" 221), and historical sense dictates that we should connect Emerson, as philosopher, poet, and essayist, as much with Coleridge, Wordsworth, Bacon, and Carlyle as with any of his American contemporaries. Spengemann is doubtless correct, too, in observing that the key terms by which critics like Matthiessen define the distinctiveness of American literature—"democracy," for instance—are terms that pertain to many so-called American texts that are not usually considered "literary" at all and that, furthermore, are terms that characterize many literary texts not written by Americans.

Matthiessen is, however, less guilty of an undue (and inaccurate) literary nationalism than some of his successors have been. Matthiessen does draw extensively upon Coleridge in his analysis of Emerson's formulation of the "organic principle," and he cites a great many other English and European writers as sources or analogies for the American writers he interprets. He is admittedly engaged in an enterprise that is nationalistic, yet he modifies this somewhat through his reliance on the English and European traditions that Eliot featured in his critical prose. Matthiessen was eager to expand the possibilities for democracy in America through a celebratory analysis of America's greatest writers; but he was also devoted to the highest in "art" in general—in particular, the best books and the best painting (which, he tells us, Russell Cheney helped him to appreciate more fully and describe). Matthiessen ranged widely in his teaching —his regular courses included world drama, Shakespeare, and major British poets—and, for all his "euphoria of America," he wrote books about Eliot and James, "the most notoriously transatlantic of America's great writers" (Arac 95; Rowe 39–40). His passion for art at its best moderated any tendency to elevate American literary texts at the expense of (or in wholesale isolation from) the literary texts of other nations and languages. Like the Emerson he describes, Matthiessen "knew that an American renaissance needed the encouragement of great writers and thinkers. His timelessness took for granted his country's immediate share in the whole cultural heritage" (631). Recent critics have more fully treated Anglo-American literary relations (Kasson; Weisbuch), but perhaps one could regard them as expanding upon and fully clarifying matters that Matthiessen sometimes slighted because he took them for granted.

Another objection to *American Renaissance* is harder to discount, however. It bears upon the announcement, much disputed by feminist critics, that Matthiessen delivers on the first page of his preface:

> The half-decade of 1850–55 saw the appearance of *Representative Men* (1850), *The Scarlet Letter* (1850), *The House of the Seven Gables* (1851), *Moby Dick* (1851), *Pierre* (1852), *Walden* (1854), and *Leaves of Grass* (1855). You might search all the rest of American literature without being able to collect a group of books equal to these in imaginative vitality. (vii)

This list, we are now abundantly aware, omits Stowe, Susan Warner, Maria Cummins, and other "sentimental" novelists. Matthiessen's "group of books," consisting only of books by white male authors, ignores the "imaginative vitality" that these women writers exemplified in their enormously popular novels of the antebellum period. Nina Baym and Mary Kelley have effectively argued for the cultural and literary value of these novels, but perhaps the most stinging rebuke to Matthiessen (and most adept testimony to the merit of the books he omits) has been presented by Jane Tompkins. Her argument needs to be quoted at length, for it sums up a common (and generally apt) criticism of Matthiessen's judgment and procedure.

Matthiessen determined the books that students would read and critics would write about for decades to come. More important, he influenced our assumptions about what kind of person can be a literary genius, what kinds of subjects great literature can discuss, our notions about who can be a hero and who cannot, notions of what constitutes heroic behavior, significant activity, central issues. Matthiessen, who believed that criticism should "be for the good and enlightenment of all the people, and not for the pampering of a class," believed that the books he had chosen were truly representative of the American people, for these works, more than any others, called "the whole soul of man into activity."

Matthiessen's list is exclusive and class-bound in the extreme. If you look at it carefully, you will see that in certain fundamental ways the list does not represent what most men and women were thinking about between 1850 and 1855, but embodies the views of a very small, socially, culturally, geographically, sexually, and racially restricted elite. None of the works that Matthiessen names is by an orthodox Christian, although that is what most Americans in the 1850s were, and although religious issues pervaded the cultural discourse of the period. None deals explicitly with the issues of abolition and temperance which preoccupied the country in this period, and gave rise to such popular works as *Uncle Tom's Cabin* and T. S. Arthur's *Ten Nights in a Barroom*. None of the works on the list achieved great popular success, although this six-year period saw the emergence of the first American best-sellers. The list includes no works by women, although women at that time dominated the literary marketplace. The list includes no works by males not of Anglo-Saxon origin, and indeed, no works by writers living south of New York, north of Boston, or west of Stockbridge, Massachusetts. . . . These exclusions are a more important indicator of the representativeness of literary works than their power to engage "the whole soul of man." (199–200; see also Lauter)

Tompkins is right: Matthiessen's concern for democracy is not sustained by his distinctly undemocratic list of great writers. But how far should we press this against Matthiessen himself as an individual? Tompkins' claim that he "determined" the books that students and critics would study may be a rather exorbitant indictment to bring against him. His book *was* enormously influential. Yet to suggest that he alone structured the field leaves out the ways in which others chose to reiterate his conclusions and repeat his errors. Matthiessen did not include texts by women and blacks; nobody else did either.

Matthiessen recognized that he excluded much from *American Renaissance* yet did not ponder the nature of these exclusions. This is where the real problem, and the major reason for disappointment, lie. One might have hoped that, given his politics, he would have been able to perceive the class, gender, and race restrictions of his canon. But while he was a socialist, he was also, like nearly all other academic critics of the same era, a critic whose educational background, interests and influences, and artistic attitudes disposed him toward high culture and a predominantly white and male literary canon. As his preface shows, Matthiessen knew that he was making choices in shaping the "American renaissance" and excluding texts which, as he reports, an intellectual historian or an interpreter of social and economic forces might treat. He states that if he were pursuing the nature of radical reform in the 1850s, he would be obliged to "stress the fact that 1852 witnessed not only the appearance of *Pierre* but of *Uncle Tom's Cabin*" (viii). It simply did not occur to him that by omitting Stowe and the women writers, he was going to end up with a list that was entirely male; and it apparently did not even enter his mind that the list was defective because it was wholly white.

Here, as elsewhere, one wonders about missed opportunities and roads not taken. Possibly American literature and criticism might have taken a different turn if Matthiessen had expanded his vision to include Stowe, Douglass, and Garrison. But it is probably the case that if he had done this, his book would not have been as influential as it was: his audiences would not have "heard" him in the same manner and might not have been as laudatory in their response. This may seem to lessen our esteem for Matthiessen's courage and deepen the antidemocratic charge against him, but it also reminds us that his book was written and read within literary and educational institutions that determined him as much as he determined them.

The troubling feature of Matthiessen's canon, then, concerns his unreflective use of terms in making his argument for it. "The one common denominator of my five writers, uniting even Hawthorne and Whitman, was their devotion to the possibilities of democracy" (ix). One could reply that Stowe and Douglass were as actively interested, if not more so, in "the possibilities of democracy" as were Emerson and the others Matthiessen selects. Matthiessen's key "denominator" does not adequately differentiate his group of writers from others of the 1850s. Nor, for that matter, is it evident that Matthiessen can persuasively claim that Hawthorne, whom he examines at length, really qualifies as a writer truly devoted to democratic values and aspirations. In his party affiliation, Hawthorne was a Democrat, and he was a friend, supporter, and biographer of the Democratic candidate for president in 1852, Franklin Pierce. But only through special pleading can we translate Hawthorne's party loyalties into a general allegiance to "democracy." Ruland has judged Matthiessen's "effort to bring Hawthorne into the fold" to be "the baldest instance of thesis-riding in his otherwise honest book" (241). Even George Abbott White, one of Matthiessen's most tolerant readers, feels obliged to label the view of Hawthorne's politics presented in *American Renaissance* "a blatant mis-reading of history," an "ideological distortion" (479).

Matthiessen is not altogether uncritical toward the writers he admires, and he does highlight Hawthorne's limitations in his section on the novelist's politics (316–37), referring in particular to the unreality and complacency that mar the ending of *The House of the Seven Gables* (334). But Matthiessen usually seeks to redeem Hawthorne and his other favorites, to superintend the texts so that they will be eminently usable and instructive. This sometimes causes his criticism to seem sloppy or disingenuous, as his terms expand in order to make writers more zealous about the "possibilities of democracy" than they actually are. When Matthiessen begins his survey of Hawthorne's politics, he does address the question of this writer's conservatism (317). But he then moves fairly quickly to Hawthorne as a "Democrat" with a capital *D* (318) and then "democrat" in general with a small *d*. Soon the political issues get even more blurred, as Matthiessen, invoking James, commends Hawthorne as a writer deeply interested in history and in possession of a profound "sense of the past" (320). Matthiessen loosely translates Hawthorne's "sense of the past," not his actual politics or even the politics implicit in his texts, into a faith in democracy. One could conceivably maintain that Matthiessen succeeds in making Hawthorne safe for democracy, but he manages to do so only by shuffling and exchanging terms that are not equivalent.

Matthiessen's tactics in the Hawthorne section, and in other parts of the book where he hymns his writers' democratic vision, prompt many readers today to be all the more sensitive to the act of canon formation he undertakes in the preface. Why is he bending Hawthorne's politics to link this writer to "democracy" when he could have made a better case by including Stowe or Douglass? Another, related shortcoming in the preface occurs when, in distinguishing his approach from Parrington's, Matthiessen again takes up the question of his choice of authors. Parrington had stated in *Main Currents*, Matthiessen reminds us, that "with aesthetic judgments I have not been greatly concerned. I have not wished to evaluate reputations or weigh literary merits, but rather to understand what our fathers thought." "My concern," Matthiessen retorts, "has been the opposite." He portrays himself as a literary critic, not as a historian, and he is therefore committed to aesthetic judgments and analyses of literary meaning (ix). This is all well and good, yet Matthiessen's aims become confused when he adds that, as a critic, he seeks to minister to the "common reader," the reader engaged in reading books because they have "an immediate life of their own" (x). Just who is the "common reader"?—the term is more open and problematic than Matthiessen allows. And how do the pleasures of the "common reader" connect with the critic's willingness to state and argue for his own "aesthetic judgments"?

Each of Matthiessen's sentences in this part of the preface is firm, but his overall argument is dubiously presented. In his next paragraph, the problems worsen as he describes the popularity of Susan Warner, Maria Cummins, and other women writers of the antebellum period and contrasts their phenomenal sales with the low sales of the books by Thoreau, Whitman, and Melville. This would seem to suggest that the "common reader" of the 1850s, though inattentive to the male authors Matthiessen highlights in *American Renaissance*, nevertheless did possess, understand, and respond significantly to a body of literary texts. Matthiessen rejects the judgment of these "common readers," quoting Hawthorne's complaint about the "damned mob of scribbling women" who divert the public "with their trash." The historian or sociologist may be interested in sentimental novels, Matthiessen remarks, but the literary critic, following Thoreau's injunction, wants to "read the best books first." Now it emerges that "common" does not actually carry the democratic meaning we normally associate with it. We should respect common readers, Matthiessen appears to be saying, but only when their taste meets with the critic's sanction.

It would be one thing for Matthiessen simply to declare that Stowe, Warner, and the others are bad writers compared with Emerson, Thoreau, Hawthorne, Melville, and Whitman. Readers of the 1980s might dislike this, but at least they would know that Matthiessen has made, and hence must take responsibility for, his own aesthetic judgments. But Matthiessen implies that he is not so much propounding independent judgments as relying upon the accumulated wisdom of literary history and the common democratic sensibility. "During the century that has ensued" since the 1850s, he states, "the successive generations of common readers, who make the decisions, would seem finally to have agreed that the authors of the pre–Civil War era who bulk largest in stature are the five who are my subject" (xi). The common readers of the 1850s do not count, but the common readers who come afterward do and Matthiessen is their representative.

One is tempted to say that Matthiessen is being dishonest in his shaky handling of his argument here. Surely he must glimpse the precariousness of his professed reliance upon "common readers," and surely, too, he must be aware—despite his talk of "successive generations"—that the generation prior to his own held a very different conception of which writers of the pre–Civil War era (and which of their texts) were the most significant. But the issue is not finally one of dishonesty in presenting a critical argument. Matthiessen is blind to the nature of the terms he employs and their implications. He naturalizes his own judgments—or rather, and more accurately, he naturalizes the judgments (the "decisions") of the intellectual and critical class to which he belongs. He draws upon and expresses the views of *uncommon* readers as though their vocabulary and values were indeed "common," the shared property of American democrats.

Matthiessen's canon began to unravel by the 1960s, as critics and teachers active in the New Left objected to the class, gender, and race biases current in the academy. More recent theoretical and practical work (it has been remarkable in its scope) has both illuminated the failings of earlier definitions of the canon and recovered many texts, particularly by blacks and women, that are now inscribed in the new American literary history (Sollors). From this vantage point, Matthiessen's judgments and choices in *American Renaissance* appear to stand as a classic case of straitened canon formation and warrant the attack that Tompkins launches against them. But perhaps we should acknowledge that *American Renaissance* itself helped to authorize the changes we now see in the canon. In its extreme white male formulation, Matthiessen's list of authors forecast the beginnings of its own refutation. By referring to the women writers he will not discuss and by devoting hundreds of pages of analysis and celebration to five white male authors, Matthiessen unwittingly prefigured in his book what later readers would dispute and labor to correct.

One additional sign of the monumentality of *American Renaissance* is, then, the enormously inviting target it presents to its ideological and critical opponents: they are able to capitalize upon its mistakes as they could not capitalize upon a less prodigiously authoritative work. This may seem to be a forced positive conclusion, one that backhandedly gives Matthiessen's book a kind of credit it does not truly deserve. Yet it does speak to a truth about Matthiessen's achievement in *American Renaissance*, whatever its errors and omissions. The moral, democratically grained urgency with which it is written has survived and flourished in the critiques launched against it.

SIX

Reading American Renaissance, *Part* 2

Democracy . . . a great word, whose history, I suppose, remains
unwritten, because that history has yet to be enacted.
—Whitman, *Democratic Vistas* 960

OBVIOUSLY THERE is much more that can and should be
said about *American Renaissance* itself, as the ample commentary
on it testifies. Giles Gunn, Frederick Stern, and George Abbott
White, among others, have written well about the book, and in part
my concerns in Chapters 5 and 6 reflect my desire not to cover
the same ground. All of these critics have examined the structure
of Matthiessen's book as a whole, studied his influential sections
on "organic form" and "artistic expression," explored his account
of "allegory" and "symbolism," and thoroughly investigated his
lengthy assessments of Melville and Hawthorne. All of them, in addition, in focusing on Hawthorne and Melville, necessarily address
Matthiessen's views on tragedy, democracy, and Christianity. Gunn
nicely records, for example, how Matthiessen tends to "turn literary questions about form and technique into moral and religious
questions about the nature of reality" (106); and he documents the
impact of Yeats and Eliot (and behind them, of Shakespeare and
Keats) on Matthiessen's notion of tragedy.

Stern also deals interestingly with Matthiessen's "tragic" reading
of Hawthorne and Melville, and indicates how Matthiessen sometimes misinterprets texts—*The Scarlet Letter* is a notable instance
—to align them with his definition of tragedy. White is less incisive
on these matters, but he provides a valuable survey of influences
on Matthiessen's thought, including Arnold, the New Humanists,

Richards, Lawrence, Parrington, Brooks, and, above all, Eliot. He also inquires into the reasons for the omission of Poe (477), whom Matthiessen later wrote about for the jointly authored *Literary History of the United States*, but whose attitudes toward "democracy" were so openly and bitterly hostile that Matthiessen had no choice but to expel him from his canon in *American Renaissance*.

As all of these critics show, Matthiessen's chapters on Hawthorne and Melville are impressive and absorbing. But to my mind, Matthiessen's hundred-page survey of Whitman illustrates perhaps even more clearly his characteristic strengths and limits as a critic. It is unfortunate, if unsurprising in view of the overt drama of the Hawthorne and Melville chapters, that neither Gunn, Stern, nor White says anything in detail about it. Matthiessen's critical intelligence is keenly displayed in this part of the book: he examines Whitman sympathetically, but is not unmindful of his weaknesses as a poet and thinker. He also makes excellent use of his interdisciplinary skills, relating Whitman's landscapes to the genre painting of W. S. Mount and the poet's realism to that of Millet and Eakins. He furthermore undertakes some challenging comparisons, bringing Whitman into stimulating connection with Hopkins in particular. The entire treatment of Whitman is informed by Matthiessen's avid interest in this writer's celebrations, extending from revelry to ritual, of American democracy. So much does Matthiessen respond to Whitman's political spirit, with its resonant implications for all American democrats and "common men," that he tends to underrate the poetry itself. He values Whitman's language, his "language experiment," yet doubts whether it emerges in aesthetically satisfying forms.

Matthiessen regards Whitman's language as the inescapable point of departure for analyses of this verbally prolific writer. Echoing Whitman's words in the essay on "slang in America," he terms language " 'the universal absorber and combiner,' the best index we have to the history of civilization" (519). Matthiessen ties this central subject to a daunting range of topics, including—this is only a partial list—Whitman's diction, interest in Quakerism, connection with Emerson, sexual symbolism, analogies for poetry (oratory, opera, the ocean), rhythm, revisions, and political themes. He also makes pertinent remarks about Whitman's relation to writers who preceded and followed him, such as Wordsworth, Burns, Jeffers, and Sandburg. On the level both of overarching argument and of concretely observed detail, Matthiessen's performance, keyed to Whitman's language, is a commanding one, as he moves proficiently from the particular to the general and back again. His typical procedure is to weave together details and discoveries about the nature of Whitman's language and to attach them to numerous citations, after which he then adjusts his pace in order to enlarge upon what all of this points to.

There are many telling generalizations in this chapter, and these are all the more persuasive because of the amount of precise questioning and observation arrayed behind them.

> On the one hand, [Whitman's] desire to grasp American facts could lead him beyond slang into the rawest jargon, the journalese of the day. On the other, his attempts to pass beyond the restrictions of language into the atmosphere it could suggest often produced only the barest formulas. His inordinate and grotesque failures in both directions throw into clearer light his rare successes, and the fusion upon which they depend. (526)

> Interior gestures were the bridge by which he passed from declamation to lyricism. Whitman ordinarily assumed that in his songs he was talking to everybody, and liked to think of his voice withering the pretensions of the thinly cultivated and radiating out to all the common people of these States. Yet even he granted at times that he wasted no ink, that his words were only for those few who had gone through enough experience to be able to apprehend them. And when he signed himself, "from me to you, whoever you are, we twain," he reached the audience he has actually held. For though he deliberately broke through all barriers of class to a degree that has hardly yet been surpassed, the fact remains that he has never spoken to wide groups. In his best poetry his favorite oratorical figures, the questions and exclamations, the apostrophes and parenthetical asides, have all become personal: they imply the presence not of many but of one. (557)

> The more you examine his way of expressing his reception of all life, his feeling that he could represent an object adequately only by identifying himself with it, the more you are struck by his constant repetition of almost the same phrasing: "Myself effusing and fluid, a phantom curiously floating, now here absorb'd and arrested." From his counterbalancing desire also to embrace what had absorbed him sprang his typical groupings of lines, long paragraphs without a main verb and yet with a distinct structural wholeness. He seems to have felt that his identification with the object made a verb unnecessary,

that present participles or infinitives with a vocative urge could best convey immediate reality—a continuous present enfolding both past and future. By this means his notes for declamation were given the suppleness, or, to adopt one of his favorite words, the nonchalance of expression that he wanted. (571)

Matthiessen is not an elegant or exciting stylist, and sometimes he seems labored. But he is usually very careful and measured in his crafting of sentences, as these passages betoken. His style's distinction results from his earnest effort to be accurate, to be precise and responsible in the ways that he states his response to the poetry and expounds the writer's theory and practice. You will not see in Matthiessen the intimidating critical artistry of Blackmur, the mix of sprightliness and startling severity of Randall Jarrell, the sly and scathing ironies of Leavis. But you will see a form of critical seriousness and care that merits a high appraisal for the virtues it embodies and the rewards it provides.

Matthiessen's style mirrors his attitude toward criticism, which identifies the critic's text as subordinate to the texts that it serves. In this sense Matthiessen is not the kind of "creative critic" to whom Geoffrey Hartman and others in our poststructuralist age have paid tribute—the critic who crosses the line that separates "commentary" from "literature" and who is consequently as demanding in his style as any author of "primary" texts (189–213). But Matthiessen perhaps is still a "creative critic" in another sense. He wants the clarity of his prose, and the richness of the evidence it gathers, to help pointedly to elucidate major American texts and to recreate from them the terms for a renewed criticism and democracy. It is possible, in this way, to perceive the demands—critical and creative—that Matthiessen places upon his readers although he does not have recourse to the densely allusive and enigmatic style for which Hartman appeals. Matthiessen seeks to fire sympathy for his writers, and to arouse a sense of solidarity and purpose among his readers. This double aim requires from him an informative and invigorating, but unprepossessing, style. He harbors ambitiously creative hopes for the imaginative work that his critical writing, plain yet poised, will foster. So intense are these hopes that he will not fashion a critical language that might deflect himself and his readers from realizing them.

Matthiessen's style is nevertheless not serious and sober at the entire expense of other effects. Occasionally it acquires considerable majesty, as Matthiessen strives to make his own commentary rise to the wondrous prose of the writers themselves. There are not compelling examples of this reach of his style in the Whitman chapter, but noteworthy instances do occur in his treatment of Thoreau and Melville. One thinks, perhaps above all, of his observations upon Thoreau's famous sentences in *Walden* about the ice company engaged in the export trade to the East Indies:

> The places to which the ice is carried in the holds of ships carry [Thoreau's] mind from Concord to the Orient, and the transition to its philosophy is sustained by turning the refreshing water into a metaphor. But having thus passed from the near to the remote, to a point so far distant both in space and time that his own world seems trivial, Thoreau prolongs his metaphor still farther and brings to the present a comparable magnificence. For the man who draws his living water from the well of the *Bhagvat-Geeta* possesses the same dignity irrespective of whether his image is reflected in Walden or Ganges. The waters have become mingled in a double experience: as the ships of the ice company complete their route around Africa, a further chapter in the history of transportation, in the conquest of space which has been progressing since the Renaissance, Thoreau also affirms his conquest—that of time—which can empower the provincial New Englander, while firmly rooted by his own green pond, to make the remote near, to embrace the richness of antiquity and also to land "in ports of which Alexander only heard the names." (118)

The essential modesty of this passage is as remarkable as its amplitude—a modesty which is evident when Matthiessen returns to Thoreau's language at the end of his complex final sentence and thus respectfully acknowledges the true begetter of these sweeping thoughts.

The Whitman chapter confirms that Matthiessen can also be wry and understated, as when he notes that Yvor Winters writes about Eliot, Pound, Crane, and Whitman "out of the unique flavor of his distaste for all concerned" (592). There are also occasions, especially at the beginning of paragraphs, when Matthiessen gives colloquial bite to his prose, saying, for instance, that Whitman, often invoked by socialists as their poet, "would at no period have satisfied a strict

Marxist for more than ten minutes" (616). Generally Matthiessen does seek to devise a style suited to summarizing details, arranging quotations, outlining patterns and relationships, and putting ideas and insights in their proper order. He seeks to be authentic, to get things right; he is a hardworking writer, not an inspired one. But he does modulate and vary the mostly middle-toned and academically appropriate movements of his language. And sometimes he develops phrases that, however restrained and unflamboyant, have a touch of polished authority, as when he states that some readers have labeled Whitman's verse "a muddy encroachment on the domains of prose" (549), or when he reflects that the "dawning of elemental consciousness [in "On the Beach at Night"] is the state that Whitman could portray most convincingly, since it is akin to the simple half-mature feelings in which he himself habitually lived" (577).

Given his absorption in the nature of Whitman's language, and given, too, his reputation as an adroit "close reader," one might have expected to find a sizable number of explications of poems in Matthiessen's treatment of Whitman. Except, however, for the pages devoted to "The Sleepers," "On the Beach at Night," and "When Lilacs Last in the Dooryard Bloom'd," Matthiessen bypasses the sustained "close reading" of texts. He does not deal in a prolonged way with "Song of Myself," "As I Ebb'd with the Ocean of Life," or "Crossing Brooklyn Ferry." This is partially the consequence of the kind of poetry Whitman writes, where expansive effects count for more than they do in the poems of other writers, and where there is not the local life that New Critical exegesis is designed to plumb. Yet the absence of close readings also signifies Matthiessen's own hesitancies about Whitman's poems. Matthiessen has a sharp sense of Whitman's poetic theory and practice, and several poems and sections from others mean a great deal to him. But though he salutes what Whitman shoots for, he finally fails to find in this poet's verse the kind of structural precision and craftsmanship that he detects in Eliot. Sometimes, in fact, Matthiessen appears not really to possess a true appreciation of Whitman's gifts as a writer, however much he values Whitman as a democratic voice. This same failure of sympathetic understanding is even more marked, it should be added, in the chapters on Emerson that open *American Renaissance*. Matthiessen quotes and works with Emerson as a provocative theorist, but since he does not have high regard or feeling for Emerson as a writer, he almost never attends to the demanding, suggestive nature of the sentences and passages he cites (see Poirier).

What, then, is Matthiessen's evaluation of Whitman? He esteems Whitman's love of language and reverence for the common facts of everyday life, and he looks upon Whitman as able through these resources to attain in his verse a level of competence that his mentor and model Emerson—too much the idealist in his poetry—fails to achieve. But Whitman is not on a par with Melville or Hawthorne, in Matthiessen's judgment. The critical emphasis in *American Renaissance* falls finally on Whitman's shortcomings: his successes are "rare" (526). Whitman is, first, a faulty, inconsistent craftsman, and, second, a stunted thinker who cannot grasp the necessary, if sometimes difficult, distinction between "good and evil." Endlessly open to possibility, his mind is uncomplicated by the tragic vision of life.

Invested as he is in the exhilarations of "democracy," Whitman rarely manages, says Matthiessen, to control his language and shape poetic "forms." He does not have the patient artistic sensibility of Thoreau in *Walden*, does not proceed attentively from concrete thing and fact to idea and ideal. Whitman leaps headlong into the cosmos, and depends too much, and in too many poems, on vehement injunctions to transport his reader there with him. "Whitman was so pleased with his journeys, and with exciting a similar attitude in his reader, that often he did not bother to write his poems but just left them heaps of materials" (568). Matthiessen misses in Whitman not only what, as a critic, he values highly in the dedicated formalism of James and Eliot, but also virtues that Matthiessen himself embraced in his life as well as in his critical pursuits. Whitman lacks perseverance in his writing; he cannot stick to the task of seeing the poem through to its proper termination. At his best, his poetry is robust, sometimes delicate, poignant, and generous, but, as a whole, it is too often self-infatuated and does not show "sustained craftsmanship" (577). The price Whitman paid for his democratic faith, his loving gathering to himself of everyone and everything, comes out in the balked achievement of his verse. "His desire to be inclusive," Matthiessen concludes, echoing George Santayana and Van Wyck Brooks, "above all robbed him of the severe choice between alternatives, which the craftsman knows as his greatest difficulty and reward" (594).

Limited as an artist, Whitman is also defective as an interpreter of nineteenth-century America: Whitman sings lustily in praise of American democracy but is blind to the evil of unchecked individualism. Whitman could not perceive why Matthew Arnold decried the corruption and leveling that were appearing as the by-products of democracy, and this signals a crucial difference between Whitman and Melville:

> The strength of Whitman's democratic faith made the strength of his poetry, but his inability even to discern the meaning of Arnold's analysis of the age is one sign of how different a level from Melville's Whitman's mind habitually moved on. Melville found many passages in Arnold to support his own discriminations between good and evil. In *Billy Budd* he worked towards a resolution of the tragic problem of life in the very years when Whitman was benevolently dismissing its existence. (625)

Whitman's complacency, his refusal to face America and human nature at their worst, troubles Matthiessen—there is something shallow and unreflective, to him, about the poet's rejoicings in man's potential. In this passage, as often in *American Renaissance*, Matthiessen cites Melville to show up the inadequacies of Whitman and other writers. Melville plays a powerful role in the book, not only in his unmasking of appearances that Whitman failed to probe behind—"Whitman rode through the years undisturbed by such deep and bitter truths as Melville had found" (179)—but in his terrible revelation, in the monomania of Ahab, of the naiveté of Emersonian individualism and Whitmanian optimism.

Here we move from the specifics of Matthiessen's treatment of Whitman to the authoritative themes, centered in Melville and his texts, that inform *American Renaissance* as a whole. Matthiessen somewhat identifies with Melville, whom one might suggest Matthiessen reads through Eliot's terms about personality and through his own private and public longings. What Matthiessen admires, and aspires toward, in Melville is what he reveres in Eliot—and in the metaphysical poets of unified sensibility Eliot wrote about. This is their virtue of "wholeness," the "integrity" that enables a man to treat all of his experiences as one, and that provides him with the courage and resourcefulness to confront hard truths about good and evil which other men cannot recognize or from which they flee. Matthiessen also finds Melville's social and political pre-occupations to mirror his own, as is evident in his taking particular note of "Melville's hopes for American democracy, his dread of its lack of humane warmth, his apprehension of the actual privations and defeats of the common man, and his depth of compassion for courageous struggle" (444).

This line of interpretation of Melville is not always convinc-ing—not so much because Matthiessen is essentially wrong about Melville's political views as because he seems to be describing them in terms that issue more from Matthiessen's own desires than from Melville's novels and stories. Matthiessen himself brings out efficiently the intricately structured, soaring language of Ahab's speeches in *Moby Dick* and explores the metaphysical density of the novel; in doing so, he creates for us a complex sense of Melville's voice that exposes the thinness of a phrase like "lack of humane warmth." That sounds like a phrase Matthiessen has employed to evoke his own needs and feelings, not Melville's art.

The more one reads *American Renaissance*, the more one is struck by repeated conjunctions between Melville and the other writers Matthiessen considers, always serving to dramatize where the others fall short. Melville "knew so much more about ordinary life than Emerson did," Matthiessen observes (401). "Unlike Hawthorne, he did not confine himself to moral and psychological observation, but launched out into metaphysics. . . . A far more passionate tem-perament than Hawthorne's drove him to speculate" (435). There are many similar sentences about Emerson, Thoreau, Hawthorne, and Whitman, and additional sentences that briefly contrast Mel-ville with writers such as Emily Dickinson who are marginal to Matthiessen's primary concerns:

> Though Emily Dickinson's comprehension of Shakespeare's treat-ment of good and evil was undoubtedly as keen as Melville's, her own drama, however intense, remained personal and lyric. Melville's greater horizon of experience, the vigorous thrust of his mind, and the strength of his passion carried him, as similar attributes had carried Blake, into wider and more dangerous waters. (434)

In speaking in this way about Melville's differences from his contem-poraries, with the added feature of a gender-coded preference for

Melville's "vigorous thrust" and "strength of passion," Matthiessen is exalting Melville at the expense of the rest of American literature. Matthiessen sometimes seems, in truth, to be setting Melville above American literature to join company with the truly great writers of England and the world. As soon as I say this, I have to qualify it, remembering what Matthiessen says on the final page of his book: "Melville did not achieve in *Moby-Dick* a *Paradise Lost* or a *Faust*. The search for the meaning of life that could be symbolized through the struggle between Ahab and the White Whale was neither so lucid nor so universal" (656). But the drive of *American Renaissance* nevertheless does locate *Moby Dick* on a different level from the other texts that Matthiessen probes. A triumphantly organic display of symbolic richness, verbal power, and acute cultural critique, it measures the era and the other masterworks of the "American renaissance." One of the peculiarly revealing ironies in *American Renaissance* is that as Matthiessen heightens his claims for Melville, he is led implicitly to pinpoint the shortcomings of the American literature he devotes his book to celebrating.

Moby Dick counts enormously for Matthiessen as a work of literary art because it teaches central, universal truths, and on an epic scale, about "human nature" and mankind's fragile emotional economy: Ahab exposes the perils of individualism, the loss of sympathy and compassion, and the wounds that afflict the soul when it denies fellowship. But this is not to imply that Matthiessen wholly fails to place *Moby Dick* within nineteenth-century American history and culture: the novel also counts for him because of what it reveals to readers about democracy in America. Ahab's career

> is prophetic of many others in the history of later nineteenth-century America. Man's confidence in his own unaided resources has seldom been carried farther than during that era of this country. The strong-willed individuals who seized the land and gutted the forests and built the railroads were no longer troubled with Ahab's obsessive sense of evil, since theology had receded even farther into their backgrounds. But their drives were as relentless as his, and they were to prove like him in many other ways also, as they went on to become the empire builders of the post–Civil War world. They tended to be as dead to enjoyment as he, as blind to everything but their one pursuit, as unmoved by fear or sympathy, as confident in assuming an identification of their wills with immutable plan or manifest destiny, as liable to

regard other men as merely arms and legs for the fulfillment of their purposes, and, finally, as arid and exhausted in their burnt-out souls. Without deliberately intending it, but by virtue of his intense concern with the precariously maintained values of democratic Christianity, which he saw everywhere being threatened or broken down, Melville created in Ahab's tragedy a fearful symbol of the self-enclosed individualism that, carried to its furthest extreme, brings disaster both upon itself and upon the group of which it is part. He provided also an ominous glimpse of what was to result when the Emersonian will to virtue became in less innocent natures the will to power and conquest. (459)

Matthiessen speaks from the center of his political and personal being here. He is angered at the plundering of the land—and the ravaging of human nature—that the nineteenth-century captains of industry perpetrated; and he is saddened and embittered by the tragic consequences of self-enclosure and isolation. In American history is writ large the cruel patterns of the human will at its most ruthless, a craving for power that violates and transforms other selves into objects for a dominant passion and plan.

This is one of Matthiessen's sublime moments, as his organic ideal achieves powerful expression in his prose. The individualism of Ahab makes clear the importance of humane organization, a democratic collectivity in which men are more than mere instruments, are more than "arms and legs." *Moby Dick*, for Matthiessen, comes boldly, strikingly alive here as a literary indictment of capitalist society and American expansionism. Defining the dangers of Emersonianism and emphasizing the evil inscribed in America's past, Matthiessen, following Melville, brings home the manner in which criticism can demonstrate the lessons that literature teaches about history.

The problem with this passage and others like it is not that Matthiessen is saying something demonstrably untrue—though one might quarrel with the reference to Melville's valuation of democratic Christianity. The problem is, instead, that his grand mode of address in them about power, cruelty, suffering, and exploitation makes us today aware of a dimension of American history he neglected in his book—slavery and its aftermath. Matthiessen does not see the Negro in his survey of American literature and culture during the antebellum years, even though the 1840s and 1850s were

dominated by debates about slavery and riddled by proslavery polemics and antislavery writing. Not only does Matthiessen leave out
Uncle Tom's Cabin, but even more curiously, he also avoids dealing
with slavery as an issue in the work of the very writers he highlights.
From the perspective of the 1980s, the result is a book that is un-
faithful to the full literary and historical actuality of the years when
the "American renaissance" bloomed.

Perhaps Matthiessen judged that Emerson's and Thoreau's essays,
letters, and comments about the Fugitive Slave Law, John Brown's
execution, and other related matters belong more to the annals of
history than to literature. Perhaps, too, he wished not to introduce
material—Emerson's reservations about, and Greenough's opposition to, the abolitionists, Whitman's dislike of Negroes—that would
undercut, or at least complicate, his stirring democratic themes.
Neither of these possible explanations for the incompleteness of
Matthiessen's study, however, clarifies his failure to analyze *Benito
Cereno*, a text that engages slavery in extraordinarily complex ways,
and a text that Matthiessen himself judged to be one of Melville's
best. "Anything like the fusion in *Moby Dick* of the inner and the
outer world," he contends, "was to be recovered only in two stories
of about a hundred pages, *Benito Cereno* and, after a lapse of more
than three decades, *Billy Budd*" (286). "Among *The Piazza Tales*,"
he later remarks, "was *Benito Cereno*, one of the most sensitively
poised pieces of writing he had ever done" (373). Yet for all his
praise of the story, Matthiessen says very little about it, and his
scanty commentary contrasts with the ample analysis he supplies for
both *Moby Dick* and *Billy Budd*. He does pause at one point to
note that the handling of the narration in *Benito Cereno* prefigures
the ambiguity of James and the method of Conrad (476–77), yet he
leaves this insight undeveloped. His only other, and his longest, reference to *Benito Cereno* occurs in the section on *Billy Budd*, where
he indicates that the symbolism of the earlier story is more limited
than that in the later one:

> The embodiment of good in the pale Spanish captain and of evil in
> the mutinied African crew, though pictorially and theatrically effec-
> tive, was unfortunate in raising unanswered questions. Although the
> Negroes were savagely vindictive and drove a terror of blackness into
> Cereno's heart, the fact remains that they were slaves and that evil
> had thus originally been done to them. Melville's failure to reckon

with this fact within the limits of his narrative makes its tragedy, for all its prolonged suspense, comparatively superficial. (508)

This seems, for Matthiessen, oddly imperceptive. He simplifies Melville's narrative, misses or ignores its multiple ironies, and asserts against the evidence of the text that Melville "fails to reckon" with the fact of the Negroes' enslavement. Melville's text achieves its power not because it adheres to a simple dichotomy between good and evil but, rather, because it discloses the crossings between these terms and the impossibility of distinguishing between them as neatly as Matthiessen does in his brief remarks about the tale.

Where might such an analysis of *Benito Cereno* lead? What might Matthiessen have done? There is an obvious danger here in seeming to divert attention away from Matthiessen's book itself, but it seems important to indicate the better alternative in some detail, particularly because it bears so crucially on two urgent questions: who in America comprises "the people" Matthiessen aspired to serve? and how effectively does American literary history minister to their needs?

Critics have often pointed out, with much valuable historical detail, the relation of *Benito Cereno* to the slavery crisis and, more generally still, to the entire drama of slavery and colonialism in the Americas (Karcher; Sundquist; Adler; Rogin; Emery). But the story depicts as well the crisis of perception and knowledge that accompanies, indeed constitutes and disfigures, white and black behavior together. Allan Emery is right to say, in an excellent essay ("Topicality"), that Melville is employing the deviously managed rebellion of the slaves aboard the *San Dominick* to expose and attack southern and northern myths of black amiability. But even more, Melville seeks to show just how double are myths of, and images for, black speech and action.

Defenders of slavery proposed two contradictory arguments to help buttress their system. Blacks, it was alleged, were totally childlike, dependent, affectionate, subservient, in need and desirous of the white paternal care and benevolence which the slaveholders provided. Blacks, it was also claimed, were barbaric, prone to rape and violence, and, in such episodes as the San Domingo revolt and Nat Turner's rampage, made terrifyingly explicit themselves how much they required constant white supervision and tight control. In his monumental 1935 study *Black Reconstruction*, W. E. B. Du Bois assessed the double bind that confronted blacks in terms similar to these:

> Everything Negroes did was wrong. If they fought for freedom, they were beasts; if they did not fight, they were born slaves. If they cowered on the plantations, they loved slavery; if they ran away, they were lazy loafers. If they sang, they were silly; if they scowled, they were impudent. (125)

To put the matter simply but accurately: when a white person looked at a black man, he could see either a supremely tractable child (a Sambo, an Uncle Tom) or a cunning savage (an incipient Bigger Thomas); he could see one of these images at a time or both at once, depending upon the kind of justification for black bondage called for at a particular moment. What, to white eyes, produced the change from child to beast was the possibility of freedom: if given freedom, the black man would instantly abuse it, his uncivilized instincts leaping into view. When whites looked at enslaved blacks, then, they already saw what he "would be like" if freed, and hence they were all the more adamant about preventing the horrible image from becoming literalized, made real.

Slave revolt, Melville's subject in his tale, was an extremely vexing worry for whites, not merely for the threats it posed, but also because it belied the commonplace that blacks were contented children who welcome their lot in life. If blacks were contented, then why would they wish to rebel against and murder their masters? They must therefore not be contented. Yet it is the seeming absoluteness of such logic that whites sought to evade, moving from one image of black behavior and identity to the next, or allowing one momentarily to erase the other from consciousness, or even maintaining both while staying blind to the critique that each presents to the other.

Melville seeks to bring out the movements of such perception and misperception throughout *Benito Cereno*, as when the stupendously benign Captain Delano ponders the reason for Benito Cereno's questions about the *Bachelor's Delight*:

> But those questions of the Spaniard. There, indeed, one might pause. Did they not seem put with much the same object with which the burglar or assassin, by day-time, reconnoitres the walls of a house?

But, with ill purposes, to solicit such information openly of the chief person endangered, and so, in effect, setting him on his guard; how unlikely a procedure was that? Absurd, then, to suppose that those questions had been prompted by evil designs. Thus, the same conduct, which, in this instance, had raised the alarm, served to dispel it. In short, scarce any suspicion or uneasiness, however apparently reasonable at the time, which was not now, with equal apparent reason, dismissed. (699)

Benito Cereno's words cause Delano's concern; they also make it seem wholly unwarranted. When Benito asks his questions about the *Bachelor's Delight*'s crew and weaponry, he prompts Delano to suspect a malign logic behind them; but the same questions also trigger a different logic that undoes the pattern and seeming rightness of the first.

Delano cannot believe he is truly in danger, and in this way he is rather unusual. It is often argued that Melville paints Delano as the representative or typical white (especially northern white) man who does not suspect the violence of which enslaved men might be capable. But slave revolt and insurrection was a constant topic of discussion among Northerners as well as Southerners; Southerners kept insisting upon the necessity of protecting themselves against revolt, while Northerners responded that while this fear might be legitimate, it simply testified to the evils of slavery and to the righteous vengeance that the slaveholding states might someday suffer at the hands of the oppressed. Possibly my distinction is too fine, but Delano is, I think, not so much meant to be a typical white man as he is meant to be revelatory of kinds of thinking, ranging from approximately correct but ungrasped insight to gross naiveté, that define and condition American consciousness about "the Negro."

Not only does Delano fail to discern the danger in Benito Cereno's questions. He does not, furthermore, even imagine that the doubleness of his response to Benito Cereno might be "doubled over" again: the questions are, of course, he eventually discovers, not Benito Cereno's but Babo's. Babo is speaking and acting doubly, too, playing his part in the "spectral marionette show" (Rogin, *Subversive Genealogy* 209) he has designed and into which he has cast Benito Cereno as his slave puppet and master in appearance only. Babo, one could even suggest, is not so much outside Benito Cereno, directing him, as he is inside, black inhabiting white.

That this suggestion is part of Melville's strategy in his story becomes evident the more one considers the "two-ness" with which so many of his sentences resonate. Near the end of the shaving scene, for example, Delano faces Babo, whose cheek is bleeding from, it seems, a cut delivered by his angry master:

> "Ah, when will master get better from his sickness; only the sour heart that sour sickness breeds made him serve Babo so; cutting Babo with the razor, because, only by accident, Babo had given master one little scratch; and for the first time in so many a day, too. Ah, ah, ah," holding his hand to his face.
>
> Is it possible, thought Captain Delano; was it to wreak in private his Spanish spite against this poor friend of his, that Don Benito, by his sullen manner, impelled me to withdraw? Ah, this slavery breeds ugly passions in man.—Poor fellow! (721)

Retrospectively, the "ugly passions" are seen here to be the slave's rather than the slaveholder's. Slavery does kindle cruelty in the heart of the master, but it also creates resentment, anger, and rebellious energy in the enslaved. Despite what Matthiessen says, Melville *is* indicting the slavery system; he is demonstrating it is wrong, and he does so by illustrating what slavery does to black and white. He is additionally portraying how whites avoid perceiving what slavery is doing to them and to the black people they hold in bondage. On the one hand, Melville theatrically presents the images according to which whites believe they know blacks; and, on the other hand, he makes complicatedly clear that whites like Delano do not really know the implications of what they know. They unwittingly touch on knowledge that they do not possess.

Melville may have even more radical meanings in mind, as is implied perhaps by the fact that Delano, as noted above, looks at and hears Benito Cereno but is in fact (though he does not realize it) responding to Babo. In his story, Melville is exploring the doubleness of language and image and also the doubleness of bodies, the two-ness of white and black bodies, each living within the other. A number of critics since Matthiessen have shrewdly observed the manifold ways in which white and black actions mirror one another; having rebelled and taken control of the *San Dominick*, the blacks treat the Spaniards barbarically, and they, in turn, once they regain command, display their own brand of barbarism toward the blacks.

But the analogous behavior bespeaks more than critics have suggested. The behavior is similar because the two races themselves, and not just their forms of behavior, are essentially the same. When, in a word, we deeply inquire into racial difference, we reach racial sameness. Skin color, in all its hues, is merely a tissue through which we readily pass. White and black dwell within, bear, and incorporate one another.

These implications of *Benito Cereno* loom everywhere in the story, and with special visibility in the conversation between Delano and Benito Cereno about the mulatto Francesco:

> Captain Delano observed with interest that while the complexion of the mulatto was hybrid, his physiognomy was European; classically so.
>
> "Don Benito," whispered he, "I am glad to see this usher-of-the-golden-rod of yours; the sight refutes an ugly remark once made to me by a Barbadoes planter; that when a mulatto has a regular European face, look out for him; he is a devil. But see, your steward here has features more regular than King George's of England; and yet there he nods, and bows, and smiles; a king, indeed—the king of kind hearts and polite fellows. What a pleasant voice he has, too."
>
> "He has, Señor."
>
> "But, tell me, has he not, so far as you have known him, always proved a good, worthy fellow?" said Captain Delano, pausing, while with a final genuflexion the steward disappeared into the cabin; "come, for the reason just mentioned, I am curious to know."
>
> "Francesco is a good man," a sort of sluggishly responded Don Benito, like a phlegmatic appreciator, who would neither find fault nor flatter.
>
> "Ah, I thought so. For it were strange indeed, and not very creditable to us white-skins, if a little of our blood mixed with the African's, should, far from improving the latter's quality, have the sad effect of pouring vitriolic acid into black broth; improving the hue, perhaps, but not the wholesomeness."
>
> "Doubtless, doubtless, Señor, but"—glancing at Babo—"not to speak of negroes, your planter's remark I have heard applied to the Spanish and Indian intermixtures in our provinces. But I know nothing about the matter," he listlessly added. (722)

Francesco is both black and white; he has the "white" features of the king of England and yet coloring that stamps him as not wholly white. Mulattoes, however, are as not anomalous as Delano's curious questions denote. Mulattoes graphically exhibit what is already the case in every "pure" black and white, and the truth of which Melville's story reveals—that there is no pure race, no race that is not free from, that does not partake of, the other. The stunning crudity of Delano's phrase for his race, "us white-skins," drives home just how superficial a white face is: it might be perceived, upon closer inspection, to be mixed with black; it can be grained with black, though perhaps too subtly for us ever to see it; or its apparently clear whiteness might be merely the index to the blackness beneath.

As the reference to the king of England intimates, Melville also wants here to entwine his narrative of race with a narrative of authority and revolution. When one man keeps another enslaved, he is enslaving himself; more than that: he is fashioning the figure who will eventually rise up violently against him. In this regard, the murder of masters by slaves is really a murder the masters perpetrate against themselves. Murder, it transpires, emerges as a form of violence launched by whites against their own race and offspring. This is something that not only Melville but other writers and statesmen before and after the Civil War glimpsed. Thomas Jefferson, slaveholder himself and rebel against kingly authority, warned at the time of the San Domingo uprising that "if something is not done and soon done, we shall be the murderers of our own children" (Rogin, *Subversive Genealogy* 213). Whites, Jefferson proposed, were working toward their own undoing, maintaining a mastery over blacks that would at some point translate into a rebellion of blacks against whites, or, more precisely, of whites against whites, blacks against blacks, white and black sons against their figurative—and, in some cases, such as Jefferson's perhaps—*literal* fathers. Two races would appear to be at war, whereas in fact—here Jefferson's own probable mixed offspring again bear witness— two mixed races would be murdering themselves. My term "two mixed races," if anything, veils the point. There is one merged race killing itself as it simultaneously clings to unjust authority and rightly wages war to overthrow it.

Frederick Douglass, in *My Bondage and My Freedom*, tendered a similar argument:

> Slaveholders have made it almost impossible for the slave to commit any crime, known either to the laws of God or to the laws of man. If he steals, he takes his own; if he kills his master, he imitates only

the heroes of the revolution. Slaveholders I hold to be individually and collectively responsible for all the evils which grow out of the horrid relation, and I believe they will be so held at the judgment, in the sight of a just God. . . . The slaveholder, kind or cruel, is a slave-holder still–the every hour violator of the just and inalienable rights of man; and he is, therefore, every hour silently whetting the knife of vengeance for his own throat. He never lisps a syllable in commendation of the fathers of this republic, nor denounces any attempted oppression of himself, without inviting the knife to his own throat, and asserting the rights of rebellion for his own slaves. (191, 269–70)

In winning and vaunting its independence from colonial bondage, white America authored the indictment of its own crimes and prepared for its own day of death: by claiming freedom for themselves, they have empowered blacks to rebel against them. Whites may believe they are masters of a different race, but, states Douglass, they are indubitably creating versions of themselves, replicating white revolutionaries even as they assume they are justly ruling over black slaves.

Stowe advances a comparable notion in *Uncle Tom's Cabin* when she has the mulatto George Harris invoke the revolutionary fathers to justify his escape and rebellion: "I'll fight for my liberty to the last breath I breathe. You say your fathers did it; if it was right for them, it is right for me!" (187; see also 298–99). Stowe, however, both prophesies the nation's fate and tries to forestall it, conceding the fact of race intermixture but then laboring to reconstitute racial difference. The "masses" of oppressed blacks in America, Augustine St. Clare warns his brother, will some day follow the lead of their present rulers, as the "people of Hayti" followed the lead of the Frenchmen who were their masters and revolutionary models.

> "O, come, Augustine! as if we hadn't had enough of that abominable, contemptible Hayti! The Haytiens were not Anglo-Saxons; if they had been there would have been another story. The Anglo Saxon is the dominant race of the world, and *is to be so*."
>
> "Well, there is a pretty fair infusion of Anglo Saxon blood among our slaves, now," said Augustine. "There are plenty among them who have only enough of the African to give a sort of tropical warmth and fervor to our calculating firmness and foresight. If the San Domingo hour comes, Anglo Saxon blood will lead on the day. Sons of white fathers, with all our haughty feelings burning in their veins, will not

always be bought and sold and traded. They will rise, and raise with them their mother's race." (392)

Stowe perceives the white blood that courses through the black man's veins: she sees how white lives in black. What she does not want to acknowledge is the black blood that runs through white bodies. Nor does she want to face the consequences of her own position about racial intermingling. Which is why she highlights the revolutionary rightness of George Harris' cause and his mixed whiteness/blackness only to script for him an African destiny, as though colonization might somehow liberate America from the complex truths about racial oneness and twoness to which George Harris' body and life attest.

The passages from Jefferson, Douglass, and Stowe, as well as the action of Melville's own text, help to clarify the ironies of the conversation between Delano and Benito Cereno with which the story concludes—ironies which cannot but resonate for us when we consider the omissions in Matthiessen's pages on Melville:

> "You were with me [said Benito Cereno] all day; stood with me, sat with me, talked with me, looked at me, ate with me, drank with me; and yet, your last act was to clutch for a monster, not only an innocent man, but the most pitiable of all men. To such a degree may malign machinations and deceptions impose. So far may even the best man err, in judging the conduct of one with the recesses of whose condition he is not acquainted. But you were forced to it; and you were in time undeceived. Would that, in both respects, it was so ever, and with all men."
>
> "You generalize, Don Benito; and mournfully enough. But the past is passed; why moralize upon it? Forget it. See, yon bright sun has forgotten it all, and the blue sea, and the blue sky; these have turned over new leaves."
>
> "Because they have no memory," he dejectedly replied; "because they are not human."
>
> "But these mild trades that now fan your cheek, do they not come with a human-like healing to you? Warm friends, steadfast friends are the trades."
>
> "With their steadfastness they but waft me to my tomb, señor," was the foreboding response.
>
> "You are saved," cried Captain Delano, more and more astonished and pained; "you are saved; what has cast such a shadow upon you?"

"The negro."
There was silence, while the moody man sat, slowly and unconsciously gathering his mantle about him, as if it were a pall. (754–55)

What is initially most striking here is the transcendent naiveté of Delano and the deathly insistence with which Benito Cereno affirms the psychological devastation wrought by "the negro." But Melville has in mind other, darker meanings, too. One of these grows apparent when we remember that Delano's "last act" was not to clutch at Benito Cereno but was, instead, to smite the dagger from Babo's hand. Melville knows that we will seek to straighten out his meanings: we know the person to whom Benito Cereno refers by his terms "monster" and "innocent man." Yet Melville wants us to pause as we get these meanings straight, wants us to linger over ambiguities and sound the depths of "eternal similitude" (Dillingham 266) that bond men. Which act of Delano's was his "last act," and which man is truly the monster and which truly "innocent"—the captain of the Spanish slave ship or the rebellious slave? One recalls Melville's meaningfully ambiguous syntax at the climactic scene: "Not Captain Delano, but Don Benito, the black, in leaping into the boat, had intended to stab" (734). "The black" seems, for a moment, a noun in apposition to Don Benito, as though he were the "black" figure who had indeed leaped into the boat. Melville makes us work to separate Don Benito and "the black"; he could have written the sentence another way, but was intent upon making us linger over it so that we first elided two terms. Even after we seek to separate them, if we can, the meaning of the sentence still reverberates ironically; "black" means the literally black Babo; it could say something, too, about the blackness of the man who kept him enslaved.

Delano's final question, "what has cast such a shadow upon you?" is thus both apt and misleading. The "shadow" does not come from the outside; it does not loom over Benito Cereno as much as it extends from him. "The negro" is the shadow he casts himself, for a man's shadow is his own. The menace comes from within, from what the "white" man is and has done.

To press these points about racial intermixture and interpenetration may seem to some ingenious, and Matthiessen, for one, may not have found them persuasive. But they derive not only from Melville's daring art but also from a field of insight about race rela-

tions to which other important texts, notably *Pudd'nhead Wilson,
Light in August,* and *Native Son,* also belong. All of these texts—
Matthiessen never wrote about them—depict the determined, sometimes frenzied effort to keep apart what cannot be kept apart: the
two different races, and the manifestly different bodies, are in fact
one. It is a perception like this to which the landmark film *Birth of
a Nation* also bears extravagant, if not fully acknowledged, witness
when it chronicles white Ku Klux Klansmen pursuing Negro rapists
and brigands who are plainly white actors in blackface: "the ob-
viousness of blackface, which fails to disguise, reveals that the Klansmen are chasing their own negative identities, their own shadow
sides" (Rogin, " 'The Sword Became a Flashing Vision' " 181). Such
a perception is similarly evoked, if again not wholly perceived, in
the southern historian Ulrich Phillips' hugely influential 1918 study
American Negro Slavery, as when he remarks about plantation life:
"The separate integration of the slaves was no more than rudimen-
tary. They were always within the social mind and conscience of the
whites, as the whites in turn were within the mind and conscience
of the blacks" (327).

Visions of two races, white and black, merging into and dependent upon one another, have a predictably double potential. They
can signify a problem to be purged by feverish and murderous attempts to restore difference; or they can force a radical confrontation
with a simple truth—that race hatred is folly, is counterproductive
and self-destructive. Contrary to prevailing white sentiment in both
the nineteenth and twentieth centuries, there is no "Negro problem."
There was and remains, as Douglass, for one, was shrewd and sensi-
ble enough to see, "not a Negro problem, but in every sense a great
national problem" ("Why Is the Negro Lynched?" 518), a problem
of a single nation of indissolubly united black and white bodies.

For all his appreciation of Melville's artistry, and despite his own
profound investment in brotherhood and justice, Matthiessen did
not see the complex truths to which Melville gestures in *Benito
Cereno.* Matthiessen resisted reckoning with this text, even though
he ranked it as one of its author's best writings. Really to engage
Benito Cereno, as it "comprehends the complex history and knotted
contemporary issues of black bondage in America" (Sundquist,
"Slavery, Revolution" 26), would have involved examining the
slavery crisis in depth and detail. It would have called graphic atten-

tion to social and political facts about America before, during, and after the 1850s which, Matthiessen professed, lay outside a "literary-critical" treatment. Or, to put the point more accurately still, it would have entailed seeing how the feverish capitalism and destructive individualism to which Matthiessen draws attention in Ahab also display their power in the system of slavery.

Matthiessen seeks to connect his literary analyses in *American Renaissance* with the culture from which they emerged. But his understanding of that culture is too limited, and his criticism is incomplete and unduly, narrowly literary even when it reaches beyond the texts themselves. For a full cultural critique to emerge successfully, Matthiessen would have had to connect Melville's text with others, like those written by Stowe and Douglass, that did not fall within artistic categories as Matthiessen understood them. Such an approach would have generally undermined, as it enlarged, the meaning of "literature" and the tasks of criticism and teaching. Both critically and with some human sympathy, one can only conclude that Matthiessen *had* to write about *Benito Cereno* as he did: to do otherwise would have meant exposing the serious limitations of his literary commitments and spotlighting the powerful things that *American Renaissance* excluded.

Seen from this angle, the monument that is *American Renaissance*, though still magnificent, begins to look less impregnable. There are other, related occasions in the book when Matthiessen's handling of texts is suspect, and his faithfulness to the literary and historical record troublingly partial. In his chapter on Thoreau, to cite a revealing instance, Matthiessen states that

> *Walden* was also one of our books that bulked largest for Tolstoy when he addressed his brief message to America (1901) and urged us to rediscover the greatness of our writers of the fifties: "And I should like to ask the American people why they do not pay more attention to these voices (hardly to be replaced by those of financial and industrial millionaires, or successful generals and admirals), and continue the good work in which they made such hopeful progress." (172)

The preceding paragraph of Tolstoy's letter, which Matthiessen omits, demonstrates that his roster of important writers of the fifties differed sharply from Matthiessen's:

If I had to address the American people, I should like to thank them for their writers who flourished about the fifties. I would mention Garrison, Parker, Emerson, Ballou, and Thoreau, not as the greatest, but as those who, I think, specially influenced me. Other names are Channing, Whittier, Lowell, Walt Whitman—a bright constellation, such as is rarely to be found in the literatures of the world." ("Message to the American People" 7)

Tolstoy's list is striking in including abolitionists, reformers, advocates of civil disobedience and political protest, and Christian socialists (Adin Ballou was the author of the 1854 text *Practical Christian Socialism*). Garrison and Parker, in particular, were notably active and eloquent in the fight against slavery. These were generally the writers and speakers, along with Stowe (another of Tolstoy's favorites) and other women authors, who aroused and angered Northerners and Southerners during the 1840s and 1850s. They reached audiences—as Matthiessen's own group, he admits, mostly did not (x)—precisely because they focused on the issues that mattered to the majority of the people. When Wendell Phillips summarized the "philosophy of the abolition movement" in 1853, he claimed that the speeches and written texts that had resulted from the antislavery cause answered the calls that had long been made for a distinctive American literature: "This discussion has been one of the noblest contributions to a literature really American" (51). Two years later, in his own review of the antislavery movement, Frederick Douglass declared that the 1850s would "be looked to by after-coming generations, as the age of anti-slavery literature" ("Anti-Slavery Movement" 356). To men like Phillips and Douglass, as well as to many who did not share their abolitionist views, it was inconceivable that an appraisal of the "literature" of the 1850s would fail to stress the contentious, astonishingly abundant literature of slavery.

It is fine for Matthiessen to assert that it is Hawthorne and Melville who should be central *to us*, in that they illuminate in their writings the "undiminished resources" we need for "our democracy" —though even here, one would still be reminded of James Baldwin's admonition about the writing of American history, "Unless I'm in that book, you're not in it either" (666). But this is not exactly in line with the historical argument that Matthiessen himself seems elsewhere to be advancing when he locates his writers in the culture and society of their age. He appears to be contextualizing his discussion, and in certain respects he does so marvelously well, but with slavery left out, the context is too restricted. It enables Matthiessen to articulate a powerful myth, but not to write wholly adequate literary and cultural history.

Possibly all of this is simply to chart the limits of Matthiessen's vision. In his criticism, he did not deal with, nor apparently did he know much about, Afro-American writers—as he also did not deal with, though he may have known more about, Freud and European Marxists and theoreticians. Every critic has groups of writers, topics, and issues that he shuns or is blind to: everyone can be shown up. One knows this, yet can still find Matthiessen's limits to be especially disappointing, since he had political allegiances that might have led him to be cognizant of the historical shortcomings and omissions of his mapping of America during its period of "renaissance" and to extend his literary categories. Though departing somewhat from the New Critics, Matthiessen shared their disregard for and devaluation of certain kinds of texts as unliterary—among them, popular poetry, sentimental novels, political speeches, and autobiographies. Texts that lacked or failed to privilege particular manifestations of literary language as the New Critics understood it—irony, tension, ambiguity—did not win Matthiessen's entire sympathy and support. He did not recognize as legitimately literary many of the genres in which women and blacks have written.

By the time Matthiessen began work on *American Renaissance*, and certainly throughout the 1930s, there was already a fairly sizable amount of research on the literature of slavery, the image of the Negro in American literature, and Negro authors. As examples, I have in mind Lorenzo Dow Turner's extensive overview of "anti-slavery sentiment in American literature prior to 1865," which appeared in the *Journal of Negro History* in 1929; Vernon Loggins' thorough account, published in 1931, of work by Negro authors in literature, history, and other fields; and Sterling Brown's two books, *Negro Poetry and Drama* and *The Negro in American Fiction*, both of which appeared in 1937. With the exception of Brown's books, these writings are not critically insightful, and more recent studies have surpassed them. All nevertheless were valuable for highlighting the antislavery writings of Garrison, Stowe, Lowell, Whittier, and other whites, and, more important, for drawing attention to Gustavus Vassa, Phillis Wheatley, David Walker,

Frederick Douglass, Martin Delany, William Wells Brown, Frank J. Webb, Henry Highland Garnet, Alexander Crummell, and other black authors. Most of these men and women were productive in the 1840s and 1850s, and they labored in a wide range of genres that included poetry, drama, autobiography, essay, fiction, and polemical protest. As Turner stated, "between the passage of the Fugitive Slave Act of 1850 and the election of Lincoln in 1860, followed a few months later by the firing upon Fort Sumter, an enormous amount of anti-slavery literature was produced. . . . It found expression in all the literary forms of the period" (459, 440). Matthiessen must have been generally aware of this, as he undoubtedly was also aware— historian of the era that he was—of events such as the antislavery rally held at Framingham, Massachusetts, on the Fourth of July, 1854, at which Thoreau delivered his address on "slavery in Massachusetts" and Garrison burned copies of the Fugitive Slave Law and the Constitution. Yet he did not find slavery to be significant enough as a literary and cultural issue to explore it even in an obviously pertinent text like *Benito Cereno*.

With the considerable advantage that hindsight offers, one can note still other ironies. Even as *American Renaissance*, a book that foregrounded five white authors as embodiments of the American democratic spirit, was making its way through the final stages of production at Oxford University Press in 1940–41, A. Philip Randolph and other black leaders were busy planning a massive march on Washington, D.C., to protest job discrimination against Negroes in the defense industries—a march, Randolph declared, that would "shake up white America" (quoted in Nash 150). "More than any other single leader, organization, or event, Randolph's electrifying effort on behalf of the March on Washington catalyzed the supporters of civil rights into a mass movement that could not be ignored" (Sitkoff 316).

In exchange for a promise to call off the march, President Roosevelt signed Executive Order 8802, which required that a clause banning discrimination be included in defense contracts and established the Committee on Fair Employment Practices. This order did not wholly accomplish its purpose, but blacks saw their threatened march and its aftermath as an emphatic expression of "black militance" (Shannon 232), and they judged the order itself as "the most significant document affecting them since the Emancipation Proclamation" (J. H. Franklin 426–27; Blum, *V Was for Victory* 188). Roosevelt's discussions about the order and eventual signing of it in June 1941 coincided with the publication of Matthiessen's book and with the dinner sponsored by the Harvard Student Union and Teachers' Union held in honor of its author.

In remarking upon this conjunction, I do not wish to score an easy point against Matthiessen, but rather want to indicate the disparity between the political and the literary/academic scenes as he viewed them. Matthiessen responded intensely to national and international events (he felt their impact personally), and he viewed his scholarship as a contribution to social and political renewal. But he could not perceive how some of the trends and details of general history—those involving black people, in particular—might bear on the exigencies of scholarship, might force, that is, a reexamination of choices that he and others regularly made in the writing of literary history.

Matthiessen is not an isolated case, of course. Although American culture kept making blacks visible during the 1920s and afterward, very few literary critics, particularly within the academy, saw them. There were the writings of Jean Toomer, Langston Hughes, and Zora Neale Hurston; there was the emergence, one that flowed outward to white literary production, of the Harlem Renaissance; there were Faulkner's novels *Light in August* (1932) and *Absalom, Absalom!* (1936); there were Louis Untermeyer's two anthologies *American Poetry from the Beginning to Whitman* (1931) and *Modern American Poetry* (5th ed., 1936), which included Negro folk songs and spirituals and poetry by Dunbar, McKay, and other blacks; and there were many anthologies of Negro stories, folk songs, rhymes, and spirituals. But the Negro as a historical fact—arguably the most compelling historical fact of all about America—and the Negro as a fact of literary/critical and pedagogical importance, did not figure in Matthiessen's work or in the work of any other key academic critic from the 1930s to the 1960s.

Again with the benefit of hindsight, it becomes quite astonishing to realize that Richard Wright, Ralph Ellison, James Baldwin, and many other gifted black men and women were writing superbly— and, in some cases, receiving great acclaim from the culture-at-large —yet were not present in the anthologies of American "masters" and "major writers" that scholars compiled from the 1930s to the

1960s. Neither these writers, nor any of their black precursors, appear in the standard American literature anthologies of the 1950s and early 1960s that were often built upon Matthiessen's premises (H. B. Franklin xiii–xxii). Throughout the period, black writers were asserting their authorial rights, and blacks in general were fighting for their civil rights, but literary scholars paid them little heed and continued to focus on texts that accorded with their New Critical instruments and their own race and class interests.

It is worth remarking in this context that slow but steady changes were occurring within the historical profession, as August Meier and Elliott Rudwick have demonstrated in their fine book on this subject. The late 1930s and 1940s were still a painful, unpleasant period for black historians, and Afro-American studies remained in a marginal relation to the discipline as a whole. Institutional barriers were formidable. At Harvard, for example, not a single black person received a Ph.D. in history between 1941 and 1956; by the end of World War II, there were only about twenty black Ph.D.'s in history available for college and university positions. Blacks found it nearly impossible to publish in the major mainstream journals, and rarely appeared as speakers at professional meetings. A fair number of white historians showed disdain for, or skepticism about, "black" history, or else equated it solely with slavery, as though this were the only real dimension of black experience in America. But telling signs of a movement in a more favorable direction were visible, as surviving currents from the leftist 1930s, New Deal liberalism, and social activist and pro–civil rights sentiment emerging from the Progressive party made their impact upon the profession.

Throughout the late 1930s and throughout the 1940s, significant books that treated race relations were being published and were often winning considerable acclaim. These include C. Vann Woodward's *Tom Watson: Agrarian Rebel* (1938), Herbert Aptheker's *American Negro Slave Revolts* (1943), Vernon Lane Wharton's *The Negro in Mississippi, 1865–1890* (1947), Benjamin Quarles's biography of Frederick Douglass (1948), and John Hope Franklin's landmark overview, *From Slavery to Freedom* (1947). Towering above all of these books in its effect on the American scene was, of course, the Swedish sociologist Gunnar Myrdal's *An American Dilemma* (1944). Merle Curti, Howard K. Beale, and other white historians were also making committed efforts to further legitimize black history as a field and to open up opportunities for young black scholars to participate in the profession more fully. Within the discipline, trends for the better were starting to appear, and these were becoming increasingly known to, and consequential for, intellectuals, social theorists, and cultural critics outside it.

Matthiessen was very attentive to new work in politics and history. Perhaps he even read or knew about the books I have mentioned. But if he did, his reading did not trigger adjustments in his own scholarship. When, in one of his last scholarly ventures, Matthiessen assembled the poems for the *Oxford Book of American Verse* in the late 1940s, he did not include a single poem by a black man or woman. In fact, he omitted Paul Laurence Dunbar, the one black poet whom Bliss Carman had included in the 1927 edition. The result is very queer. In certain respects, his collection is extremely sensitive and discriminating—Allen Tate and E. E. Cummings both remarked that no one had ever made better selections of their poems. And, more generally still, his *Oxford Book* certainly marked a bold revision of literary taste in its demotion of the nineteenth-century New England gentlemen and in its emphasis upon Whitman, Dickinson, Eliot, Crane, Moore, Stevens, and others. According to an expert on poetry anthologies, Matthiessen's book constitutes "one of the most radical redefinitions of the canon ever. . . . [It] redefined the canon in almost every way imaginable: the canon of individual poems, of genres, of subject matter, of names" (Golding 298). True enough: Matthiessen did prepare an innovative and risk-taking anthology. But his canon, drawn along Eliot's and the New Critics' lines, is hardly democratic. Somehow Matthiessen was able to admire and include a poem like Crane's "Black Tambourine," which gestures toward the black man "wander[ing] in some mid-kingdom," without noticing the implications of this for the collection he himself had prepared. The omission of black poets seems all the more curious when one recalls Matthiessen's speech of welcome at the opening meeting of the Salzburg Seminar, where he had apologetically noted the absence of Negroes among the Americans (*From the Heart of Europe* 14). He thought and worried about such things in public political terms; he did not see how they should also enter into the work of the editor, critic, and scholar.

The absence of blacks from Matthiessen's anthology becomes even more puzzling in view of the special efforts made by his Progressive party to appeal for civil rights and win the support of Negro voters. The party platform of 1948 included detailed proposals on the need to combat race prejudice in employment, housing, education, and government service; campaign literature sought to connect the aims of the Progressive party with the aspirations of the Negro people; and spokesmen linked Henry Wallace to such illustrious names as Frederick Douglass, John Brown, and Wendell Phillips. W. E. B. Du Bois, Paul Robeson, and other blacks held prominent positions in the Progressive party, and still others ran for public office as its candidates. Some of Wallace's detractors, black as well as white, contended that his own performance on racial issues, while he served in the Roosevelt administration, had been disappointing (MacDougall 3: 654–62). But during his campaign, Wallace was very vocal in his attacks on Jim Crow, saying on one occasion that "it is not only desirable to break down segregation; it is an absolute necessity. We *must* meet this issue head on" (quoted in MacDougall 3: 667). He and his running mate, Glen Taylor, campaigned in the South, often meeting with virulent opposition—Taylor was even arrested at one point for breaking a segregation ordinance.

In the end, however, the Progressive party did poorly among black voters, as it did poorly among all other groups. Blacks were resistant to the influence of Communists in the campaign, and, following the lead of the NAACP, they proved unwilling to desert the liberal and labor-based Democrats for a questionable third-party alternative. But, failure though it was, Matthiessen's Progressive party does deserve credit for including civil rights in its goals for the nation, and it likely impelled the Democrats to be more forthright in their own platform than they would otherwise have been (Record 278–86). It surely contributed, too, to Truman's decision in September 1948 to issue an executive order that desegregated the armed forces and mandated "fair practices procedures throughout the federal government" (Starobin 181; Marable 174).

Matthiessen himself also took controversial stands on particular race-related issues, defending Du Bois, for example, when the NAACP removed him from his position for backing Wallace and criticizing Truman. Du Bois had decided that the Progressive party stood for communication and cooperation with the Soviet Union, peace, and civil rights, and hence was far preferable to both the Republicans and the Democrats, whom he regarded as "reactionary, militaristic, and racist" (Rudwick 292). In urging Wallace to run on a third-party ticket and in "donn[ing] a Wallace button" during the campaign, Du Bois maintained that he was expressing his political views as an individual, not as an official of the NAACP (*Autobiography* 334). But this disclaimer did not satisfy Walter White and other NAACP leaders, who felt that Wallace was altogether unacceptable, despite past NAACP support for him and despite the evidence of some early interest on the part of blacks in his candidacy (Starobin 180). They cashiered Du Bois for his labors on Wallace's behalf, labeling his activities unduly "partisan" and "political" even as they themselves worked tirelessly for Truman and the Democrats. Du Bois' dismissal from his post angered Matthiessen, and he was one of many Progressive party activists, intellectuals, and longtime NAACP members who vigorously protested against it (Horne 107). Matthiessen even appeared on a literature panel with Du Bois in March 1949, at one of the sessions of the Cultural and Scientific Conference for World Peace held in New York City (Rampersad 251–52).

There are additional examples one could cite from other moments in Matthiessen's career. In the fall of 1944, Matthiessen worked tirelessly with the American Civil Liberties Union to protest the banning in Boston of Lillian Smith's controversial novel of miscegenation and lynching, *Strange Fruit* (Summers 143; De Voto). Perhaps the issue here was more one of free speech than race relations, but there is no question that Matthiessen was sensitive to, and deeply concerned about, the racial and sexual intolerance and nightmare that Smith graphically portrays. Two years later, in 1946, he wrote a letter to the editor of the *Sewanee Review*, protesting an "extremist article" by Donald Davidson that the journal had recently printed ("Communication" 144). Davidson had assailed "the various attempts to legislate the Negro into equal status" and had maintained the right of the South, for the present at least, to preserve its "bi-racial," segregated society ("Preface to Decision" 403, 406). To Matthiessen, this piece, like others that the *Sewanee Review* had published, laid out the race question as one of "North versus the South," whereas the really fundamental question concerned racial equality and justice and the need to end discrimination against all groups—Chinese, Mexicans, Nisei, and Jews as well as Negroes. It was precisely one of the terrible lessons of Nazi Germany, he emphasized, that it exhibited the "brutalization" that results from a "doctrine of racial superiority"

("Communication"; see also Ransom 12 June 1946, *Selected Letters* 323).

All of this and much more is certainly admirable, yet it remains true that Matthiessen seems finally to have compartmentalized his literary and political values when it came to race relations. Despite all that he was doing politically in the late 1940s, he still selected only white poets for the Oxford anthology. In this light, it is suggestive to return to *American Renaissance*, in order to gloss it with the final paragraph of Richard Wright's essay "How 'Bigger' Was Born," which appeared a year before the publication of Matthiessen's book. Not only does Wright delineate the limits of the American literary tradition and direct us toward roads not taken by our eminent writers. He also corrects in advance, one might say, the approving citation, by Matthiessen and countless critics, of Hawthorne's and James's tallying up of the liabilities of American civilization for the novelist.

> Early American writers, Henry James and Nathaniel Hawthorne, complained bitterly about the bleakness and flatness of the American scene. But I think that if they were alive, they'd feel at home in modern America. True, we have no great church in America; our national traditions are of such a sort that we are not wont to brag of them; and we have no army that's above the level of mercenary fighters; we have no group acceptable to the whole of our country upholding certain humane values; we have no rich symbols, no colorful rituals. We have only a money-grabbing, industrial civilization. But we do have in the Negro the embodiment of a past tragic enough to appease the spiritual hunger of even a James; and we have in the oppression of the Negro a shadow athwart our national life dense and heavy enough to satisfy even the gloomy broodings of a Hawthorne. And if Poe were alive, he would not have to invent horror; horror would invent him. (563)

Whatever might be missing from the American scene, there *is* "something else" powerfully suited to the making of great literature and that is the tragic history of the Negro. Matthiessen could extend his critical sympathy to the art and politics of Dreiser, and could appreciate the illuminations that pairing Dreiser and James could spark. But, in common with so many critics and scholars of his day, he couldn't see and gauge black men and women as artists, and thus was not able to imagine other suggestive conjunctions—Emerson and Douglass, Melville and Wright, James and Du Bois.

What I have shown in this chapter obviously implies a limiting judgment upon Matthiessen. But simply to criticize him would not justify the degree of detail I have provided. In his neglect of Afro-American writings, Matthiessen is revealingly typical of nearly all the critics in his generation. Civil rights issues were everywhere around him, and these formed one aspect of his own political work as a socialist. But the movements on the public political scene did not prompt Matthiessen to change the nature of his criticism or enlarge the group of writers he took to be central to the American experience. Like many critics, past and present, he embraced political convictions that he would not allow to make deep contact with his literary values and canonical distinctions. If he had really read and written about literature as a socialist, he would have produced a different sort of criticism. It would not necessarily have been a criticism that he and others would have found appealing—it would have been unfamiliar and unsettling—but it would have more effectively implemented the organic vision of work undertaken "for the people" to which Matthiessen movingly subscribed.

Matthiessen's case, then, contains chastening lessons for the present, especially as it exposes kinds of inconsistency and contradiction from which few of us are free. These continue to pervade literary criticism because no matter how radical we might be in theory and in social practice, we cannot bring ourselves to endanger an understanding of literature according to which we have been trained and with which we have grown accommodated. As I shall try to explain in my Conclusion, truly dedicated democratic service for the people may require changes in criticism that will prove uncomfortable to envision and accept.

Conclusion

The problem of the Twentieth Century is the problem of the color line.

—W. E. B. Du Bois, *Souls of Black Folk* xi

CRITICS AND TEACHERS today, having more successfully absorbed the impact of black civil and literary rights, now possess somewhat more flexible notions about what literature is, and these allow for comparisons and connections that Matthiessen would likely have disdained or avoided. It is now possible to admire Whitman less as a writer in steadfast opposition to nineteenth-century popular culture than as a writer at home with the evangelical and sentimental idioms that ruled the age (Zweig). We can begin to differentiate Whitman from the sentimental tradition, as Matthiessen sought to do, even as we connect him with that tradition and with the affirmations of home and hearth, love and compassion, which Stowe expresses in *Uncle Tom's Cabin*. Now we can also move from the monomaniacal Ahab to the brooding, obsessive protagonist of Martin Delany's novel of the late 1850s, *Blake*, who defies the white man's religion and professes that he will interpret Scripture only as he himself sees fit. Finally, to take one last example, we can examine, as I have done in Chapter 6, the historical significance and racial imagery of *Benito Cereno*, performing an analysis that lies outside the bounds of *American Renaissance*. If this were a book on Melville, not Matthiessen, I could proceed to relate *Benito Cereno* to still other texts in the American and Afro-American traditions, texts such as Douglass's *The Heroic Slave*, which describes the suggestively named Madison Washington's rebellion aboard the slaveholding ship *Creole*, a rebellion staged as a reenactment of the revolutionary fathers' blow for freedom struck in 1776.

Lines of inquiry of this sort currently figure in much excellent critical and scholarly work in the academy. Not only have we benefited from the recovery of many little-known texts by black men and women writers, including William Wells Brown, Harriet Jacobs, Harriet Wilson, and Sutton Griggs, but we have also seen the upward revaluation of Charles Chesnutt, Zora Neale Hurston, and others. There has been, in addition, richly detailed attention paid to racial themes in Twain and Faulkner. The canon, in a word, has expanded dramatically, going well beyond what Matthiessen helped to create and shape, even reaching to include at last the literature of native Americans, Chicanos, and Latin Americans (Sanchez; Lincoln; Krupat; Swann and Krupat). The interpretive strategies for exploring the enlarged canon have grown and developed in sophistication as well.

Yet we should not be too quick to congratulate ourselves for our greater tolerance and sympathy. It is important to consider the elements of professional self-aggrandizement involved when white academics proceed industriously to explicate Afro-American and minority texts. If you are in an English department, you can write only so many essays on Hawthorne and James before the law of diminishing returns sets in. Afro-American texts, documents, materials—here is a fairly untouched field for critical methodologies to traverse. Nothing intrinsically evil or surprising about that; it is a familiar, if not always cheering, part of the momentum for "the new" that academic professionalism encourages. In seizing upon this particular "new" field, however, we are handling materials that many black (and some white) men and women labored hard to make respectable as a discipline in its own right. Many people fought painful battles in the late 1960s and 1970s to legitimate the study of Afro-American literature, culture, and history. Now, in often endangered, underfunded, and understaffed black studies departments, they behold white men and women in English and Romance language departments stealing their subject. Scholars at work in opening up the canon are doing something essential and valuably democratizing, but there is an exploitativeness to such work that we should acknowledge.

An even more difficult issue arises here, though, and that concerns the place—if such a place remains possible today—of critical judgment and evaluation. Often in this book, I have criticized

Matthiessen's shortcomings, including his failure to be pluralistic and his consequent inability to make his scholarship reflect the democracy he upheld in his political life. But one should ask whether Matthiessen might have been right in his judgment that there is a group of "best" writers and books even if he erred in the manner in which he made and framed his selection.

To recommend that the canon might profitably be limited as well as reoriented is certain to draw fire from the left. Needless to say, I would not want to postpone ongoing study of the canon, nor would I want to curtail the kinds of projects that critics and scholars pursue: knowledge must grow, and many interesting major and minor authors merit analysis and research. But the same principle may not hold for teaching, where the teacher has to make serious decisions about which authors his or her students ought to read and learn about in a particular course on some period or phase of American literature. I recognize that, as Richard Ohmann has argued, "to posit standards is always to engage in an ideological maneuver, to generalize the interests and values of one class or group and present them as the interests and values of all" ("Social Relations" 197); and I agree with him, too, that "excellence is a constantly changing, socially chosen value" ("Social Definition" 96). But one could accept these insights and still contend for greater selectivity and stress on judgment, for seeing the act of interpreting texts as laced with critical preferences, choices, decisions, responsibilities. Judgment does not have to mean closure; it can be a process of communal debate and exchange in the classroom, and within the department and discipline, in which political as well as literary interests and values are openly expressed. Such a debate may well prove a more fertile ground for literary study than simply adding more texts.

What I am describing is the effort to ask about the relationship between value judgments and the "opening up" of the canon. It is crucial, certainly, to scrutinize Matthiessen's canon and assess its inability to represent "the people" Matthiessen himself wished to serve. A course on the American Renaissance ought to incorporate the writings of Douglass and Stowe. My own inclination, then, is to strive for ever-greater catholicity and inclusiveness. But, again, as teachers we must often be strict about defining the field of texts, if only out of sheer pedagogical necessity—you can only do so much in a semester. It is striking how little discussion of these choices, and the literary and political assumptions behind them, enters into the business of teachers and academic intellectuals. To put the matter in rather crude, but accurate, terms: everyone makes out his or her reading list in isolation, and there is no general debate about which knowledge might be most worth having.

I have myself profited from reading many sentimental novels and slave narratives, and I am glad that scholars are tilling these texts and their contexts. But is there much warrant for teaching lots of these texts at the expense of Emerson and Whitman? *Uncle Tom's Cabin* and *My Bondage and My Freedom* are rich, suggestive examples of the sentimental and slave narrative genres, and I teach them often. And one of the reasons they figure especially largely for me is that they are markedly superior to most of the other texts which they in some ways resemble. Others doubtless disagree with me and likely could develop good arguments for their position. My point here, finally, is not so much who is right as it is the absence of critical discussion and exchange. Particularly within departments in colleges and universities, one rarely finds substantive conversation about competing values and choices, or a general ongoing discursive account of the judgments that various individuals inevitably make.

Simply expanding the literary canon does not necessarily mean that education will improve. Take, for instance, the very widely used *Norton Anthology of American Literature* (second edition), volume 1 totaling 2,535 pages and volume 2 running to 2,652 pages. Both include, as they should, minority and women writers, and hence testify to praiseworthy openness on the part of the editors. Yet neither volume cuts back at all on the sizable sections given to the various male members of the traditional pantheon. Is this really inclusiveness or a characteristic form of American inflation, in which the editors offer more choices but default on discriminating among the range of choices? Does this show a splendid pluralism or confess the impossibility of judgment—as though there were no basis for selection? What we have here are two massive books, both of which tend toward affirming bulk rather than critical thought, and both of which, whatever their copiousness, nevertheless still omit significant figures (William Lloyd Garrison and Randolph Bourne, for instance) and thus could be said to persist in being too restrictive. These books are big, but not big enough, and not necessarily better, despite laudable diversity in content, than what we have used in the past.

They include a great deal, but still leave out much, and they do not investigate the basis of selection—something a different anthology, with fewer choices, might conceivably, and productively, undertake to do.

Matthiessen's choices in *American Renaissance*, it seems plain, were undemocratic. But though we are being more inclusive as editors, anthologists, and teachers, we may not be doing a better, more disciplined and exacting job in working for democracy than he did. However familiar, overgeneralized, and inadequate Matthiessen's writing sometimes is, we still can profitably read and learn from it—above all for the manner in which Matthiessen's positions remain current, ironically reflecting the positions of those who judge they have gone beyond him. We have not resolved the tension between literature and politics that sometimes disarms and weakens Matthiessen's books. In the guise of addressing it, we have only engaged it at its highly vulnerable "literary" points and avoided the personal and political challenges that would oblige us to change what we do as critics and teachers.

The more one reflects upon the canon and critical judgment, the clearer it becomes that we are here engaging political as well as literary issues. We want to believe that we can discuss literature free from political interference and violation, but Matthiessen's case shows that this belief leads to confusion. Even more, it damages the very criticism that is trying so earnestly to stay "literary": it forestalls inquiry into questions that writing like Eliot's poetry and prose raises.

Matthiessen's criticism reveals the dangers, both intellectual and political, that result when the teacher/critic seeks to distinguish between art and politics, literary criticism and criticism of other kinds. Over and over again, from the time of his book on Eliot until the end of his life, Matthiessen ends up in untenable positions because he preserves literature in a special category. He aims to fashion a criticism inspired by a democratic politics, but, determined not to allow politics to intervene in the critic's tasks, he never can wholly achieve his goal and, indeed, sometimes badly blurs it. I would propose that the better, if riskier, way is to acknowledge one's political beliefs first, and then to make pedagogical decisions accordingly. If I claim to desire, and wish to work for, political change, then I should teach in line with my politics. At its best, this view mandates taking with full seriousness the organic vision which Matthiessen embraced; at its worst, it verges upon being unaccommodatingly dogmatic. But it follows from studying Matthiessen and trying to learn from him. It means imagining a different way of writing criticism and teaching, one that does not accept a definition of literary study that insists upon seeing certain texts and interpretive strategies as essentially beyond or outside political purposes.

In defining my own canon, as I make choices among writers and texts, I stress four terms: dissent, struggle, vision, conflict. These terms, and the texts that sustain them in my teaching, overlap with one another, but there are some differences in emphasis among them. By "dissent," I mean to refer to writers such as Douglass and Garrison, whose language functioned as crucial weapons in the abolitionist cause; they dissent from the established order, one that sanctioned slavery in the midst of American "democracy," with a fierce, unremitting verbal power. "Struggle," for me, points especially to C. L. R. James, Walter Rodney, Eric Williams, Franz Fanon, Amilcar Cabral, and other writers of the Americas and Africa who deemed their literary—and historical, sociological, and economic—labor as profoundly a part of a *political* cause, a struggle for liberation from colonialism.

"Vision" is a term that obviously pertains to such work, but it is perhaps even more apt to designate the value of writings by Du Bois, Wright, Martin Luther King, and Malcolm X, all of whom grew up within the American context and who wrote forthrightly about race relations in America's rural and urban settings; as their careers progressed, they increasingly tied the national racial situation to the international opposition to white, Western imperialism. "Conflict" is, in a sense, a more limited, even somewhat contrary term. It connects, for me, with writers such as Melville, Twain, and Faulkner, who magnificently exhibit the causes and consequences of racial injustice but who never quite manage to imagine resolutions to them in their powerful fictive forms. These writers illuminate the dilemmas of slavery, prejudice, and miscegenation with tremendously complex insight; they cannot, however, work through the contradictions they articulate in order to envision a society and culture of richer possibilities that would give greater grounds for hope.

Of all the writers I have named, W. E. B. Du Bois (1868–1963) stands out with a special kind of distinction, and I would point to him as marking a better theoretical and practical path than the one Matthiessen honorably pursued. During the course of his long career, Du Bois produced superior work in many genres. His Harvard dissertation, *The Suppression of the African Slave Trade* (1896), the first of his nineteen books, was a pioneering, minutely detailed analysis of the growth and eventual elimination of the slave trade to the United States; his absorbing rendering of African culture and Afro-American history, *The Negro* (1915), served as "the Bible of Pan-Africanism" (Rampersad 234); and his later historical book, *Black Reconstruction* (1935), bitingly challenged the traditional view of the post–Civil War period as above all a time of white suffering and Negro abuses and abominations. His sociological studies of the black family and community, especially *The Philadelphia Negro* (1899), remain valuable; his countless essays and reviews, not only in *The Crisis* but in other academic journals and popular magazines and newspapers, are extraordinary for their range and virtuosity; and his numerous articles on education, work, and, perhaps most notably of all, the Pan-African movement further testify to his national and international vision of the development of people of color. He also wrote novels, stories, and poetry, and invented mixed genres of his own, as the sociologically acute and lyrically eloquent *Souls of Black Folk* (1903) demonstrates. Du Bois' autobiographical writings, including in particular *Dusk of Dawn* (1940), are also rewarding texts that situate the life of the writer within the complex political movements of the late nineteenth and twentieth centuries.

With the exception of *The Souls of Black Folk*, Du Bois' writings are rarely taught and are rarely accorded in literary history the credit they abundantly deserve. In part this results from the fertile ways in which Du Bois' writings span and exceed generic and disciplinary categories. Who should teach him? Where should he be taught? Du Bois' astonishing range has possibly worked to his disadvantage, particularly in the academy, leaving the majority of his books unread and unstudied because it is unclear to whose departmental terrain they belong. "His contribution," concludes Arnold Rampersad, "has sunk to the status of a footnote in the long history of race relations in the United States" (291). Yet as a premier "man of letters" (Marable 215), Du Bois in fact has few rivals in this century. Edmund Wilson immediately comes to mind as a comparably compelling force in our literature. And there are intriguing stylistic and ideological connections between Du Bois and Wilson, including their reliance on nineteenth-century English prose traditions, their mutual interest in Hippolyte Taine's theory and practice of history, and their absorption in Marxist thought during the 1930s (and, in Du Bois' case, in later decades as well).

But Wilson and Du Bois—they seem, by the way, never to have read or even referred to one another—are different types of men of letters. Wilson did not possess the same degree of patience and persistent curiosity about fact and detail that Du Bois manifests and that resulted, no doubt, from Du Bois' training in (and respect for) the rigors of Germanic scholarship and the "higher learning" of the university. Wilson loved to dive into a big, new project, working it up through essays and reviews that he organized into superb books. He then habitually tackled another, different project and rarely looked back: what was done, was done. His briskly conducted surveys of many new fields signal one of his strengths but also a limit to the depth and development of his writing. With Du Bois, more so than with Wilson, there is a greater sense of a constantly revitalized organic enterprise, as new writing and political work function together to build upon, complicate, extend, and elucidate the old. Du Bois' integrated enterprise, undertaken in order to benefit "the people," exemplifies the ideal that Matthiessen held dear but could not quite manage to practice.

Du Bois always perceived his writing, in whatever form or forum, as having political point and purpose. As he noted in a diary entry on his twenty-fifth birthday, "I therefore take the world that the Unknown lay in my hands and work for the rise of the Negro people, taking for granted that their best development means the best development of the world" (*Autobiography* 171). Du Bois assembled knowledge, fired off polemics, issued moral appeals, and preached international brotherhood and peace in the hope of effecting differences in the lives of the lowly and oppressed. He stood for equality and justice, for bringing all men and women into "the kingdom of culture" as co-workers (*Souls of Black Folk* 46). So much was this Du Bois' intention that he was willing to use the explosive word "propaganda" to accent it. Viewing himself as, in everything, a writer, an artist, he affirmed that "all art is propaganda and ever must be, despite the wailing of the purists. I stand in utter shamelessness and say that whatever art I have for writing has been used always for propaganda for gaining the right for black folk to love and enjoy" ("Criteria of Negro Art" 288).

In some respects it is curious that Du Bois is still undertaught and undervalued. William James, Nathaniel Shaler, Albert Bushnell Hart, George Santayana, and others praised him during his student days at Harvard; Hart later said that he "counted [Du Bois] always among the ablest and keenest of our teacher-scholars, an American who viewed his country broadly" (Du Bois, *Autobiography* 269). Some of America's most gifted novelists, poets, and playwrights admired him. Eugene O'Neill once referred to Du Bois as "ranking among the foremost writers of true importance in the country" (Tuttle 52). Van Wyck Brooks commended him as "an intellectual who was also an artist and a prophet," a man "with a mind at once passionate, critical, humorous, and detached" and "a mental horizon as wide as the world" (*Confident Years* 548). Even earlier, no less an eminence than Henry James termed him "that most accomplished of members of the Negro race" (418). It was William James who sent his brother a copy of *The Souls of Black Folk*, referring to it as "a decidedly moving book" (2: 196). *The Souls of Black Folk* is a landmark in Afro-American culture. James Weldon Johnson, in his autobiography, stated that this book "had a greater effect upon and within the Negro race in America than any other single book published in this country since *Uncle Tom's Cabin*" (203); and Rampersad has summarized its significance even more dramatically: "If all of the nation's literature may stem from one book, as Hemingway implied about *The Adventures of Huckleberry Finn*, then it can as accurately be said that all of Afro-American literature of a creative nature has proceeded from Du Bois' comprehensive statement on the nature of the people in *The Souls of Black Folk*" (89).

But while *The Souls of Black Folk* has loomed largely within the Afro-American intellectual community, it has not received much attention within the white one. Nor has it generated a more extensive interest in Du Bois' other writings. Du Bois' black skin still bars him from attaining the stature that he had, by rights, attained through his written work. He has also suffered—and suffered literally in his life —because of his Communist sympathies and eventual membership in the Communist party (Horne). As a black man and a Communist, Du Bois has for decades been tainted, excluded from the literary and historical register of the dominant (and predominantly white) world of scholarship.

Du Bois' work is hardly perfect. His scholarship was formidable throughout his career, but it ebbed somewhat in precision and originality after *The Suppression of the African Slave Trade*, *The Philadelphia Negro*, and the best volumes in the Atlanta University Publications on the Study of Negro Problems. It is also impossible to deny the naiveté that mars Du Bois' account of his travels in the Soviet Union and the People's Republic of China, as presented in his posthumous *Autobiography* (1968). He made unfortunate mistakes, too, in his assessment of the African liberation movements of the 1950s, especially in the case of Nkrumah's Ghana. But despite these ideological and analytical errors, he still should figure significantly in American culture and for American literary studies. As scholar and teacher, his work is at one with his politics: his political interests and goals instruct him how best to shape his intellectual and pedagogical mission. In Matthiessen's case, one reaches a different conclusion: his writing gestures toward politics but is too frequently at odds with it. Matthiessen could not—he did not wish to—shake free from distinctly literary views and values, which he then sought, unsuccessfully, to couple with political aspirations and beliefs. I confess to being closer to Matthiessen than not; I would like to be more like Du Bois.

It is testimony to the writerly distinction of Du Bois and the others I have named that one would want to call them "great artists." They are that. But from another point of view, their status as artists matters less, in the classroom, than their exemplary performance as writers who project political lessons, who craft embodiments of political truth. All of them enable me to help teach students a language of resistance, and I perceive myself, in reading and attending to their texts, as not so much a "literary" critic as a teacher/critic of language. It is the language of these texts—*My Bondage and My Freedom*, *Thoughts on African Colonization*, *The Souls of Black Folk*, *The Black Jacobins*, *Benito Cereno*, *Huckleberry Finn*, *Light in August*—that fascinates and excites me, and I am drawn toward *this* language in *these* texts and others like them because of my political commitments.

I foreground race in my teaching since, with Du Bois, I regard race "as the central problem of the greatest of the world's democracies and so the problem of the future world" (Green and Smith 264). Others whose political views are similar to my own might prefer to focus upon gender and class, and on the intersections of race, class, and gender. Their choice of texts and methods will be different from, though complementary to, mine. In developing my approach to texts, I have thus learned from Matthiessen but have adapted and altered his key critical tenet. Matthiessen stated that "an artist's use of language is the most sensitive index to cultural history" (*American Renaissance* xv). I would reformulate this to read: "cultural history and work for change lead us to focus with special attention on language as it is displayed in texts we choose for political reasons."

Parrington once observed that "provocative social thinking and the American university seem never to have got on well together" (*Beginnings of Critical Realism* 124). At least within literary studies, this occurs partially because "social thinking" keeps getting balked and deflected by our allegiance to "literature as an art." This may be a fine loyalty, and many admirable men and women have supported it, but it is crucial to realize, as Matthiessen's scholarship confirms, how variable have been the boundaries that define "literature" and "art." It is simply historically wrong to speak as if literary art is, has always been, and will always be this or that particular thing. Matthiessen felt certain that he knew what literature was; yet when we read his books today, we notice right away the books (and constituencies) that lie outside his range of literary expertise and mission. Invoking the primacy of "literature" may sound with the ring of truth; and this has often proven to be a highly effective ideological and institutional flourish. But the emphasis on "literature" is regularly an exclusive and excluding one; and it obliges us to forget how different this category (and the kinds of criticism which accompanied it) looked just a decade or two ago. I prefer myself to begin, as I have emphasized, with present political interests and to proceed from there to choose writers and texts which I can examine with students to develop and express these interests.

Education does not merely have political implications; it *is* political. Borrowing from Giroux and Aronowitz's *Education under Siege*, I would maintain that

> in a radical sense, education represents a collectively produced set of experiences organized around issues and concerns that allow for a critical understanding of everyday oppression as well as the dynamics involved in constructing alternative political cultures. As the embodiment of an ideal, it refers to forms of learning and action based on

a commitment to the elimination of class, racial, and gender oppression. (132)

My labor as a teacher includes working with texts that will enable students to acquire some of the tools they need to understand the strengths of their culture and counteract its negative elements. It is not just that they are alienated, but that they lack a language for verbalizing their alienation effectively and resisting it. Furthermore, they rarely see that the critical "resources" (a fine word of Matthiessen's) for such a language lie close at hand. As currently constituted, literary study has rarely given them this language; it does not furnish them with texts that illustrate resistance and that stress the writerly acts of dissent, struggle, vision, and conflict that vitalize a main current of America's cultural tradition. Nor does literary study today instruct students in the exercise of a critical judgment that is, at once, political and literary. It frequently hands texts over to students without locating their language in specific historical situations and without clarifying the analysis (and possibly the indictment) of the contemporary American and international scene that this language supplies.

Conservative readers will doubtless object to the claims made in these final pages. Yet surely they, too, seek a better way to undertake literary study than the one presently and confusedly in place. They likely will not accept my account of the relation between literature and politics, but I hope they would offer their own, so that the debate could proceed honestly on this ground. Conservatives do not want to acknowledge the presence of ideology in their criticism, and they urge a nonpartisan appreciation of the best that has been thought and said in the Western tradition. Instead of contending that these texts, and the values identified with them, are indisputable, conservatives would perhaps do better to concede that both the texts and the values are in dispute—for political reasons—and should proceed forcefully to prosecute their case openly from a conservative direction.

The Introduction to this book contains its point of departure—that polemical advocacy of "American study" I wrote for a conference and from which Matthiessen's name is conspicuously absent. But I am no longer certain (happy discovery!) that enjoining men and women in the humanities everywhere to rally behind a particular literary cause and program for reform makes much sense. And I say this even though I would like to believe, for the general and immediate health of literary study as a whole, that conservatives, liberals, and radicals could at least agree on the powerful presence of politics in their work and could promote clear disagreement and debate on this basis. Finally, however, it may be better to take a personal stand, identifying a specific conception of radical intellectual work and seeking alliances, inside and outside a home institution, with others who might be willing to share, improve, modify it. The question now is not, What can be done to reform departments of English and change the profession as a whole? It is, instead, What facts in the "world of practice and choice and struggle" (Williams 226) impel me as an individual, and might lead others, toward particular kinds of literary judgment and pedagogical action? This is a sounder strategy, and ultimately, I hope, it will prove more productive.

Works Cited

Aaron, Daniel. *Writers on the Left.* 1961. New York: Avon, 1965.

Adler, Joyce. "Melville's *Benito Cereno*: Slavery and Violence in the Americas." *Science and Society* 38 (1974): 23–52.

Alinsky, Saul D. *Reveille for Radicals.* 1946. New York: Vintage, 1969.

Arac, Jonathan. "F. O. Matthiessen: Authorizing an American Renaissance." In *The American Renaissance Reconsidered,* ed. Walter Benn Michaels and Donald E. Pease, 90–112. Baltimore: Johns Hopkins Univ. Press, 1985.

Arvin, Newton. "The Democratic Tradition in American Letters." In *The Writer in a Changing World,* ed. Henry Hart, 34–43. Equinox Cooperative Press, 1937.

Arvin, Newton. *Walt Whitman.* New York: Macmillan, 1938.

Babbitt, Irving. *Literature and the American College.* 1908. Clifton: Augustus M. Kelley, 1972.

Babbitt, Irving. *Rousseau and Romanticism.* 1919. Cleveland: Meridian, 1964.

Baldwin, James. "In Conversation." 1966. In *Black Voices: An Anthology of Afro-American Literature,* ed. Abraham Chapman, 660–68. New York: New American Library, 1968.

Baym, Nina. *Novels, Readers, and Reviewers: Responses to Fiction in Antebellum America.* Ithaca: Cornell Univ. Press, 1984.

Baym, Nina. *Woman's Fiction: A Guide to Novels by and about Women in America, 1820–1870.* Ithaca: Cornell Univ. Press, 1978.

Benziger, James. "Organic Unity: Leibniz to Coleridge." *PMLA* 66 (March 1951): 24–48.

Bercovitch, Sacvan. "The Problem of Ideology in American Literary History." *Critical Inquiry* 12 (1986): 631–53.

Blackmur, R. P. *The Double Agent: Essays in Craft and Elucidation.* 1935. Gloucester: Peter Smith, 1962.

Blackmur, R. P. *The Expense of Greatness.* 1940. Gloucester: Peter Smith, 1958.

Bloom, Alexander. *Prodigal Sons: The New York Intellectuals and Their World.* New York: Oxford Univ. Press, 1986.

Blum, John Morton. *V Was for Victory: Politics and American Culture during World War II.* New York: Harcourt, Brace, Jovanovich, 1976.

Blum, John Morton, ed. *The Price of Vision: The Diary of Henry A. Wallace, 1942–1946.* Boston: Houghton Mifflin, 1973.

Bourne, Randolph. "The Art of Theodore Dreiser." 1917. *The Radical Will: Selected Writings, 1911–1918,* ed. Olaf Hansen, 462–66. New York: Urizen, 1977.

Bowron, Bernard. "The Making of an American Scholar." In *F. O. Matthiessen (1902–1950): A Collective Portrait,* ed. Paul M. Sweezy and Leo Huberman, 44–54. New York: Henry Schuman, 1950.

Bradbury, John M. *The Fugitives: A Critical Account.* Chapel Hill: Univ. of North Carolina Press, 1958.

Brodhead, Richard H. *The School of Hawthorne.* New York: Oxford Univ. Press, 1986.

Brooks, Cleanth. *Modern Poetry and the Tradition.* 1939. Chapel Hill: Univ. of North Carolina Press, 1967.

Brooks, Cleanth, and Robert Penn Warren, eds. *Understanding Poetry: An Anthology for College Students.* 1938. New York: Henry Holt, 1950.

Brooks, Cleanth, and William K. Wimsatt, Jr. *Literary Criticism: A Short History.* 1957. New York: Vintage, 1967.

Brooks, Van Wyck. *The Confident Years, 1885–1915.* New York: Dutton, 1952.

Brooks, Van Wyck. *The Flowering of New England, 1815–1865.* New York: Dutton, 1936.

Brown, Sterling. *Negro Poetry and Drama* and *The Negro in American Fiction.* 1937. New York: Atheneum, 1972.

Buell, Lawrence. *New England Literary Culture: From Revolution through Renaissance.* New York: Cambridge Univ. Press, 1986.

Buhle, Paul. *Marxism in the United States: Remapping the History of the American Left.* London: Verso, 1987.

Cain, William E. *The Crisis in Criticism: Theory, Literature, and Reform in English Studies.* Baltimore: Johns Hopkins Univ. Press, 1984.

Cain, William E. "English in America Reconsidered: Theory, Criticism, Marxism, and Social Change." In *Criticism in the University,* ed. Gerald Graff and Reginald Gibbons, 85–104. Evanston: Northwestern Univ. Press, 1985.

Cantor, Milton. *The Divided Left: American Radicalism, 1900–1975.* New York: Hill and Wang, 1978.

Casciato, Arthur. "Citizen Writers: A History of the League of American Writers, 1935–1942." Diss., Univ. of Virginia, 1986.

Caughey, John. "Historians' Choice: Results of a Poll on Recently Published American History and Biography." *Mississippi Valley Historical Review* 39 (1952): 289–302.

Caute, David. *The Great Fear: The Anti-Communist Purge under Truman and Eisenhower.* New York: Simon and Schuster, 1978.

Cowley, Malcolm. "Dreiser: Genius in the Raw." 1965. *The Flower and the Leaf: A Contemporary Record of American Writing since 1941*, ed. Donald W. Faulkner, 304–8. New York: Viking, 1985.

Cowley, Malcolm. *The Literary Situation.* 1954. New York: Viking, 1958.

Cowley, Malcolm. "Thirty Years Later: Memories of the First American Writers' Congress." *American Scholar* 35 (1965–66): 495–516.

Cox, James M. "The Memoirs of Henry James: Self-Interest as Autobiography." *Southern Review* 22 (1986): 231–51.

Cunliffe, Marcus, and Robin Winks, eds. *Pastmasters: Some Essays on American Historians.* New York: Harper and Row, 1969.

Cutrer, Thomas W. "Conference on Literature and Reading in the South and Southwest, 1935." *Southern Review* 21 (1985): 260–300.

Cutrer, Thomas W. *Parnassus on the Mississippi: The Southern Review and the Baton Rouge Literary Community, 1935–1942.* Baton Rouge: Louisiana State Univ. Press, 1984.

Davidson, Donald. "Preface to Decision." *Sewanee Review* 53 (1945): 394–412.

Delany, Martin R. *Blake, or The Huts of America.* 1859–61. Boston: Beacon, 1970.

De Voto, Bernard. "The Decision in the *Strange Fruit* Case: The Obscenity Statute in Massachusetts." *New England Quarterly* 19 (1946): 147–83.

Dillingham, William B. *Melville's Shorter Fiction, 1853–1856.* Athens: Univ. of Georgia Press, 1977.

Douglass, Frederick. "The Anti-Slavery Movement." 1855. *The Life and Writings of Frederick Douglass*, ed. Philip S. Foner. 5 vols. 2: 333–59. New York: International Publishers, 1975.

Douglass, Frederick. "The Heroic Slave." *Frederick Douglass: The Narrative and Selected Writings*, ed. Michael Meyer, 299–348. New York: Modern Library, 1984.

Douglass, Frederick. *My Bondage and My Freedom.* 1855. New York: Dover, 1969.

Douglass, Frederick. "Why Is the Negro Lynched?" 1894. *The Life and Writings of Frederick Douglass*, ed. Philip S. Foner. 5 vols. 4: 491–523. New York: International Publishers, 1975.

Dreiser, Theodore. *America Is Worth Saving.* New York: Modern Age, 1941.

Dreiser, Theodore. *The Color of a Great City.* New York: Boni and Liveright, 1923.

Dreiser, Theodore. *Dreiser Looks at Russia.* New York: Liveright, 1928.

Dreiser, Theodore. "Introduction to *Harlan Miners Speak*." 1932. *Theodore*

Dreiser: A Selection of Uncollected Prose, ed. Donald Pizer, 265–71. Detroit: Wayne State Univ. Press, 1977.

Dreiser, Theodore. *Letters*. Ed. Robert H. Elias. 3 vols. Philadelphia: Univ. of Pennsylvania Press, 1959.

Dreiser, Theodore. *Sister Carrie*. 1900. Norton Critical Edition, ed. Donald Pizer. New York: Norton, 1970.

Dreiser, Theodore. *Sister Carrie*. The Pennsylvania Edition. New York: Penguin, 1981.

Dreiser, Theodore. *Tragic America*. London: Constable, 1931.

Dreiser, Theodore, ed. *The Living Thoughts of Thoreau*. 1939. New York: Fawcett, 1963.

Du Bois, W. E. B. *The Autobiography of W. E. B. Du Bois*. New York: International, 1980.

Du Bois, W. E. B. *Black Reconstruction*. 1935. Millwood: Kraus-Thomson, 1976.

Du Bois, W. E. B. "Criteria of Negro Art." 1926. *W. E. B. Du Bois: The Crisis Writings*, ed. Daniel Walden, 279–90. Greenwich: Fawcett, 1972.

Du Bois, W. E. B. *The Souls of Black Folk*. 1903. New York: Signet, 1969.

Dunham, Barrows. "Statements by Friends and Associates." In *F. O. Matthiessen (1902–1950): A Collective Portrait*, ed. Paul M. Sweezy and Leo Huberman, 102–3. New York: Henry Schuman, 1950.

Dunmire, B. L. "The Development of American Literature Textbooks Used in the United States from 1870 to 1952." Diss., Univ. of Pittsburgh, 1954.

Edel, Leon. *Henry James, The Master, 1901–1916*. New York: Lippincott, 1972.

Elias, Robert H. "Review of *Theodore Dreiser*." *American Literature* 23 (1951–52): 505–8.

Elias, Robert H. *Theodore Dreiser: Apostle of Nature*. 2d ed. New York: Cornell, 1970.

Eliot, T. S. *The Idea of a Christian Society*. 1940. *Christianity and Culture*. New York: Harcourt, Brace and World, n.d.

Eliot, T. S. "On Henry James." 1918. In *The Question of Henry James: A Collection of Critical Essays*, ed. F. W. Dupee, 123–33. London: Allan Wingate, 1947.

Eliot, T. S. *The Sacred Wood: Essays on Poetry and Criticism*. 1920. London: Methuen, 1972.

Emery, Allan Moore. "*Benito Cereno* and Manifest Destiny." *Nineteenth Century Fiction* 39 (June 1984): 48–68.

Emery, Allan Moore. "The Topicality of Depravity in *Benito Cereno*." *American Literature* 55 (October 1983): 316–31.

Empson, William. *Milton's God.* 1961. London: Chatto and Windus, 1965.

Empson, William. *Seven Types of Ambiguity.* 1930. Rev. ed. New York: New Directions, 1966.

Empson, William. *Some Versions of Pastoral.* 1934. New York: New Directions, 1968.

Feidelson, Charles, Jr. *Symbolism and American Literature.* 1953. Chicago: Univ. of Chicago Press, 1970.

Fekete, John. *The Critical Twilight: Explorations in the Ideology of Anglo-American Literary Theory from Eliot to McLuhan.* London: Routledge and Kegan Paul, 1977.

Ferguson, Robert A. *Law and Letters in American Culture.* Cambridge: Harvard Univ. Press, 1984.

Fisher, Philip. "Acting, Reading, Fortune's Wheel: *Sister Carrie* and the Life History of Objects." In *American Realism: New Essays,* ed. Eric J. Sundquist, 259–77. Baltimore: Johns Hopkins Univ. Press, 1982.

Fox, Richard Wightman. *Reinhold Niebuhr: A Biography.* New York: Pantheon, 1985.

Franklin, H. Bruce. *The Victim as Criminal and Artist: Literature from the American Prison.* New York: Oxford Univ. Press, 1978.

Franklin, John Hope. *From Slavery to Freedom: A History of Negro Americans.* 5th ed. New York: Knopf, 1980.

Frohock, W. M. *Theodore Dreiser.* Minneapolis: Univ. of Minnesota Press, 1972.

Gilbert, James Burkhardt. *Writers and Partisans: A History of Literary Radicalism in America.* New York: John Wiley and Sons, 1968.

Gilbert, Martin. *Auschwitz and the Allies.* New York: Holt, Rinehart, and Winston, 1981.

Gilmore, Michael T. *American Romanticism and the Marketplace.* Chicago: Univ. of Chicago Press, 1985.

Giroux, Henry A., and Stanley Aronowitz. *Education under Siege: The Conservative, Liberal, and Radical Debate over Schooling.* South Hadley: Bergin and Garvey, 1985.

Golding, Alan C. "A History of American Poetry Anthologies." In *Canons,* ed. Robert von Hallberg, 279–307. Chicago: Univ. of Chicago Press, 1984.

Graff, Gerald. *Professing Literature: An Institutional History.* Chicago: Univ. of Chicago Press, 1987.

Green, Dan S., and Earl Smith. "W. E. B. Du Bois and the Concepts of Race and Class." *Phylon* 44 (1983): 262–72.

Greenough, Horatio. *Form and Function: Remarks on Art, Design, and Architecture.* Berkeley: Univ. of California Press, 1969.

Gunn, Giles B. *F. O. Matthiessen: The Critical Achievement.* Seattle: Univ. of Washington Press, 1975.

Habegger, Alfred. *Gender, Fantasy, and Realism in American Literature.* New York: Columbia Univ. Press, 1982.

Hartman, Geoffrey. *Criticism in the Wilderness: The Study of Literature Today.* New Haven: Yale Univ. Press, 1980.

Havard, William C. "The Search for Identity." In *The History of Southern Literature,* ed. Louis D. Rubin, Jr., 415–28. Baton Rouge: Louisiana State Univ. Press, 1985.

Hedges, William L. "The Myth of the Republic and the Theory of American Literature." *Prospects* 4 (1979): 101–20.

Hemingway, Ernest. *Selected Letters, 1917–1961.* Ed. Carlos Baker. New York: Scribner's, 1981.

Hewitt, Rosalie. "*The American Scene*: Its Genesis and Reception, 1905–1977." *Henry James Review* 1 (1980): 179–96.

Hicks, Granville. "Eliot in Our Time." 1936. *Granville Hicks in the New Masses,* ed. Jack Alan Robbins, 102–6. Port Washington: Kennikat, 1974.

Hicks, Granville. *The Great Tradition: An Interpretation of American Literature since the Civil War.* 1933. Chicago: Quadrangle, 1969.

Hicks, Granville. *Where We Came Out.* New York: Viking, 1954.

Higham, John. *History: Professional Scholarship in America.* Baltimore: Johns Hopkins Univ. Press, 1983.

Higham, John, and Paul K. Conkin, eds. *New Directions in American Intellectual History.* Baltimore: Johns Hopkins Univ. Press, 1979.

Hofstadter, Richard. "Native Sons of Our Literature." *Nation,* 28 April 1951, 398.

Holland, Laurence B. *The Expense of Vision: Essays on the Craft of Henry James.* Princeton: Princeton Univ. Press, 1964.

Hollinger, David A. "The Canon and Its Keepers: Modernism and Mid-Twentieth-Century American Intellectuals." *In the American Province: Studies in the History and Historiography of Ideas,* 74–91. Bloomington: Indiana Univ. Press, 1985.

Horne, Gerald. *Black and Red: W. E. B. Du Bois and the Afro-American Response to the Cold War, 1944–1963.* Albany: State Univ. of New York Press, 1986.

Howe, Irving. *A Margin of Hope: An Intellectual Autobiography.* New York: Harcourt, Brace, Jovanovich, 1982.

Howe, Irving. "Reply." *Partisan Review* 15 (1948): 1256.

Howe, Irving. "The Sentimental Fellow-Travelling of F. O. Matthiessen." *Partisan Review* 15 (1948): 1125–29.

Howe, Irving. *Socialism and America.* New York: Harcourt, Brace, Jovanovich, 1985.

Hubbell, Jay B. *Who Are the Major American Writers? A Study of the Changing Literary Canon.* Durham: Duke Univ. Press, 1972.

Hyde, Louis, ed. *Rat and the Devil: Journal Letters of F. O. Matthiessen and Russell Cheney.* Hamden: Archon, 1978.

I'll Take My Stand: The South and the Agrarian Tradition. 1930. Baton Rouge: Louisiana State Univ. Press, 1980.

James, Henry. *The American Scene.* 1907. Bloomington: Indiana Univ. Press, 1969.

James, William. *Letters.* Ed. Henry James. 2 vols. 1920. New York: Kraus, 1969.

Johnson, James Weldon. *Along This Way.* 1933. New York: Viking, 1961.

Jones, Howard Mumford. *The Theory of American Literature.* Rev. ed. Ithaca: Cornell Univ. Press, 1965.

Kampf, Louis, and Paul Lauter, eds. *The Politics of Literature: Dissenting Essays on the Teaching of English.* New York: Pantheon, 1972.

Kaplan, Justin. "Theodore Dreiser: The Early Years." *Boston Globe,* 5 October 1986, B125–26.

Karcher, Carolyn. *Shadow over the Promised Land: Slavery, Race, and Violence in Melville's America.* Baton Rouge: Louisiana State Univ. Press, 1980.

Kasson, Joy S. *Artistic Voyagers: Europe and the American Imagination in the Works of Irving, Allston, Cole, Cooper, and Hawthorne.* Westport: Greenwood, 1982.

Kazin, Alfred. *New York Jew.* 1978. New York: Vintage, 1979.

Kazin, Alfred. *On Native Grounds: An Interpretation of Modern American Prose Literature.* 1942. New York: Harcourt, Brace, Jovanovich, 1970.

Kelley, Mary. *Private Woman, Public Stage: Literary Domesticity in Nineteenth-Century America.* New York: Oxford Univ. Press, 1984.

Kennell, Ruth Epperson. *Theodore Dreiser and the Soviet Union, 1927–1945.* New York: International Publishers, 1969.

Kenner, Hugh. *The Pound Era.* Berkeley: Univ. of California Press, 1971.

Klehr, Harvey. *The Heyday of American Communism: The Depression Decade.* New York: Basic, 1984.

Klein, Marcus. *Foreigners: The Making of American Literature, 1900–1940.* Chicago: Univ. of Chicago Press, 1981.

Krupat, Arnold. *Those Who Come After: A Study of Native American Autobiography.* Berkeley: Univ. of California Press, 1985.

Lasch, Christopher. *The Agony of the American Left.* New York: Vintage, 1969.

Lauter, Paul. "Race and Gender in the Shaping of the American Literary Canon: A Case Study from the Twenties." *Feminist Studies* 9 (1983): 435–63.

Lawrence, D. H. *Studies in Classic American Literature*. 1923. New York: Viking, 1964.

Leary, Lewis. *American Literature: A Study and Research Guide*. New York: St. Martin's, 1976.

Leavis, F. R. *The Common Pursuit*. 1952. London: Chatto and Windus, 1972.

Leavis, F. R. *The Great Tradition*. 1948. New York: New York Univ. Press, 1969.

Leavis, F. R. *Revaluation: Tradition and Development in English Poetry*. 1936. London: Chatto and Windus, 1969.

Lehan, Richard. *Theodore Dreiser: His World and His Novels*. Carbondale: Southern Illinois Univ. Press, 1969.

Lenin, V. I. "Party Organization and Party Literature." 1905. *Lenin on Literature and Art*, 22–27. Moscow: Progress Publishers, 1970.

Levenson, J. C. *The Mind and Art of Henry Adams*. 1957. Stanford: Stanford Univ. Press, 1968.

Levin, Harry. *The Power of Blackness: Hawthorne, Poe, Melville*. 1958. New York: Vintage, 1960.

Lewis, R. W. B. *The American Adam: Innocence, Tragedy, and Tradition in the Nineteenth Century*. 1955. Chicago: Univ. of Chicago Press, 1971.

Lincoln, Kenneth. *Native American Renaissance*. Berkeley: Univ. of California Press, 1983.

Lipset, Seymour Martin, and Earl Raab. *The Politics of Unreason: Right-Wing Extremism in America, 1790–1970*. New York: Harper and Row, 1970.

Lipsitz, George. *Class and Culture in Cold War America*. South Hadley: Bergin and Garvey, 1982.

Loggins, Vernon. *The Negro Author: His Development in America to 1900*. 1931. Port Washington: Kennikat, 1964.

Lowes, John Livingston. *The Road to Xanadu: A Study in the Ways of the Imagination*. 1927. Boston: Houghton Mifflin, 1964.

Lynn, Kenneth. "F. O. Matthiessen." In *Masters: Portraits of Great Teachers*, ed. Joseph Epstein, 103–18. New York: Basic, 1981.

McCarthy, Joseph. "Speech at Wheeling, West Virginia." February 1950. In *A History of Our Time: Readings on Postwar America*, ed. William H. Chafe and Harvard Sitkoff. 2d ed. 64–67. New York: Oxford Univ. Press, 1987.

MacDonald, Dwight. *Henry Wallace: The Man and the Myth*. New York: Vanguard, 1948.

MacDougall, Curtis D. *Gideon's Army*. 3 vols. New York: Marzani and Munsell, 1965.

Marable, Manning. *W. E. B. Du Bois: Black Radical Democrat.* Boston: Twayne, 1986.

Markels, Julian. "Dreiser and the Plotting of Inarticulate Experience." 1961. In *Sister Carrie*, ed. Donald Pizer, 527–41. New York: Norton, 1970.

Markowitz, Norman D. *The Rise and Fall of the People's Century: Henry A. Wallace and American Liberalism, 1941–1948.* New York: Free Press, 1973.

Marx, Leo. "Double Consciousness and the Cultural Politics of F. O. Matthiessen." *Monthly Review* 34 (1983): 34–56.

Marx, Leo. "The Harvard Retrospect and the Arrested Development of American Radicalism." In *A Symposium on Political Activism and the Academic Conscience: The Harvard Experience, 1936–1941*, ed. John Lydenberg, 31–42. Hobart and William Smith Colleges, December 5 and 6, 1975.

Marx, Leo. *The Machine in the Garden: Technology and the Pastoral Ideal.* 1964. New York: Oxford Univ. Press, 1974.

Marx, Leo. "The Teacher." In *F. O. Matthiessen (1902–1950): A Collective Portrait*, ed. Paul M. Sweezy and Leo Huberman, 37–43. New York: Henry Schuman, 1950.

Matthiessen, F. O. *The Achievement of T. S. Eliot: An Essay on the Nature of Poetry.* 1935. 2d ed., 1947. 3d ed., with additional chapter by C. L. Barber. New York: Oxford Univ. Press, 1960.

Matthiessen, F. O. *American Renaissance: Art and Expression in the Age of Emerson and Whitman.* 1941. New York: Oxford Univ. Press, 1972.

Matthiessen, F. O. "A Communication." *Sewanee Review* 54 (1946): 144.

Matthiessen, F. O. "Edgar Allan Poe." In *Literary History of the United States*, ed. Robert E. Spiller et al., 321–42. 1948. 3d ed. New York: Macmillan, 1972.

Matthiessen, F. O. "An Excited Debater." 1933. *The Responsibilities of the Critic: Essays and Reviews by F. O. Matthiessen*, ed. John Rackliffe, 184–89. New York: Oxford Univ. Press, 1952.

Matthiessen, F. O. "*The Flowering of New England.*" 1936. *Responsibilities of the Critic*, 199–208.

Matthiessen, F. O. *From the Heart of Europe.* New York: Oxford Univ. Press, 1948.

Matthiessen, F. O. "*The Great Tradition*: A Counterstatement." 1934. *Responsibilities of the Critic*, 189–99.

Matthiessen, F. O. *Henry James: The Major Phase.* New York: Oxford Univ. Press, 1944.

Matthiessen, F. O. "In the Tradition from Emerson." *New Republic*, 6 April 1938, 279–80.

Matthiessen, F. O. *The James Family: A Group Biography.* 1947. New York: Knopf, 1961.

Matthiessen, F. O. "New Standards in American Criticism: 1929." 1929. *Responsibilities of the Critic,* 181–83.

Matthiessen, F. O. "Record of Our Education." *New Republic,* 13 July 1938, 285.

Matthiessen, F. O. "The Responsibilities of the Critic." 1949. *Responsibilities of the Critic,* 3–18.

Matthiessen, F. O. *Sarah Orne Jewett.* Boston: Houghton Mifflin, 1929.

Matthiessen, F. O. *Theodore Dreiser.* 1951. New York: Delta, 1966.

Matthiessen, F. O. *Translation: An Elizabethan Art.* Cambridge: Harvard Univ. Press, 1931.

Matthiessen, F. O. "Whitman: Sanguine Confused American." 1938. *Responsibilities of the Critic,* 215–17.

Matthiessen, F. O., ed. *The American Novels and Stories of Henry James.* New York: Knopf, 1947.

Matthiessen, F. O., ed. *Henry James: Stories of Writers and Artists.* New York: New Directions, 1944.

Matthiessen, F. O., ed. *The Oxford Book of American Verse.* New York: Oxford Univ. Press, 1950.

Matthiessen, F. O., and Kenneth Murdock, eds. *The Notebooks of Henry James.* 1947. New York: Oxford Univ. Press, 1961.

Meier, August, and Elliott Rudwick. *Black History and the Historical Profession, 1915–1980.* Urbana: Univ. of Illinois Press, 1986.

Melville, Herman. *Benito Cereno.* 1856. New York: Library of America, 1984.

Mencken, H. L. "Theodore Dreiser." 1917. In *The American Scene: A Reader,* ed. Huntington Cairns, 111–56. New York: Vintage, 1982.

Michaels, Walter Benn. "*Sister Carrie*'s Popular Economy." *Critical Inquiry* 7 (1980): 373–90.

Morris, Wesley. *Toward a New Historicism.* Princeton: Princeton Univ. Press, 1972.

Mumford, Lewis. *The Golden Day: A Study in American Experience and Culture.* New York: Boni and Liveright, 1926.

Nash, Gerald D. *The Great Depression and World War II: Organizing America, 1933–1945.* New York: St. Martin's, 1979.

National Cyclopaedia of American Biography. Vol. 46. New York: James T. White, 1956.

Nelson, Truman. *The Sin of the Prophet.* Boston: Little, Brown, 1952.

Nevin, Thomas R. *Irving Babbitt: An Intellectual Study.* Chapel Hill: Univ. of North Carolina Press, 1984.

Newby, I. A. *The South: A History.* New York: Holt, Rinehart, and Winston, 1978.

Niebuhr, Reinhold. "For Peace, We Must Risk War." *Life*, 20 September 1948, 38–39.

Niebuhr, Reinhold. *The Irony of American History*. New York: Scribner's, 1952.

Niebuhr, Reinhold. "The Presidential Campaign." *Christianity and Crisis*, 1 November 1948, 137–38.

Norton, Anne. *Alternative Americas: A Reading of Antebellum Political Culture*. Chicago: Univ. of Chicago Press, 1986.

Nuhn, Ferner. "Teaching American Literature in American Colleges." *American Mercury* 13 (1928): 328–31.

Ohmann, Richard. "The Social Definition of Literature." In *What Is Literature?* ed. Paul Hernadi, 89–101. Bloomington: Indiana Univ. Press, 1978.

Ohmann, Richard. "The Social Relations of Criticism." In *What Is Criticism?* ed. Paul Hernadi, 189–98. Bloomington: Indiana Univ. Press, 1981.

O'Neill, William L. *The Great Schism: Stalinism and the American Intellectuals*. New York: Simon and Schuster, 1982.

Parker, Hershel. *Flawed Texts and Verbal Icons: Literary Authority in American Fiction*. Evanston: Northwestern Univ. Press, 1984.

Parrington, Vernon Louis. *The Beginnings of Critical Realism in America, 1860–1920*. 1930. New York: Harcourt, Brace, and World, 1958.

Parrington, Vernon Louis. *The Colonial Mind, 1620–1800*. 1927. New York: Harcourt, Brace, and World, 1954.

Parrington, Vernon Louis. *The Romantic Revolution in America, 1800–1860*. 1927. New York: Harcourt, Brace, and World, 1954.

Pearce, Roy Harvey. *Historicism Once More: Problems and Occasions for the American Scholar*. Princeton: Princeton Univ. Press, 1969.

Pease, Donald E. "*Moby Dick* and the Cold War." In *The American Renaissance Reconsidered*, ed. Walter Benn Michaels and Donald E. Pease, 113–55. Baltimore: Johns Hopkins Univ. Press, 1985.

Pells, Richard H. *The Liberal Mind in a Conservative Age: American Intellectuals in the 1940s and 1950s*. New York: Harper and Row, 1985.

Pells, Richard H. *Radical Visions and American Dreams: Culture and Social Thought in the Depression Years*. New York: Harper and Row, 1973.

Perl, Jeffrey M. *The Tradition of Return: The Implicit History of Modern Literature*. Princeton: Princeton Univ. Press, 1984.

Phillips, Ulrich B. *American Negro Slavery*. 1918. Louisiana State Univ. Press, 1966.

Phillips, Wendell. "Philosophy of the Abolition Movement." 1853. *Wendell Phillips on Civil Rights and Freedom*, ed. Louis Filler, 28–71. New York: Hill and Wang, 1965.

Pierson, George Wilson. *Yale: The University College, 1921–1937*. New Haven: Yale Univ. Press, 1955.

Pizer, Donald. *The Novels of Theodore Dreiser: A Critical Study*. Minneapolis: Univ. of Minnesota Press, 1976.

Poirier, Richard. *The Renewal of Literature: Emersonian Reflections*. New York: Random House, 1987.

Posnock, Ross. "Henry James, Veblen, and Adorno: The Crisis of the Modern Self." *Journal of American Studies* 21 (1987): 31–54.

Pound, Ezra. "Henry James." 1918. *Literary Essays of Ezra Pound*, 294–338. New York: New Directions, 1968.

Pound, Ezra. "How to Read." 1929. *Literary Essays*, 15–40.

Rahv, Philip. "Our Country and Our Culture." *Partisan Review* 19 (May–June 1952): 304–10.

Rahv, Philip. "The Unfuture of Utopia." 1949. *Literature and the Sixth Sense*, 331–38. Boston: Houghton Mifflin, 1970.

Rampersad, Arnold. *The Art and Imagination of W. E. B. Du Bois*. Cambridge: Harvard Univ. Press, 1976.

Ransom, John Crowe. "The Esthetic of Regionalism." 1934. In *Literary Opinion in America*, ed. Morton Dauwen Zabel, 106–21. New York: Harper and Brothers, 1937.

Ransom, John Crowe. *Selected Letters*. Ed. Thomas Daniel Young and George Core. Baton Rouge: Louisiana State Univ. Press, 1985.

Ransom, John Crowe. "The Teaching of Poetry." *Kenyon Review* 1 (1939): 81–83.

Ransom, John Crowe. *The World's Body*. 1938. Baton Rouge: Louisiana State Univ. Press, 1968.

Record, Wilson. *The Negro and the Communist Party*. 1951. New York: Atheneum, 1971.

Reising, Russell. *The Unusable Past: Theory and the Study of American Literature*. New York: Methuen, 1986.

Report of the Committee on Trends in Research in American Literature, 1940–1950. New York: MLA, 1951.

Richards, I. A. *Coleridge on Imagination*. 1934. Bloomington: Indiana Univ. Press, 1969.

Rock, Virginia. "The Making and Meaning of *I'll Take My Stand*: A Study in Utopian Conservatism, 1925–1939." Diss., Univ. of Minnesota, 1961.

Rogin, Michael Paul. *Subversive Genealogy: The Politics and Art of Herman Melville*. New York: Knopf, 1983.

Rogin, Michael Paul. " 'The Sword Became a Flashing Vision': D. W. Griffith's *The Birth of a Nation*." *Representations* 9 (Winter 1985): 150–95.

Roszak, Theodore, ed. *The Dissenting Academy: Essays Criticizing the Teaching of the Humanities in American Universities*. New York: Pantheon, 1968.

Rourke, Constance. *American Humor: A Study of the National Character*. 1931. New York: Doubleday, n.d.

Rowe, John Carlos. *The Theoretical Dimensions of Henry James*. Madison: Univ. of Wisconsin Press, 1984.

Rubin, Louis D., Jr. *The Wary Fugitives: Four Poets and the South*. Baton Rouge: Louisiana State Univ. Press, 1978.

Rudwick, Elliott. *W. E. B. Du Bois: Voice of the Black Protest Movement*. 1960. New York: Univ. of Illinois Press, 1982.

Ruland, Richard. *The Rediscovery of American Literature: Premises of Critical Taste, 1900–1940*. Cambridge: Harvard Univ. Press, 1967.

Sanchez, Marta Ester. *Contemporary Chicana Poetry: A Critical Approach to an Emerging Literature*. Berkeley: Univ. of California Press, 1985.

Sarton, May. *Faithful Are the Wounds*. New York: Rinehart, 1955.

Schapsmeier, Edward L., and Frederick H. Schapsmeier. *Prophet in Politics: Henry A. Wallace and the War Years, 1940–1965*. Ames: Iowa State Univ. Press, 1970.

Schrecker, Ellen W. *No Ivory Tower: McCarthyism and the Universities*. New York: Oxford Univ. Press, 1986.

See, Fred G. "The Text as Mirror: *Sister Carrie* and the Lost Language of the Heart." *Criticism* 20 (1978): 144–66.

Shakespeare, William. *The Complete Signet Shakespeare*. Ed. Sylvan Barnet. New York: Harcourt, Brace, Jovanovich, 1972.

Shannon, David A. *Between the Wars: America, 1919–1941*. 2d ed. Boston: Houghton Mifflin, 1979.

Sitkoff, Harvard. *A New Deal for Blacks: The Emergence of Civil Rights as a National Issue, The Depression Decade*. New York: Oxford Univ. Press, 1978.

Skotheim, Robert Allen. *American Intellectual Histories and Historians*. Princeton: Princeton Univ. Press, 1966.

Smith, Henry Nash. *Virgin Land: The American West as Symbol and Myth*. 1950. New York: Vintage, n.d.

Sollors, Werner. *Beyond Ethnicity: Consent and Descent in American Culture*. New York: Oxford Univ. Press, 1986.

"The South Gets Rough with Wallace." *Life*, 13 September 1948, 33–35.

Spengemann, William C. "American Things/Literary Things: The Problem of American Literary History." *American Literature* 57 (1985): 456–81.

Spengemann, William C. "American Writers and English Literature." *ELH* 52 (1985): 209–38.

Works Cited

Spiller, Robert E. Review of *American Renaissance*. *American Literature* 13 (1941–42): 432–35.

Spiller, Robert E., et al., eds. *Literary History of the United States*. 1948. 3d ed. New York: Macmillan, 1972.

Starobin, Joseph R. *American Communism in Crisis, 1943–1957*. Cambridge: Harvard Univ. Press, 1972.

Stern, Frederick C. *F. O. Matthiessen: Christian Socialist as Critic*. Chapel Hill: Univ. of North Carolina Press, 1981.

Stevens, Wallace. *Letters of Wallace Stevens*. Ed. Holly Stevens. 1966. New York: Knopf, 1977.

Stewart, John L. *The Burden of Time: The Fugitives and the Agrarians*. Princeton: Princeton Univ. Press, 1965.

Stowe, Harriet Beecher. *Uncle Tom's Cabin*. 1852. New York: Viking Penguin, 1981.

Sullivan, Louis H. *The Autobiography of an Idea*. New York: W. W. Norton, 1926.

Summers, Joseph. "Statement." In *F. O. Matthiessen (1902–1950): A Collective Portrait*, ed. Paul M. Sweezy and Leo Huberman, 141–44. New York: Henry Schuman, 1950.

Summers, Joseph, and U. T. Miller Summers. "F. O. Matthiessen." In *Dictionary of American Biography*. Supplement 4, 1946–1950. New York: Scribner's, 1974.

Sundquist, Eric J. "*Benito Cereno* and New World Slavery." In *Reconstructing American Literary History*, ed. Sacvan Bercovitch, 93–122. Cambridge: Harvard Univ. Press, 1986.

Sundquist, Eric J. "Slavery, Revolution, and the American Renaissance." In *The American Renaissance Reconsidered*, ed. Walter Benn Michaels and Donald Pease, 1–33. Baltimore: Johns Hopkins Univ. Press, 1985.

Susman, Warren I. "The Culture of the Thirties." 1983. *Culture as History: The Transformation of American Society in the Twentieth Century*, 150–83. New York: Pantheon, 1984.

Sutton, Walter. *Modern American Criticism*. Englewood Cliffs: Prentice-Hall, 1963.

Swann, Brian, and Arnold Krupat, eds. *Recovering the Word: Essays on Native American Literature*. Berkeley: Univ. of California Press, 1987.

Sweezy, Paul M. "Labor and Political Activities." In *F. O. Matthiessen (1902–1950): A Collective Portrait*, ed. Paul M. Sweezy and Leo Huberman, 61–75. New York: Henry Schuman, 1950.

Sweezy, Paul M., and Leo Huberman, eds. *F. O. Matthiessen (1902–1950): A Collective Portrait*. New York: Henry Schuman, 1950.

Tawney, R. H. *The Acquisitive Society*. 1920. New York: Harcourt, Brace, and World, n.d.

Thomas, Brook. "The Legal Fictions of Herman Melville and Lemuel Shaw." *Critical Inquiry* 11 (September 1984): 24–51.

Thomas, Norman. *After the New Deal, What?* New York: Macmillan, 1936.

Tolstoy, Leo. "A Message to the American People." 1901. *Tolstoy on Civil Disobedience and Non-Violence.* New York: New American Library, 1967.

Tompkins, Jane. *Sensational Designs: The Cultural Work of American Fiction, 1790–1860.* New York: Oxford Univ. Press, 1985.

Trilling, Lionel. *The Middle of the Journey.* 1947. New York: Avon, 1976.

Trilling, Lionel. "*The Princess Casamassima.*" 1948. *The Liberal Imagination: Essays on Literature and Society.* 1950. 69–101. New York: Penguin, n.d.

Trilling, Lionel. "Reality in America." 1940, 1946. *The Liberal Imagination: Essays on Literature and Society.* 1950. 17–34. New York: Penguin, n.d.

Turner, Lorenzo Dow. "Anti-Slavery Sentiment in American Literature Prior to 1865." *Journal of Negro History* 14 (1929): 371–492.

Tuttle, William M., ed. *W. E. B. Du Bois.* Englewood Cliffs: Prentice-Hall, 1973.

Vanderbilt, Kermit. *American Literature and the Academy: The Roots, Growth, and Maturity of a Profession.* Philadelphia: Univ. of Pennsylvania Press, 1987.

Van Doren, Carl. "Toward a New Canon." *Nation,* 13 April 1932, 429–30.

Walker, J. Samuel. *Henry A. Wallace and American Foreign Policy.* Westport: Greenwood, 1976.

Wallace, Henry. *Democracy Reborn: Selected from Public Papers.* Ed. Russell Lord. New York: Reynal and Hitchcock, 1944.

Wallace, Henry. *Sixty Million Jobs.* New York: Reynal and Hitchcock, 1945.

Walton, Richard J. *Henry Wallace, Harry Truman, and the Cold War.* New York: Viking, 1976.

Webster, Grant. *The Republic of Letters: A History of Postwar American Literary Opinion.* Baltimore: Johns Hopkins Univ. Press, 1979.

Weisbuch, Robert. *Atlantic Double-Cross: American Literature and British Influence in the Age of Emerson.* Chicago: Univ. of Chicago Press, 1986.

Wellek, René. *American Criticism, 1900–1950.* New Haven: Yale Univ. Press, 1986.

White, George Abbott. " 'Have I Any Right in a Community That Would So Utterly Disapprove of Me If It Knew the Facts?' " *Harvard Magazine* (September–October 1978): 58–62.

Whitman, Walt. *Complete Poetry and Collected Prose.* New York: Library of America, 1982.

Works Cited

Williams, Raymond. *Writing in Society*. London: Verso, 1983.

Winters, Yvor. *Maule's Curse: Seven Studies in the History of American Obscurantism*. 1938. *In Defense of Reason*. 3d ed. Denver: Alan Swallow, 1947.

Wright, Frank Lloyd. *The Future of Architecture*. 1953. New York: Meridian, 1970.

Wright, Richard. "How 'Bigger' Was Born." 1940. In *Black Voices: An Anthology of Afro-American Literature*, ed. Abraham Chapman, 538–63. New York: New American Library, 1968.

Wyman, David S. *The Abandonment of the Jews: America and the Holocaust, 1941–1945*. New York: Pantheon, 1984.

Young, Thomas Daniel. "Editors and Critics." In *The History of Southern Literature*, ed. Louis D. Rubin, Jr., 407–14. Baton Rouge: Louisiana State Univ. Press, 1985.

Ziff, Larzer. *Literary Democracy: The Declaration of Cultural Independence in America*. New York: Viking, 1981.

Zweig, Paul. *Walt Whitman: The Making of the Poet*. New York: Basic, 1984.

Index

Index

Index